The Minister's Task and Calling in the Sermons of Jonathan Edwards

Helen Westra

Studies in American Religion
Volume 17

The Edwin Mellen Press
Lewiston/Queenston

Library of Congress Cataloging-in-Publication Data

Westra, Helen.
The minister's task and calling in the sermons of
Jonathan Edwards.

(Studies in American Religion ; v. 17)
Bibliography: p.
1. Edwards, Jonathan, 1703-1758--Contributions in
pastoral theology. 2. Pastoral theology--History of
doctrines--18th century. I.   Title II.   Series.
BV4006.W47 1986   253'.092'4   85-29694
ISBN 0-88946-661-0 (alk. paper)

BV
4006
.W47
1986

This is volume 17 in the continuing series
Studies in American Religion
Volume 17 ISBN 0-88946-661-0
SAR Series ISBN 0-88946-992-X

The Edwin Mellen Press   The Edwin Mellen Press
Box 450   Box 67
Lewiston, New York   Queenston, Ontario
USA 14092   CANADA L0S 1L0

Printed in the United States of America

For Nettie C. Petter
whose life reflects the living Word

ACKNOWLEDGEMENTS

Yale University's Beinecke Rare Book and Manuscript Library houses the Jonathan Edwards Manuscript Collection, the primary source of material for this study. Several things should be noted about my transcriptions of sermons and notes from this collection. To keep these transcriptions as close as possible to the original text, I have chosen not to normalize Edwards' spelling or punctuation. Furthermore, in my transcriptions I have used a question mark in brackets [?] to indicate an undeciphered word, and I have placed a question mark in parentheses (?) to indicate that the preceding word is tentatively deciphered. In addition, I have placed brackets around a biblical text reference when I wish to indicate the unpublished Edwards sermon based on that text. Thanks and acknowledgements are due to Beinecke Library for access to the Edwards Manuscript Collection and specifically for permission to quote from the unpublished sermons in that collection and to reproduce pages 25 and 26 from Edwards' manuscript sermon on Acts 20:28.

Though Edwards' handwriting is minute and in some instances exceedingly difficult to decipher, I take full responsibility for any errors I may have made in transcribing. I offer my efforts humbly with a confession similar to that of Rev. Isaac Watts, editor of A Faithful Narrative, who remarked that Edwards' manuscript was "written in so small a hand and so hard to read . . . [that] I am sure I was forced to guess at several words in it." Happily, present-day scholars can anticipate studying some of Edwards' hitherto unpublished sermons when they appear in the forthcoming Yale edition of sermons edited by Wilson Kimnach.

I also wish to express warm thanks to friends and colleagues along the way who have significantly stimulated and encouraged my efforts in this work—to Thomas Werge, James Dougherty, and Nathan Hatch for their generous time and interest; to Wilson Kimnach, whose expert knowledge and command of the Edwards manuscript sermons were an enormous inspiration to me in my research at Yale; to Thomas Schafer for kind permission to use his typescripts of Edwards' "Miscellanies"; to the Zahm Foundation for a research and travel grant; to the University of Notre Dame English Department for a fellowship providing the resources and opportunity to expedite my investigation without delay or interruption; to Hope College for its generosity and facilities enabling me to complete this work; and to Myra Kohsel, Diane Krikke, Pam Pater, and Lisa Van Wyhe for their competence and patience in meeting deadlines and seeing my manuscript through several drafts.

But first and last I owe profound thanks to my husband and children for their loving support and to my father, Rev. Andrew Petter, for his personal example of meticulous scholarship and gospel ministry.

TABLE OF CONTENTS

INTRODUCTION

In the two hundred and fifty years since Jonathan Edwards' first publications and the New England religious "awakenings" which he vividly described to the world,[1] critical analysis and considerations of his thought have accumulated steadily. Recent book-length bibliographies, notably M. X. Lesser's Jonathan Edwards: A Reference Guide[2] and Nancy Manspeaker's Jonathan Edwards: Bibliographical Synopses,[3] thoroughly document the numerous and wide-ranging studies on Edwards which have been produced by generations of theologians, philosophers, and students of American culture. Current scholarly interest, a veritable Edwardsean "Renaissance," remains strong as it builds on seminal twentieth-century research and manuscript studies.[4]

There are healthy indications that attention to Edwards' life and thought will not ebb quickly. Much of Edward's writing is yet unpublished, and the Editorial Committee of the Yale edition of The

****

[1] Edwards' first published sermons were God Glorified in the Work of Redemption, by the Greatness of Man's Dependence upon him in the Whole of it (Boston, 1731), and A Divine and Supernatural Light, Immediately imparted to the Soul by the Spirit of God, Shown to be both a Scriptural and Rational Doctrine (Boston, 1734). He preached God Glorified upon invitation in Boston on July 8, 1731, before the Boston clergy at the Public Lecture. On November 6, 1736, Edwards wrote a letter to Rev. Benjamin Coleman of Boston documenting revival activities and awakenings in Northampton and thirty-two other Connecticut River Valley communities. This was published in Boston in 1737 under the title of A Faithful Narrative of the Surprising Work of God in Conversion of many Hundred Souls in Northampton and the Neighboring Towns and Villages.

[2] (Boston: G. K. Hall & Co., 1981).

[3] (New York: Edwin Mellen Press, 1981).

[4] Clarence Faust and Thomas Johnson both contributed foundational twentieth-century scholarship on Edwards in Jonathan Edwards: Representative Selections, with Introduction, Bibliography and Notes

Works of Jonathan Edwards is presently laboring with "the massive body of Edwards' manuscripts" so as to offer "a full and complete exposure of his ideas in a manner never before possible."[5] Originally under the general editorship of Perry Miller and now directed by John E. Smith, the committee has already produced seven volumes: Freedom of the Will, ed. Paul Ramsey (1957); Religious Affections, ed. John E. Smith (1959); Original Sin, ed. Clyde Holbrook (1970); The Great Awakening, ed. C. C. Goen (1972); Apocalyptic Writings, ed. Stephen Stein (1977); Philosophical Writings, ed. Wallace Anderson (1980); The Life of David Brainerd, ed. Norman Pettit(1985). Forthcoming volumes will represent eight more categories of Edwards' writings: the "Miscellanies," ethical writings, The History of Redemption, writings on typology, biblical writings, church history, correspondence, and early sermons.[6] Each volume will include a substantial "Editor's Introduction" providing elaborate research on the context, influences, and sources of the works. In addition to the contributions anticipated from the manuscript editors, other scholars and writers will no doubt also continue to challenge, modify, counterbalance, and expand assessments of a man often described with superlatives—"America's greatest

****

(Footnote 4 Continued From Previous Page)
(1935; rpt. New York: Hill & Wang, 1962). Thomas Johnson's writing also include "Jonathan Edwards' Background of Reading," Publications of the Colonial Society of Massachusetts, 28 (1931), 193-222. Perry Miller's Jonathan Edwards is considered by many to be "the single most important volume in modern Edwards scholarship and now the inevitable starting point for any consideration of Edwards as a thinker," Manspeaker, p. 131.

[5]Stephen Stein, The Works of Jonathan Edwards (New Haven; Yale University Press, 1977), V, x.

[6]John E. Smith, "A Summary Report on the Progress of the Yale Edition of The Works of Jonathan Edwards," Early American Literature, 14 (Winter 79-80) 352-53.

metaphysical genius," [7] America's leading theologian,"[8] "the greatest master in false philosophy,"[9] and the "most bitter hater of man the American pulpit ever had."[10]

Edwards' influential leadership and preaching during New England's Great Awakening have indeed become commonplace parts of our knowledge of American's cultural history. Scholars have written prolifically on Edwards' revivalist activities, his sulfurous sermons, and his sinewy treatises. As successive generations of writers have probed his thought, the complexity and range of his mind appear in multifarious studies and bibliographic entries on Edwards as philosopher, scientist, theologian, ethicist, logician, typologist, psychologist, proto-romanticist, revivalist, historian, mystic, and literary artist.[11]

Obvious gaps remain, however, along the way of Edwardsean scholarship. For more than thirty years Edwards sought to fulfill the

****
[7]Miller, "Jonathan Edwards on the Sense of the Heart," Harvard Theological Review, 41 (1948), 123.

[8]Arthur Cushman McGiffert, Jonathan Edwards (New York, 1932), p. 4.

9 George Santayana, Character and Opinion in the United States (New York, 1920), p. 9.

[10]Charles Angoff, A Literary History of the American People (New York, 1935), p. 299.

[11]See bibliographic essays in M. X. Lesser, Jonathan Edwards, vii-xviii; and Manspeaker, Jonathan Edwards, vii-xviii. See also: Everett H. Emerson, "Jonathan Edwards," Fifteen American Authors before 1900: Bibliographic Essays on Research and Criticism, eds. Robert A. Reese and Earl N. Harbert (Madison: University of Wisconsin Press, 1971); Clarence H. Faust and Thomas H. Johnson, "Selected Bibliography," Jonathan Edwards: Representative Selections, rev. ed., American Century Series (New York: Hill & Wang, 1962); Richard Sliwoski, "Doctoral Dissertations on Jonathan Edwards," Early American Literature, 14 (1979-80), 318-327; William Scheick, "Introduction," Critical Essays on Jonathan Edwards, ed. William J. Scheick (Boston: G. K. Hall & Co., 1980); Thomas Werge, "Jonathan Edwards and the Puritan Mind in America: Directions in Textual and Interpretative Criticism," Reformed Review, 23 (1970), 153-56; Daniel

"sacred work and office of a minister of the gospel"[12] prophetically, authoritatively, and chastely as he understood that office. Yet his probing, deliberate examinations of the task and qualifications of gospel ministry have received scant treatment. Few studies have been directed systematically toward the theology and doctrines that shaped his conception and enactments of that office.

In addressing Edwards' sermons, scholars have often limited their analyses to discussions on his rhetorical strategy or on sociological and psychological theories by which to explain or denounce the impact sermons such as Sinners in the Hands of an Angry God had on colonial audiences.[13] A long history of limited accessibility to Edwards' full sermon canon as well as disproportionately heavy emphasis on his imprecatory sermons has perpetuated the notion that in Edwards there is a peculiar "absence of pastoral and communal sensibilities."[14] His controversy with his Northampton congregation resulting in his dismissal has also left him open to the general charge that "his pastoral sense was not keen."[15] In her investigations of Edwards' ministerial career Patricia Tracy rightly notes that while his

****

(Footnote 11 Continued From Previous Page)
Shea, "Jonathan Edwards: The First Two Hundred Years," Journal of American Studies, 14 (1980), 181-98.

[12] Jonathan Edwards, The Church's Marriage to Her Sons and to Her God, in The Works of President Edwards, ed. Sereno E. Dwight, 10 vols. (New York: S. Converse, 1829-30), III, 562. This edition is hereafter cited as Works (Dwight).

[13] This sermon was preached at Enfield, July 8, 1741, and printed in Boston, 1741.

[14] Daniel Shea, "Jonathan Edwards: The First Two Hundred Years," Journal of American Studies, 14 (1980), 197-98.

[15] David W. Waanders, "The Pastoral Sense of Jonathan Edwards," Reformed Review, 29 (1976), 124-25.

achievements as philosopher and theologian have been studied extensively, his vocation as pastor has received "only minimal attention."[16] Studies focusing on Edwards' pastoral theology or doctrines of ministry have indeed been infrequent.

In Edwards' manuscripts and writings there are, nevertheless, a great many evidences of his continuing interest and sensitivity to the biblical doctrines underlying gospel ministry and pastoral responsibilities. Though he was an articulate and powerful ecclesiastical leader, he did not produce works paralleling John Calvin's systematic examination of the ministerial office[17] or Cotton Mather's manual for the practice of ministry.[18] But Edwards' discussions on gospel ministry appear scattered widely throughout his "Miscellanies," notebooks, dissertations, correspondence, and especially his published and unpublished sermons. Examining these multiform comments on ministry can bring to light a more complete and finely-detailed theological and pastoral picture than we presently have respecting his doctrines and views of ministry.

There remains much to be discovered about Jonathan Edwards as gospel minister. Of the close to twelve hundred extant manuscript sermons, only a fraction have been published. The sermon corpus, claims Wilson Kimnach, sermon editor of the Yale edition of Edwards Works, stands "unrivaled as a chronicle of the man and his art in the midst of life."[19] Certainly if one wishes to illuminate or detail the deeply held vocational principles and beliefs which shaped Edwards'

****

[16]Jonathan Edwards, Pastor (New York, 1979), 4.

[17]Institutes of the Christian Religion (Book IV).

[18]Manuductio ad Ministerium (Boston, 1726).

[19]"The Literary Techniques of Jonathan Edwards" (Dissertation, University of Pennsylvania, 1971), 197.

ministry, the form and content of his preaching, his ministerial
reactions to the events of his life and time, and his personal and
professional relationship to his divine master, the many sermons he
wrote and preached from 1722-1758 are an exceedingly rich source of
light.

I do not wish to suggest that other writers have altogether
ignored the pastoral dimensions of Edwards' theology or his sermons on
gospel ministry. In my investigation of Edwards I have benefited from
a number of fine studies of Edwards' complex theology; of his sermonic
utterances; and of the social, intellectual, and spiritual climate in
the colonies as it influenced and was influenced by Edwards.[20]

Perry Miller has done much to reveal the intricate patterns in
Jonathan Edwards' thought and to go beyond external biography to expose
the creative life of his mind. Miller focuses most rigorously on the
ramifications of Edwards' philosophy, psychology, and rhetorical
theory; he also insists that to understand Edwards, one must "seek to
ascertain not so much the peculiar doctrines in which he expressed his

****

[20]Following are books valuable for understanding Edwards' position
in eighteenth-century colonial history and thought. Most treat
Edwards' doctrines of ministry in a limited way, if at all, but remain
useful as engaging, insightful explorations of the man and his ideas:
Conrad Cherry, The Theology of Jonathan Edwards: A Reappraisal (N.Y.,
1966); Edward H. Davidson, Jonathan Edwards: The Narrative of a
Puritan Mind (Boston, 1966); Roland Delattre, Beauty and Sensibility
in the Thought of Jonathan Edwards: An Essay in Aesthetics and
Theological Ethics (New Haven, 1968); Douglas Elwood, The
Philosophical Theology of Jonathan Edwards (N.Y., 1960); Alan Heimert
Religion and the American Mind (Cambridge, 1966); David Harlan, The
Clergy and the Great Awakening in New England (Ann Arbor, 1979);
Samuel Hopkins, The Life and Character of the Late Reverend Mr.
Jonathan Edwards (Boston, 1765); Wilson Kimnach, "The Literary
Techniques of Jonathan Edwards" (Doctoral Dissertation, University of
Pennsylvania, 1971); Perry Miller, Jonathan Edwards (N.Y., 1949);
Harold Simonson, Jonathan Edwards: Theologion of the Heart (Grand
Rapids, 1974); Patricia Tracy, Jonathan Edwards, Pastor (N.Y., 1980);
Ola Winslow, Jonathan Edwards, 1703-1758: A Biography (N.Y., 1940).

meaning as the meaning itself."[21] Without repudiating Miller, I would however remark that one cannot afford in the search for the meaning of gospel ministry, as Edwards understood it, to slight the doctrines that informed Edwards' vision, theology, and perceptions of gospel ministry. If any vocational principle consistently directed Edwards' work, it was his dogmatic belief that a faithful minister is called apart from others to be an honored participant in God's glorious work of redemption. My interest in Edwards, more theological than Miller's, lies particularly in discerning the nature, source, intent, qualifications, and form of that participation as Edwards himself studied, understood, and attempted it.

I am also indebted to Ola Winslow's solidly researched biographical volume for its wealth of material relating to Edwards' ecclesiastical leadership in Northampton and the New England colonies.[22] In contrast to Winslow's historical study, Conrad Cherry's work on Edwards is largely theological.[23] Cherry's chapter on "Word and Spirit" provides instructive discussions on the crucial distinctions between saving grace and the preacher as a vital yet mysterious "means of grace." But in scrutinizing Edwards' theory of faith as an informing force or principle in ministerial life and work, Cherry makes little use of the unpublished sermons.

Books by Ralph Turnbull and John Gerstner on Edwards' ministry offered slight usefulness for my purpose.[24] Turnbull's Jonathan Edwards: The Preacher provides only superficial examination of Edwards' ministerial activities. Gerstner does draw frequently on the

****

[21]Miller, Jonathan Edwards, xii.

[22]Jonathan Edwards, 1703-1758, A Biography (N.Y., 1940).

[23]The Theology of Jonathan Edwards: A Reappraisal (N.Y., 1966).

[24]Turnbull, Jonathan Edwards: The Preacher (Grand Rapids, 1958); Gerstner, Steps to Salvation: The Evangelical Message of Jonathan Edwards (Philadelphia, 1959).

sermons, published and unpublished, to analyze Edwards' evangelistic
message. But his references to unpublished sermons seldom go beyond
citing the sermon text and doctrine; thus we look in vain to Gerstner
for penetrating exposure of the content of Edwards' manuscript sermons
on gospel ministry.

By combining historical, sociological, and demographic methods,
Patricia Tracy significantly contextualizes Edwards' successes and
failures in the Connecticut River Valley community which initially
accepted him as Solomon Stoddard's assistant, then supported and
respected him as their principal pastor, came to love and revere him
highly, but finally contested him vehemently and rejected him. In
adding new details and insights to the traditional picture of Edwards'
career in Northampton, Tracy fulfills her aim of drawing out some
"neglected pastoral implications of his ideas and activities,"
particularly his relationships with various groups and individuals in
his parish.

The work of Wilson Kimnach on Edwards' sermon manuscripts has been
especially encouraging to me in my approach to understanding Edwards'
vision of ministry through the sermons he wrote, preached, labeled,
preserved, and occasionally published. Kimnach sees Edwards' sermon
corpus as the "pre-eminent genre and primary vehicle for the
articulation of his thought"[25] and observes that many of his best, most
cogent theological expressions are yet to be uncovered in the
unpublished sermons. Kimnach's manuscript research provides valuable
keys to Edwards' habits of mind and sermon preparation, his adroit and
varied use of the Puritan sermon form, and his high consciousness of
his duty as God's messenger to souls.

My attempts to increase understanding of Edwards have been
directed particularly to the theological, pastoral, and aesthetic

****
[25]Kimnach, "Literary Techniques," p. 1. In addition, Kimnach
discusses the sermon manuscripts in several excellent essays: "The
Brazen Trumpet: Jonathan Edwards' Conception of the Sermon" in

formulations of his views of gospel ministry. My study thus includes treatment of relevant passages expatiating on the minister's charge and task wherever these passages appear in Edwards' writings. However, I examine most closely nine ministerial sermons—the ordination and installation sermons he delivered between 1736 and 1757—as well as other important unpublished sermons on preaching and ministry. These sermons are notably informed by Edwards' staunch belief that Christ, in appointing gospel ministers to a sacred vocation, endows them with spiritual gifts and graces and delegates them above all others to be guardians of the Scriptures and watchmen in God's Kingdom.

In exploring the elements of Edwards' ministerial vision, I have attempted to shed further light on Edwards' view of the minister as "a kind of subordinate savior,"[26] and on his apostolic tendencies and Calvinist confidence in the efficacy of preaching as a means of grace. This light comes most often from the hundreds of sermons he prepared during his thirty-six year preaching career. These sermons, most of them unpublished, constitute the most regular, public, and extensive exercise of his pastoral office. A significant number of them focus directly on gospel ministry. As Edwards writes and preaches sermons about preaching, ministry, and ministers, these "ministerial" sermons become tenor and vehicle in his efforts to enact and articulate his conviction that a minister is Christ's proxy and co-worker in the care of souls.

****

(Footnote 25 Continued From Previous Page)
Jonathan Edwards: His Life and Influence, ed. Charles Angoff (New Jersey, 1975) 29-44; "Jonathan Edwards' Early Sermons: New York, 1722-1723," Journal of Presbyterian History, 55 (1977), 255-266; "Jonathan Edwards' Sermon Mill," Early American Literature, 10 (1975), 167-178.

[26]Unpublished sermon on Acts 20:28, preached May 28, 1754, and July, 1756, Edwards Manuscript Collection, Beinecke Rare Book and Manuscript Library at Yale.

Further shaping Edwards' pastoral efforts is his belief that ministers, like Old Testament kings and prophets and like New Testament apostles, are lively types of Christ "the eternal personal word." In typifying or imaging the Logos, ministers stand as "God's significations," their express purpose being to prepare hearts for the Word and to communicate with utter integrity the vital relationships and connections between words, spoken and heard, and their ultimate meanings in the mind and will of God, who is both creative and redemptive Word. Accordingly, Edwards views the minister's task as pivotal in bringing together sinful humans and sovereign deity. In preaching, the minister faithfully attempts to externalize the spiritual world of God's will and mind and at the same time to demonstrate an obedient, gracious, personal response to God's infinite perfection and glory.

Also related to his vision of gospel ministry is Edwards' exegesis and application of biblical images of ministry--the minister as steward, messenger, husbandman, proxy bridegroom, light, watchman, soldier, and anointed "son of oil." His treatments of these images become lively attempts to embody the faithful minister's great authority, dignity, honor, responsibility, love for souls, and fidelity to Christ.

Edwards' repeated aesthetic celebration and elevation of the place of gospel minister in God's "grand design" for the church, society, and the world are vivid indications that the sermons are not only doctrinal and theological vehicles. They are literary works embodying telling patterns of exposition and application; powerfully managed images and examples; a wide range of style and expression; and pointed commentary on social, historical, and ecclesistical issues.

As history reveals, Edwards' patriarchal, autocratic leadership and ecclesiastical direction came into increasingly painful conflict with the latitudiniarian, egalitarian impulses growing among the

colonists.   Consequently, his final "ministerial" sermons vividly
enlarge upon the agony as well as the joy of gospel ministry.   In
contrast to earlier sermons, the later ordination sermons heavily
identify gospel ministry with the self-sacrificing, suffering work of
Christ.   In Christ as prototype and in faithful minister as mimesis,
the great design of redemption is accomplished and made visible by
painful, patient, self-abnegating love.   Because ministry is grounded
in Christ, ministers can be faithful only if they are transformed into
the image of Christ the mediating, suffering prophet and Savior.

A chronological survey of the ministerial and ordination sermons
suggests that Edwards' sermonic efforts to uphold the honor and
authority of gospel ministry gradually shift from the detailed use of
biblical analogies and secondary images of ministry--minister as
steward, messenger, olive branch, etc.--to a more focused, direct
apprehension of Christ as the incarnation of benevolence, humility, and
spiritual beauty.   For all believers but especially for gospel
ministers Christ stands as the perfect professional model and exemplar.
This for Edwards was the great challenge but also the heavy burden of
his years of ministry.

CHAPTER I
EDWARDS AND THE SCOPE OF THE GOSPEL MINISTRY

"A faithful minister," said Jonathan Edwards, "is to be joyfully received and beloved by the people under his care as a precious gift of their ascending Redeemer."[1] As a devout, assiduous student of the Scriptures, Edwards undoubtedly knew that the biblical name of Jonathan meant "Jehovah's gift." Certainly he was acquainted with the two most notable Old Testament Jonathans, namely, prince Jonathan the son of Saul and priest Jonathan the son of Gershon. Princely Jonathan, whose tender story appears in the books of Samuel and Chronicles, is an Old Testament example of Christ-like love and faithfulness. Priestly Jonathan, whose history is recorded in Judges, is repugnantly ambitious. He exploits his ministerial office, sanctions materialism and heresy, and even condones idolatry among God's people. In the contrast between the lives of these two biblical Jonathans, it must have appeared clearly to Edwards that neither name, title, family lines, nor religious traditions offer immunity to disobedience or infidelity in one's vocation. One's name can be a graceful token aptly adorning a godly life; it can also be an ironic reminder of its bearer's failures. Throughout his many years of preaching and gospel ministry, Edwards prayerfully dedicated himself to being "Jehovah's gift" to the souls in his care. He did so wholeheartedly believing that a faithful minister as a means of grace can be "the greatest blessing of anything in the world that ever God bestows on a people."[2]

****
[1] The Church's Marriage to Her Sons, and to Her God, Works (Dwight) III, 564.

[2] The True Excellency of a Gospel Minister, The Works of Jonathan Edwards, M.A., ed. Edward Hickman, 2 vols. (London: William Tegg & Co., 1879), II, 960. This edition is hereafter cited as Works (Hickman).

Edwards' Ministerial Vision

Edwards was convinced that in God's providential plan each person has a place, particular gifts, and a task in the world. In The Nature of True Virtue Edwards remarks that God's design is apparent in the "beauty of order in society . . . as when the different members of society have all their appointed office, place and station, according to their several capacities and talents, and every one keeps his place, and continues in his proper business."[3] God is the giver of human talents and gifts, the ordainer of offices and stations, and the conceiver of individual identities. By the light of grace, each believer "reflects the Image of Christ, tho each one has his particular gift and there be some particular gift and there be some particular grace or spiritual beauty that is most conspicuous in him."[4] Applying this concept of gifts directly to the pastoral vocation, Edwards indicates in a funeral sermon (Sept. 2, 1741) for Rev. William Williams that it is Christ who bestows "all those gifts and graces whereby ministers do become faithful, eminent and successful."[5] Dutifully understanding one's place and role in the world is, for Edwards, part of comprehending and cooperating in God's larger, cosmic design in the church, in society, and in the history of the world.

If the "beauty or order of society" comes through a fulfillment of God's design in which people serve Him and each other in their appointed places and offices according to their several capacities "and

****

[3] A Dissertation on the Nature of True Virtue, Works (Hickman), I, 129.

[4] "Notes of Scripture," Works (Dwight), IX, 181.

[5] The Sorrows of the Bereaved Spread Before Jesus, Works (Hickman), II, 967.

each one keeps his place," it should certainly not surprise us that Jonathan Edwards frequently examined and probed the pastoral office to which he had dedicated himself by "the most sacred vows."[6] This meticulous attention to the role and responsibility of the minister in the church, New England society, and the world loomed large in Edwards' life, not only because he was intensely introspective, conscientious, and scrupulous, but also because for him the line between his personal and vocational life at times became virtually indistinguishable: the office absorbed the man, the man the office. For him it was a vocation which more than any other vocation had enormous and eternal consequences. The same unrelenting zeal and perfectionism which pressed the young Edwards to engage in agonizingly regular self-scrutiny[7] and later prodded his powerful genius to clarify the most abstract, knotty Calvinist doctrines, also moved him to pursue the office of gospel ministry with a persistence and application so intense that it prompted many—including Edwards himself at times—to note comparisons between his ministry and that of the apostles and early church leaders.

Edwards' vocational intensity breaks through tellingly in a brief dramatic dialogue he includes in a 1743 ordination sermon. He presents a verbal exchange between God and a faithful pastor who stands before the heavenly throne on "the day of judgment before Christ"[8]—that event Edwards ominously calls in his Farewell Sermon the "last great day of accounts."[9] The minister appears, as all ministers must ultimately

****
[6]Works (Hickman), I, 587.

[7]See Jonathan Edwards' "Resolutions" and "Diary" in Works (Hickman), I, lxii - lxxviii.

[8]The Watchman's Duty and Account, Works (Dwight), VII, 190.

[9]Farewell Sermon, Works (Hickman), I, ccxliii.

appear, to answer for his work on behalf of God and the souls entrusted
to his pastoral care. The Master questions; the minister responds in
words at once self-conscious and deferential, self-confident and
direct:

> Lord, . . . I have not neglected . . . [the] souls thou
> didst commit to me, to gratify my sloth, or pursue my
> worldly interest; I have given myself wholly to this work,
> labouring therein night and day; I have been ready, Lord,
> as thou knowest, to sacrifice my own ease and profit, and
> pleasure, and temporal convenience, and the good will of
> my neighbors, for the sake of the good of the souls I had
> the charge of . . . ; I sought out acceptable words, and
> studied for the most likely means to be used.

The details of Edwards' life history and the force of his sermons
reveal how autobiographical and strikingly prophetic were these words
he assigned to his exemplary pastor. Certainly it is ironic that
Edwards is most remembered for the sulfurous warnings which he believed
were "acceptable words" but which some in later generations came to
view as hideous, sadistic, or at best, manipulative.[10] Ironic or
prophetic as Edwards' sermon scenario appears to modern readers,
however, it leaves no doubt that he believed minister's words are
impressive means by which grace is revealed to God's people.

It is in the "acceptable words" and "most likely means" of his
sermons that Edwards' vision of gospel ministry comes to richly
concrete expression. The dialectical interaction between Edwards'
ministerial doctrines and his ministerial duties issues most
dramatically in the homiletic form. During his many years of ministry,
the approximately twelve hundred sermons he composed and preached
constitute no doubt the most frequent and systematic exercise of his

****
[10]In a check of 17 high school and college anthologies of American
literature, the 15 which include selections from Edwards chose <u>Sinners
in the Hands of an Angry God</u> for the intensity of its terrifying imagery.

pastoral office. Among these sermons the most elaborate and energetic treatments of ministry occur in those he prepared for pastoral ordinations and installations.

As part of an eighteenth-century New England trend toward making ordination and installation sermons available to readers,[11] Edwards published four such sermons during his lifetime.[12] At least seven other sermons related directly to ordination and "instalment" remain in manuscript in the Yale Beinecke Library collection of Edwards' works.[13] There are many other ministry-related sermons, some published but many unpublished, including funeral sermons for fellow ministers, fasts for special occasions, sermons for notable ecclesiastical events, and addresses for clerical or synodical gatherings. These ministerial sermons, along with relevant miscellanies and numerous observations in other works, point unmistakably to Edwards' personal preoccupation as well as his theological elevation and lively celebration of the role of

****

[11]William T. Youngs, Jr., God's Messengers: Religious Leadership in Colonial New England, 1700-1750 (Baltimore, 1976), p.132. Youngs indicates that the first published New England ordination sermon appeared in 1709, the next in 1716, seventy-eight appeared from 1716 through 1740, and from 1741 to 1750 forty-four ordination sermons were published.

[12]These sermons were published under the following titles: The Great Concern of Watchman for Souls, In a Sermon Preach'd at the Ordination of the Reverend Mr. Jonathan Judd, June 8, 1974 (Boston, 1743); The True Excellency of a Minister of the Gospel: A Sermon preached at Pelham, Aug. 30, 1744 at the ordination of the Rev. Mr. Robert Abercrombie (Boston, 1744); The Church's Marriage to her Sons, and to her God: A Sermon Preached at the Instalment of the Rev. Mr. Samuel Buell as Pastor . . . at East-Hampton on Long-Island, September 19, 1746 (Boston, 1746); Christ the Great Example of Gospel Ministers: A Sermon Preach'd at Portsmouth, at the ordination of the Reverend Mr. Job Strong . . . June 29, 1749 (Boston, n.d.). See Appendix for the texts of these sermons.

[13]Luke 10:17-18   May 17, 1736   Ordination at Lambston

    Romans 12:4-8   1739   Ordination of Deacons

ministers in God's "grand design"[14] for the church, for society, and
for world history.

Edwards' sermons embody significantly developed patterns of
exposition, exegesis, and application. They also demonstrate a rich
range of style and expression as well as powerfully managed metaphors,
images, and exempla. I therefore consider the ministerial sermons and
observations not only as evident theological vehicles for Edwards'
doctrines of ministry but also as literary works—even as "performative
utterances."[15] The philosopher J. L. Austin in How to Do Things With
Words uses this term "performative utterance" to indicate "that the
issuing of the utterance is the performing of an action." We have here
a view of speech as "not . . . just saying something."[16] The words of

****
(Footnote 13 Continued from Previous Page)

I Cor. 2:11-13	May 7, 1740	Ordination of Mr. Billing
Acts 14:23	Jan. 1740/41*	Fast at Hadley preceding Ordination
Zech. 4:12-14	Nov. 11, 1747	Instalment of Rev. J. Ashley
Acts 16:9	Aug., 1751	Instalment Fast at Stockbridge
Acts 20:28	Mar. 28, 1754	Instalment of Mr. Billing
	July 3, 1756	Mr. Jones' Ordination

*Until about 1750 in America, March 25 marked each year's official
beginning, and dates for January, February, and March were often written with a slash, e.g., Jan. 1740/41. My references to sermon dates
will hereafter be regularized to follow modern dating form.

[14]This phrase is used repeatedly in A History of the Work of
Redemption in Works (Hickman) I, 532-619. The "grand design" in God's
work of redemption is like the blueprint for a magnificent palace
built gradually "by many successive works and dispensations of God,
all tending to one great effect . . . all together making up one great
work" (p. 535).

[15]J. L. Austin, How to Do Things with Words (London, 1962), p. 6.

[16]Ibid., pp. 6-7.

Edwards' sermons are in this sense not to be considered as static or abstract truths, detached from action. What Edwards thinks or says is not remote or detached from what he does; his words are spoken deeds; his deeds are incarnate words or thoughts.

The personal word of God is, of course, quintessentially performantive in Edwards' view; that is, Christ's word and work are utterly inseparable. Christ's Word is active: his works speak. God's Word spoken and inscripturated is always associated with God's active, effectual power. By God's Word the world exists and continues. As James Daane, a twentieth-century Calvinist insists, "Divine words always release an energy that actuates what they say. Events occur because of the divine saying of them."[17] Likewise, the words of the minister, as he is God's instrument and voice, are powerfully active, and as such demand notice and response. Faithful preaching is never inconsequential or ineffective; it is a power, for good or for ill, to those that hear it. The minister's word is deed; his word as a word of God impresses the hearers one way or another and becomes part of the compelling circumstances of their lives.

Edwards' view of the minister's performantive word appears graphically in his reiterated image of the minister as one who sounds the trumpet of the Lord,[18] one who "does what a horn does to speak so as to influence and affect its hearers."[19] Indeed, trumpeting as a metaphor for preaching informs Edwards' entire sermon on Isaiah 27:13; this sermon's express "design" is "to show how the preaching of the

****

[17]Preaching With Confidence: a Theological Essay on the Power of the Pulpit (Grand Rapids, Eerdmans, 1980), p. 20.

[18]Works (Hickman), I, 584.

[19]Nov., 1733, unpublished Micah 2:11 manuscript sermon at Yale University's Beinecke Rare Book and Manuscript Library, where the Edwards MSS collection of sermons is housed and filed by biblical text.

word may fitly be compared to the blowing of a trumpet."[20]   Thus, the
minister's trumpeted words do not merely describe God's promises, warnings, or callings to men and women. The minister's words actively are
God's promises, warnings, callings.   In his Isaiah 27:13 "trumpet"
sermon preached only weeks before the famous Enfield sermon on Sinners
in the Hands of an Angry God, Edwards exhorts his congregation to hear
the sound of God's trumpet blown by his appointed messengers.   The
unpublished sermon is filled with passages describing the trumpet's
glorious sound, the means God uses to sound it, the imperative to
listen and respond, and the blessedness of those who are brought to
salvation by it:

> We may observe the means by which they [souls] shall be
> brought unto this state of salvation, viz by the
> preaching of the word of God here called blowing the
> great trumpet.
>
> ------------------------
>
> We all of us are favoured with the impressive and joyful
> sound. We sit within the hearing.
>
> ------------------------
>
> We are peculiarly favoured in this beyond many millions of
> mankind that dwell out of the hearing of the sound.   It
> never once reached their ears . . . They are perishing and
> they have no joyful trumpet to give 'em notice of a Savior
> and to call 'em to this Savior as we have. But we have the
> . . . trumpet very plainly sounding in our ears. We have
> the joyful . . . sound of the gospel, [the] sound of the
> silver trumpet calling to the great gospel feast, [the]
> jubilee proclaiming Christ the king that God has set on his

****
[20] June, 1741, unpublished manuscript sermon (Beinecke).

holy hill of Zion.

This is a day wherein this trumpet is sounding in an extraordinary manner. God has raised up some that he has fitted with an extraordinary zeal and fervency of spirit to warn and invite hearers. So that the trumpet has been heard of late more frequently and loudly than ordinary here in this land . . . .

Consider that this is the trumpet of God that you have heard and therefore should hear. Isaiah 18:3 . . . And now especially is God himself sounding the silver trumpet.

When the great God speaks it becomes all heaven and earth most devoutly and solemnly to attend.

Gather yourselves to the mountain of the house of the Lord. Come and worship at his holy mountain in Jerusalem. Hear also the joyful trumpet at Mount Zion that offers mercy and calls you and invites you to come.

That trumpet in Mount Zion is the voice of Christ.
Christ is sounding a trumpet now to call you.

Therefore hearken to this voice and come to this glorious person that was dead and is alive, that died for sinners.

In Pressing into the Kingdom of God Edwards likewise says to his hearers, "Salvation is offered to you . . . in the word and ordinances," and "I therefore beseech you in Christ's stead now to press into the kingdom of God." Accordingly Edwards addresses his

congregation in full confidence that his words are also God's words:
"God is now calling you . . . and it is agreeable to the will and word
of Christ, that I should now, in his name, call you, as one set over
you, and sent to you to that end; so it is his will that you hearken to
what I say, as his voice."[21]

Edwards' sermons also manifest his essential vocational "onlooks,"
the ways in which he looks upon himself as a minister. I borrow this
coined   word—"onlooks"--from   Donald   Evans,   whose   Logic   of
Self-Involvement[22] is a valuable study especially applying Austin's
ideas on performative utterance to religious language. For identifying
Edwards' considerations of himself relative to God and to humans, the
term "onlooks" is less vague and more inclusive and accurate than
"views," "opinion," "conceptions," "perspectives," or "outlooks." To
investigate Edwards' "onlooks," most notably his ministerial onlooks,
will be to deepen our understanding of Edwards significantly, for, as
Evans indicates, onlooks are "the core of many attitudes" and are
"extremely important in the analysis of evaluative language generally,
and of religious language in particular."[23]   One's onlooks are an
integral part of one's belief system. Such a contention is also the
thrust of Herbert Butterfield's remark that through faith in God the
believer "acquires a vision for working purposes in the world." A
believer's vision shapes his or her vocational expressions, for
ultimately, says Butterfield, the believer's "interpretation of the
whole human drama depends on an intimately personal decision concerning
the part that [he or she] mean[s] to play in it."[24]

****
   [21]Works (Hickman), I, 660.

   [22](New York, 1969), pp. 124-41.

   [23]Ibid., pp. 124-125.

   [24]Christianity and History (London, 1949), p. 86.

A brief preliminary example may serve to demonstrate the complex interrelationships between Edwards' vocational onlooks, his homiletic utterances, and his religious beliefs. Let us suppose Edwards reads in I Corinthians 4:1 that Christ's ministers are counted as "stewards of the mysteries of God," and Edwards accepts this as a divine prescription for his task of minister. We can then say, using Evans' terminology, that Edwards has the following onlook: "I, a minister of Christ, look on myself as a steward of the mysteries of God." Moreover, Edwards' sermons and ministerial writings reveal that this onlook actively informs his utterances. Clearly, then, an onlook contains important linguistic, theological, social and psychological implications.[25] These complexities are even further multiplied when we recognize that Edwards also looks vocationally on himself as—among other things—a shepherd, a trumpet, a spiritual father, God's mouth or voice, God's ambassador, keeper of God's oracles, officer in God's kingdom, the people's mouth to God, the church's proxy husband, the church's physician, God's watchman, and a burning and shining light.[26]

Placed within the context of Edwards' religious heritage and traditions, his vocational onlooks in particular and his sermons in general reveal the fundamental authority, grandeur, intricacies, and difficulties of his office. His treatment of the ministry is indeed lofty. This elevated view places Edwards in a long line of Puritans such as William Ames, Robert Parker, Thomas Shepard, and John Norton

****

[25] Evans considers onlooks as characteristically possessing values, identifiable in their context, which are Commissive (involving an expression of personal commitment or involvement), Autobiographical (referring "both to behavior and to a way of looking"), Expressive (involving "various feelings"), Behabitive-postural (involving opinions and attitudes), and Verdictive (placing the "I" within a structure or scheme, or ascribing a status or function to "I"). Logic of Self-Involvement, p. 126.

[26] David Hall's treatment of early New England ministry in The Faithful Shepherd: A History of the New England Ministry in the Seventeenth Century is one of the finest, but his emphasis on the

who stressed the sacerdotal rank of the ministerial office and viewed the nature of the minister's authority as "superior" to that of the authority of laymen in a gathered church.[27] Edwards believes himself directly appointed by Christ to serve God and mankind in an office which carries with it "honour that is . . . in some respects greater than that of the Angels."[28] According to Edwards, the minister serves and participates, as do the angels, in preparing and purifying the church to be the holy bride of Christ. Ministers also participate, as the angels do not, in communal membership of the joyful, sanctified body to whom Christ will be united in spiritual marriage. Thus Edwards' complex ministerial role of representing God to mankind and mankind to God requires mixed, if not paradoxical, duties of him. In representing God, he must as a trumpet be confident, assertive, oracular. In representing mankind, he must as a sinner in profound need of salvation, be meek, submissive, and self-consciously humble.

The Minister's Role in the Church

Like the apostle Paul, Edwards views the minister as God's holy, ordained agent, fulfilling the highest possible office, devoted to

****
(Footnote 26 Continued From Previous Page)
"middle way" between a prophetic and sacerdotal ministry as a "vital presence" remaining in New England as part of the Reformed tradition, although correct, does not do full justice to the complexities of Edwards' vocational onlooks, pp. 4, 6, 9, 10.

[27]See Hall's Faithful Shepherd for a discussion on the history of England's debates and discussions on the relationship between church and minister and between ecclesiastical officers and lay brethren, pp. 102-120.

[28]Christ the Example of Ministers, Works (Hickman), II, p. 964.

matters of greatest importance to humans and to God. Says Edwards,
"Ministers are his messengers, sent forth by him; and, in their office
and administrations among their people, represent his person, stand in
his stead, as those that are sent to declare his mind, to do his work,
and to speak and act in his name."[29] Edwards looks on himself as God's
proxy, speaking "the mind and will of God."[30] In this vocational
onlook Edwards follows the position of Richard Baxter—to preach
faithfully is "to stand up in the face of a congregation and deliver a
message from the living God."[31] As he articulates the gospel, the
minister is God's mouth. Thus Edwards claims in Some Thoughts
Concerning the Revival, "Preaching of the Word of God is commonly
spoken of in Scripture in such expressions as seem to import a loud and
earnest speaking." When Christ is being brought forth in the church,
"Christ cries by his ministers . . . and 'tis worthy to be noted that
the word commonly used in the New Testament that we translate 'preach,'
properly signifies to proclaim aloud like a crier."[32] Speaking for
God, the minister reveals and defends God's just requirements for
humanity. He declares God's intentions in the work of redemption. He
warns of God's awful judgments against sin. He articulates God's
covenant promises and love to His saints. Speaking as God's agent
before a solemnly gathered auditory, the minister to whom God "has
committed his holy oracles"[33] makes God's momentous decrees audible and

****

[29] Farewell Sermon, Works (Hickman), I, ccxlv.

[30] Edwards uses this phrase repeatedly to designate what he believes
is the substance of his sermons. See his pair of sermons on The
Perpetuity and Change of the Sabbath, Works (Hickman), II, 93, 94, 96,
100, 101.

[31] The Reformed Pastor (New York, 1860), p. 75.

[32] Works (Yale), III, pp. 388-389.

[33] Jonathan Edwards, The Watchman's Duty and Account, Works (Dwight),
VII, 183.

unequivocal: the minister makes the obscure plain and the mysterious comprehensible.

As Christ in his ministry on earth spoke with authority and revealed the will of his Father, so ministers, appointed by Christ to stand in Christ's place, must confidently proclaim the gospel and carry on the work of redemption. We cannot overestimate the importance in Edwards' pastoral theology, of his assumption that Christ's earthly ministry is the visible, audible demonstration of the words and work He has since delegated to his ministerial ambassadors. Christ the Logos is the prototype of vital ministry and performative language; Christ is the Word which God speaks. Christ's word materializes in his deeds. His preaching, exhorting, teaching, and healing are magnificent in their authority. To his hearers Christ proclaimed, "Now ye are clean through the word which I have spoken unto you" (John 15:3). As Christ forcefully spoke to people, says Edwards, he "more clearly and abundantly revealed the mind and will of God than ever it had been revealed before."[34] Christ brought light into darkness, made visible what had been obscure, and made substantial what had been foreshadowed verbally and typically by the Old Testament prophets. The words Christ spoke on earth, says Edwards, "are God's words which union is the consequence of God's communicating his spirit without measure to [Christ's] human nature, so as to render it the same person with him that is God."[35] Christ compellingly declared doctrines and truths which were not only "the doctrines of God the Father, but his own doctrines."[36] Christ embodied the gospel, qualifying his statements

****

[34] Works (Hickman), I, p. 567.

[35] "Miscellanies" #764. All of Edwards' miscellanies have been transcribed by Thomas Schafer, the editor of the forthcoming volume of Miscellanies in the Yale series of Edwards Works. I am indebted to Thomas Schafer and the Beinecke Library for the use of the transcripts.

[36] Ibid., p. 576.

with nothing more than his complete integrity as the Word of God: "I say unto you," "This is my commandment," and "Verily, verily I say unto you." Christ's words are powerful and life-giving,[37] and as Christ's emissary, a minister cherishes, proclaims, and reenacts the Master's words of eternal life.

But not only does the minister actively declare and proclaim God's word. A minister also demonstrates the appropriate response to the word's power: "Ministers are to be ensamples, not only teachers."[38] God's word--sent into the world as the Logos, the Scriptures and the gospel ministry--as it is heard requires acknowledgement; that is, God not only desires "to have converse with us," but He also "hath commanded us. . . to have converse with him."[39] Thus, in the role of a representative believer, the minister responds as the people's "mouth to God."[40] In this capacity, the minister attempts to embody the humility and gratitude of the redeemed saint who submits to God's sovereignty. A contrite heart, true meekness, and religious affection in God's minister exemplify the right posture of creaturely dependence and reverence before the Creator. Accordingly, Edwards' sermons-- shaped by the traditional three-part Puritan sermon form[41]--focus, especially in the application, not only on what the word of God says but what it does as a force which creates, directs, and stimulates

****

[37]James Daane in Preaching with Confidence (Grand Rapids, Mich., 1980), p. 26, notes this power pointedly in his statement that "the Word itself creates its own hearing, as it once created its own world, by re-creating those through faith who once had no faith."

[38]Works (Hickman), II, 958.

[39]Works (Hickman), II, 945.

[40]The Sorrows of the Bereaved Spread Before Jesus, Works (Hickman), II, 967.

[41]The Puritan sermon form, used throughout the seventeenth and early eighteenth century in England and New England, was taught in Puritan divinity schools and described as early as 1592 by William

activity in the life of the believer. Demonstrating this principle at work within himself, Edwards' words in the application of the sermon Pressing into the Kingdom of God are responsive exclamations to the Lord: "Praised be the name of God that he has stirred you up . . . !" and "Glory be to his name!"[42] In acknowledging the power of the word of God, Edwards believes that congregations ought to follow the good examples of their pastors.[43]

In his warm praises and solemn, penitential gratitude addressed to the Heavenly Father who has condescended to gather wretched sinners as beloved children into his bosom, the minister leads the people in "converse" with God. The minister thus embodies an "evangelical obedience"[44] in his expressions of meekness and awakened love to God. And further, as Christ in his public ministry appeared obedient, humble, and responsive to His Father's will, resigning himself to God's redemption designs, so the minister by demonstrating these saintly excellencies teaches his people to imitate Christ in their approach to God. Edwards' role as a representative believer or "people's mouth to God" informs not only his sermon applications but also his

****

(Footnote 41 Continued From Previous Page)
Perkins. For a discussion of this form see W. Fraser Mitchell's English Pulpit Oratory (New York: Russell, Inc., 1962). Typically the Puritan sermon moved from Scripture to Doctrine to Application or, as Wilson Kimnach indicates, from "Holy Writ to abstract principle to personal values and actions, "Jonathan Edwards' Early Sermons: New York, 1722-23," in Journal of Presbyterian History, 55 (Fall 1977), p. 257.

[42] Works (Hickman), I, 659.

[43] See Works (Hickman), II, 855-866. The thrust of this sermon on Philippians 3:17 is that God appoints preachers "to be a pattern for Christians to follow" (855).

[44] Sabbath, Works (Hickman), II, 101.

congregational prayers which were generally <u>ex tempore</u>. According to
Samuel Hopkins' report, Edwards' public prayers were marked by "a
spirit of real and undissembled devotion," and his pious expressions to
God "were much to the acceptance and edification of those who joined
with him."[45]

Edwards' ministerial role is clearly pivotal, bringing together
and representing the holy deity and needful humans. "In the preaching
of the word, holy doctrines and the divine will are exhibited," says
Edwards in a sermon on worship; "in prayers and praise, and in the
attendance on the word and sacraments are represented our faith, love,
and obedience."[46]   Indeed, Edwards' sermons are on the one hand an
objectification or externalization of the spiritual world of God's will
and ideas.   On the other hand, they are a saint's expressive response
to God's perfection, an acknowledgement of God's sovereignty, beauty,
and justice.   Doctrinal exegesis and profound religious expression
together become the tenor and vehicle for Edwards' intensely personal
attempt to embody the ideal saint and ideal minister.

According to B. W. Anderson, "man's role . . . is to perform the
task which is given him by his Creator."[47] The enormous responsibility
of his ministerial task never fell lightly on Edwards. Thomas Prince,
an eighteenth-century ecclesiastical historian, remarks that Edwards in
the pulpit exuded an "habitual and great solemnity, looking and
speaking as in the presence of God, and with a weighty sense of the
matter delivered."[48]   His bearing signified his profound efforts not

****

[45]Cited in <u>Memoirs of Jonathan Edwards</u> by Sereno Dwight in <u>Works</u>
(Hickman), I, ccxxxii.

[46]<u>A Warning to Professors</u>, <u>Works</u> (Hickman), II, 186.

[47]"The Earth is the Lord's" <u>Interpretation</u> (1955), p. 15.

[48]<u>The Christian History</u> (Boston, n.d.), II, 390-91.

merely to balance the official functions of his ministerial role but to
embody them.   In this process, his language takes on "performative
force,"[49] for Edwards, like the New Testament apostles and writers,
believed that the ministry is enacted "especially [by] those who labour
in the word and doctrine" (I Timothy 5:17).   Words sent forth as
messages from God "are words which produce results, which are
established, verified, or performed, words which go out and do not
return empty-handed . . . ; such words could not reach their objective
without the help of God."[50]   In and through his official flow of words
--exhortations, admonitions, proclamations, invocations, publications
--Edwards vigorously exercises his role as God's ambassador, believing
that salvation comes to God's people in the word and ordinances, that
when God's word is preached, "then is the likeliest time to have the
Spirit accompanying it."[51]   Accordingly, in the following discussions,
we will view Edwards' preaching as practice, his sermons and writings
as deeds.   Clearly Edwards' words are his actions.

The Minister's Role as Christ's Workman

   In The History of the Work of Redemption--a series of 30 sermons
preached in 1739 and published posthumously--and in Christ the Great
Example of Gospel Ministers Edwards makes explicit his belief that

****
[49]Evans, "The Performative Force of Language" in Logic of Self-
Involvement, pp. 26-78.

[50]G. B. Cairn in "The Biblical Doctrine of the Word" cited by
D. Evans in Logic, pp. 163-164.

[51]Perpetuity and Change of the Sabbath, Works (Hickman), II, 103.

Christ's work of redemption is "the most important of all his works."[52] Christ expressly established the office of gospel minister shortly after his resurrection when he appeared to his followers, "commissioning and sending forth his apostles to teach and baptise."[53] As it proceeds through history, this gospel ministry is, according to Edwards, the cohesive strength of the church, or, as Calvin had called it, "the chief sinew" of the church.[54]

The ministry of redemption begins with Christ and continues in and through all the other messengers Christ calls to be his co-laborers. Says Edwards: "Christ called many disciples, whom he employed as ministers. He sent seventy at one time in this work: but there were twelve that were set apart as apostles, who were the grand ministers of his kingdom, and as it were the twelve foundations of his church. . . . These were the main instruments of setting up his kingdom in the world."[55] Edwards notes that "this commission which Christ gives to his apostles, in the most essential parts of it, belongs to all ministers; and the apostles by virtue of it, were ministers or elders of the church."[56] Clearly, it is from the highest and holiest source that apostles and pastors receive their authority in "respect to that

****

[52] History of Redemption in Works (Hickman), I, 616; Christ the Example (Hickman), II, 964.

[53] (Hickman), I, 586.

[54] Institutes of the Christian Religion, ed. John T. McNeill, trans. Ford Lewis Battles (Philadelphia, 1960), II, Bk. IV, chap. iii, sec. 2, cited hereafter as Calvin, Institutes (II), IV.iii.2.

[55] (Hickman), I, 577.

[56] Ibid., I, 586. Here Edwards seems to be acknowledging a narrow sense of the term "apostle" without denying the broader use of the term. Edwards here follows the pattern used by Paul who, as Adolf Harnack explains in The Mission and Expansion of Christianity (New York, 1960), "holds fast to the wider conception of the apostolate, but the twelve disciples form in his view its original nucleus." However, while the primitive usage of "apostle" indicates that the

great errand"[57] of gospel ministry to God's people.

In performing their "great errand" for God, Christ's apostles and ministers serve as the primary guardians of the means of grace—God's ordinances relating to sabbath, public worship, sacraments, and preaching of the word. Mandated by Christ, the early church apostles and leaders established these means of grace during the post-resurrection age of gospel light. In this great age of apostolic leadership, many "dispensations of Providence"[58]—miracles, inspired writings, missionary travels, pentecostal gifts, numerous conversions—distinguished Christ's ministers as remarkable agents in extending God's kingdom and advancing the work of redemption. Speaking in behalf of Christ, the spirit-filled apostles instituted the Christian sabbath as "the day of the week on which Christ arose" and thus "the day of the church's holy rejoicing to the end of the world."[59] Further, the apostles, and especially Paul, who calls himself an apostle in addition to "the twelve" mentioned in Acts 1, were the vocal agents in abolishing burdensome Jewish ceremonial laws in order to promote "a church of God dwelling in all parts of the world."[60]

But most important, the original apostles had observed the particulars of Christ's redeeming work and had walked and lived with

----

****

(Footnote 56 Continued From Previous Page)
narrow and broad conception of the term existed side by side, Harnack notes that the narrower sense generally dominated, although in the second century some of the church fathers did bear the title of apostle, pp. 322-323.

[57](Hickman), I, 961.

[58]Works (Hickman), I, 584.

[59]Ibid., 586.

[60]Ibid.

Christ; Paul had seen and heard Christ in the Damascus road experience. It was to the apostles that Christ revealed the meaning of his life, death, resurrection, and ascension in accomplishing the salvation, reconciliation, and justification of sinful creatures before God. To the apostles came infallible guidance in understanding the dim Old Testament foreshadowings and prophecies which had previously been hidden under a veil of types and shadows. During Christ's life and especially in the events of his death and resurrection, the apostles beheld the very substance of the doctrines of redemption "fully and plainly."[61] They saw and heard the Logos; consequently they were made the inspired "penmen of the Scriptures," to proclaim "for all ages"[62] Christ the visible, performative Word through whom "the vail [sic] of the temple is rent from top to bottom. Christ the antetype of Moses, shines; his face is without a vail . . . . Now these glorious mysteries, which were in a great measure kept secret from the foundation of the world, are clearly revealed."[63]

Describing the work of the early "grand ministers" and "foundations of the church," Edwards demonstrates a strong sense of kinship with them. Like them, he has experienced the "providential dispensation" of being called by God at a time and place where Christ's church is being awakened in an "extraordinary" manner.

Indeed, Edwards' apostolic identifications and sensibility accord with his theological insistence that all ministers principally receive their personal call and commission directly from Christ,[64] not from a

****

[61]Works (Hickman), I, 587.

[62]Sermon on Philippians 3:17 (February 1740) in Works (Hickman), II, 864.

[63](Hickman), I, 587.

[64]We recall that Edwards in History of Redemption said the "commission which Christ gives to his apostles, in the most essential parts of it, belong to all ministers." Works (Hickman), I, 577.

human agency or organized church. Edwards, following Calvin,[65]
believes that ministers _first_ receive an inward call to ministry from
the Savior; this call is only confirmed outwardly by the congregation
that calls and ordains a minister into a public exercise of his Christ-
appointed office. Edwards here differs with the Catholic church's
doctrine of apostolic succession. In History of Redemption he
disclaims the tradition among Catholic Christians that the pope is
"Christ's viceregent on earth" invested with "the very same power that
Christ would have [claimed], if he was present on earth reigning on his
throne."[66]   Edwards likewise strongly disapproved of the successive,
perpetuated ordinations of bishops in the Anglican church, and most
recently for him, the authority the English bishops represented to the
Connecticut Congregational ministers who seceded to the Episcopal
church in 1722.

Always fearful of humanly-devised hierarchies which might deny the
personal spirit and proclamation of Christ's call to ministers, Edwards
in "Miscellanies" #40 gives clear indication of his uneasiness toward
ecclesiastical power structures that might serve man rather than God.

> 'Tis a thousand pities that the world's church office and
> power should so tear the world to pieces and raise such a
> fog and dust about apostolic office, power, and succession,
> pope's, bishop's, and presbyter's power. It is not such a
> desperately difficult thing to know what power belongs to
> each of these, if we will let drop those words that are
> without fixed meanings [that is, meaning fixed by
> Scriptures].[67]

****

[65]Institutes (II), IV.iii.11.

[66](Hickman), I, p. 595.

[67]"Miscellanies" entry #40 on "ministers," in The Philosophy of
Jonathan Edwards from His Private Notebooks, ed. Harvey G. Townsend
(Eugene, Oregon, 1955), p. 200.

In his concern for searching out biblically-constituted and God-ordained principles for the ministerial office, Edwards stands close to Calvin, who remarked that "in indiscriminately calling those who rule the church 'bishops,' 'presbyters,' 'pastors,' and 'ministers,' I did so according to the Scriptural usage, which interchanges these terms. For to all who carry out the ministry of the Word it accords the title of 'bishops'."[68]

Many more connections between Edwards and Calvin come to light in a study of the historic doctrines of ecclesiastical office and ministerial authority. Following Calvin in the Reformed tradition, Edwards defines ministers as selected by God to be His special officers. In A Warning to Professors Edwards asserts that "when the word is preached by authorized ministers, they speak in God's name, as Christ's ambassadors."[69] According to Calvin, God "uses the ministry of men . . . as a sort of delegated work . . . that through their mouth he may do his own work."[70] Says Calvin in the Institutes, "This human ministry which God uses to govern the church is the chief sinew by which believers are held together in one body . . . . Through the ministers to whom he has entrusted this office and has conferred the grace to carry it out, he dispenses and distributes his gifts to the church."[71]

In describing the ministerial task as a lofty and awesome one, Calvin notes that "God often commended the dignity of the ministry by all possible marks of approval in order that it might be held among us

****

[68]Institutes (II), IV.iii.8.

[69]Works (Hickman), II, 186.

[70]An Harmony of the Confessions of the Faith of the Christian and Reformed Churches (London, 1586), 186.

[71](II), IV.iii.3.

in highest honor and esteem, even as the most excellent of all things."[72] Edwards likewise elevates the office of ministry: "the work that ministers are called and devoted to, is no other than the work of Christ, or the work Christ does," and thus "the honour that is put upon faithful ministers is, in some respects, greater than that of the angels."[73] Edwards also follows Calvin's view that in governing the church and holding it together, the minister in his sinewy role of leadership among the officers of the church acts on God's behalf in admitting persons to membership in the church: "the officers of the church when they admit are to act in the name of God in admitting; to them are committed the keys of the kingdom of heaven . . . and what they do is done in heaven."[74] As God's agents to the church, ministers are especially chosen to reveal God's secret mind and will, to protect and build the church, and to bring unity among believers. In Edwards' theology of ministry, there is no doubt that "when a true minister preaches, he speaks as the oracles of God, . . . and he is to be heard as one representing Christ."[75]

Edwards' doctrines of ministry hold the gospel minister to be a principal interpreter or steward of God's word for the church and the world. Speaking "as the oracles of God" in their commission to preach the full gospel, ministers are painstakingly to search the Scriptures they are especially chosen to safeguard and transmit to God's people. Theirs is the task of uncovering the spiritual wonders behind the "images or shadows of divine things." Edwards accepts as a vocational

****

[72]Commentaries on the Epistles of Paul the Apostle to the Corinthians, trans. John Pringle (Edinburgh, 1848-1849), II, 172.

[73]Christ the Example of Ministers, Works (Hickman), II, 964.

[74]"Miscellanies" #689. Early 1736 is the date suggested by Thomas Schafe

[75]A Warning, Works (Hickman), II, 186.

directive the biblical text he includes in <u>The True Excellency of a</u>
<u>Gospel Minister</u>[76]: "Therefore every scribe which is instructed unto
the kingdom of heaven is like unto a man that is a householder, which
bringeth forth out of his treasure things new and old" (Matthew 13:52).
The minister is to bring to light the full, original treasure and
riches contained in God's Word; he is not to develop groundless
doctrines or ingenuous schemes. Consequently, in commenting on the
extraordinary stirrings among the people of Northampton, Edwards
insists that in his preaching "there were no new doctrines embraced,
but people have been abundantly established in those that we account
orthodox."[77]

As a student of divinity and searcher of the Word of God, the
gospel minister becomes expert in "that science of doctrine which
comprehends all those truths and rules which concern the great business
of religion."[78] Thus enlightened, he harvests the Scripture, labouring
reverently to bring its ancient biblical truths and realities to new
apprehension, its eternal doctrines to timely expression. According to
Edwards' understanding of the threshing metaphor which he acknowledges
in the margin of his interleaved Bible, God's minister's "chief work"[79]
is to mill the precious kernels of biblical truth, removing them from
the obscuring husks or "veils" of their historic, cultural matrix. The
preacher in this way makes God's truths palatable and nourishing for

****

[76]<u>Works</u> (Hickman), II, 955.

[77]May 30, 1735, letter to Rev. Dr. Benjamin Colman, pastor of the
Brattle Street Church in Boston, in <u>Great Awakening</u>, ed., C. C. Goen
(New Haven, 1972), p. 108.

[78]<u>Importance and Advantage of a Thorough Knowledge of Divine Truth</u>,
<u>Works</u> (Dwight), IV, 1-3.

[79]Along the margin of p. 814 of Edwards' interleaved Bible, he
comments relative to I Cor. 9:9 that a minister's preaching "the Word
of God" serves "as it were [to] bring out that spiritual food from the

the salvation of the souls in his keeping.

Along the margin of his Bible, Edwards also observes that the most important "business and labours of a minister of the gospel" is "to explain and apply the word of God to his hearers."[80] This revealing and applying the word is essential to spiritual growth and sanctification, for "the Scriptures, in all their parts," notes Edwards, "were made for the use of the church here on earth."[81] Revelation is a dynamic process: "God will, by degrees, unveil their [the Scriptures'] meaning to his church . . . that his church might make progress in the understanding of it . . . and in unfolding its mysteries."[82] Moreover, the performative power of Scripture when read, studied, and applied produces an irresistible pull, a peculiar spell, or in Edwards' words, "a strange and unaccountable kind of enchantment, if I may so speak, . . . that we seem to be actually present; and we invisibly fancy, not that we are readers, but spectators, yea, actors in the business."[83] As the minister-spectator unveils the Bible's mysteries and both reveals and applies them, he becomes through his performative utterances, his preaching and writing, a devout "actor in the business." He becomes God's lively and authoritative means of grace, strengthening the foundation and enlarging the membership of Christ's kingdom.

****

(Footnote 79 Continued From Previous Page)
veil or husk it is wrapped up in on the plant whereon it grew, that it might be fitted for our use." This Bible is in the Edwards MSS collection at Beinecke.

[80]P. 814 of the interleaved Bible in the Beinecke Edwards MSS Collection.

[81]"Miscellaneous Observations," Works (Hickman), II, 474.

[82]Ibid., 474.

[83]Ibid.

The Minister's Role in Society

Edwards' theology of ministry, then, explores the minister's calling and work in the church of Christ and also attempts to interpret the pastoral office within a societal setting. As noted earlier, in The Nature of True Virtue Edwards points to the "beauty of order in society . . . as when the different members of society have all their appointed office, place and station according to their several capacities and talents."[84] Edwards' conceptions of his ministerial office exercised in an eighteenth-century colonial culture reflect his complex vocational onlooks and the immediate tensions he experienced in representing both God and the souls in his charge in a time of social change and intellectual enlightenment.

Fundamentally, Edwards believed that gospel ministers "especially are the officers of Christ's kingdom, who, above all other men upon earth, represent his person."[85] This definition comes exceedingly close to John Calvin's view that "from among men [God] takes some to serve as his ambassadors in the world, to be interpreters of his secret will and, in short, to represent his person."[86] There are more than two centuries between Calvin's and Edwards' ministerial statements, yet both project an essentially elitist view of ministry's importance and status. But, much had occurred between the time of Calvin and Edwards to modify the minister's social position. The Bible was no longer read and interpreted exclusively by clergy; the latitudinarian impulses in American Protestantism accentuated the Reformation view that Christian vocation is not unique to ministers; traditional hierarchical class

****

[84] Works (Hickman), I, 129.

[85] Some Thoughts on the Revival in Works (Hickman), I, 387.

[86] Institutes (II), IV.iii.1.

structures were disappearing among the colonial landowners, while
merchants, artisans, and tradespeople were gaining conspicuous wealth
and political power.

In eighteenth-century New England, colonists were increasingly
resenting the traditional pastoral office in its role as a "speaking
Aristocracy in the face of a silent Democracy."[87]   A fundamentally
democratic society was beginning to call into question the minister's
privileged relationships to God and mankind, and to ignore the
minister's patriarchal insistence that people for their own good "were
obliged to hear"[88] their minister's words.   Arminian theology and
Enlightment philosophy were at this time encouraging the attitude that
souls needed not so much to heed their "spiritual fathers" as to
develop their own natural gifts and reason so as to be worthy of
salvation.

Assessing current cultural developments as well as traditional
doctrines of ministry, Edwards endeavors on the one hand to stress the
pastor's authoritative ecclesiastical office and on the other hand to
discover a ministerial position which minimizes a wide spiritual
division between individual believers and the pastor who cares for
their souls.   Edwards indeed asserts in his ministry that all souls are
totally depraved and equally in need of grace.   Thus in a peculiar way
salvation is democratic and experiential.   A person's "new sense of the
heart" is a personal, inner experience that recognizes no distinctions
of rank, class, race, age, or sex.[89]   And as each person must finally

****

[87] Samuel Stone's description of Congregational church government,
as cited by Cotton Mather in Magnalia Christi Americana (London, 1702,
ed. Hartford, 1853-5), I, 437.

[88] Edwards' "Miscellanies" entry #40, The Philosophy of Jonathan
Edwards, ed., Townsend, p. 200.

[89] Perry Miller remarks in The Puritans, ed. Perry Miller and
Thomas H. Johnson (New York, 1938), p. 17, that the American frontier
conspired "to lessen the prestige of the cultured classes and to

give his or her own account before God, each must hear or forbear the word of God for himself or herself: "it is every man's business to choose that food which he thinks to be best for his eternal welfare." In fact, in Edwards' view congregations as well as individuals must have the freedom to choose their own pastor, "that feeder that will give the food wherewith they will be best fed."[90] For, says Edwards, "ministers are not properly Governours but only leaders, are not to make new Laws but only to teach Christ's laws."[91] Yet at the same time that he earnestly espouses lay responsibility, Edwards also insists that the minister's authority must not be ignored or denigrated. Though the minister operates within a societal context, he has authority rooted in the Word Himself, and unlike civil and temporal authority, ministerial authority ultimately transcends the here and now to be distinctly recognized and rewarded in Christ's heavenly kingdom.

Each saint, Edwards believes, has direct, immediate fellowship and communion with God.[92] But at the same time ministers are God's visible, audible means of grace, ordained for the benefit of God's kingdom as are the Scriptures, the Sabbath, and the sacraments. As the

****
(Footnote 89 Continued From Previous Page)
enhance the social power of those who wanted their religion in a more simple, downright, and 'democratic' form, who cared nothing for the refinements and subtleties of historic theology." But it was not, explains Miller, until the growing social and religious foment of the Great Awakening that the traditional conception of the aristocratic, learned, and patriarchal minister was overtly denounced by popular leaders who represented those seeking to be liberated from the controls of the theologically trained.

[90]"Miscellanies" entry qq ministers, Beinecke, Edwards MSS Collection.

[91]"Miscellanies" entry 10 Pastors, Beinecke, Edwards MMS Collection.

[92]With its insistence on immediate access to God and to God's Word, the Puritan brand of iconoclasm in the interest of godly living opened the way to eliminate creeds, church order, liturgy, and even

Bible constitutes the basis for Edwards' performative word and aura of
authority, the scriptural mandate that ministers are to represent God
takes priority over their task of representing God's people.   In
emulating the biblical prophets and preachers, Edwards denounces, as
any Isaiah or Amos speaking for God would denounce, current social
evils—tavern-haunting, gaming, materialism, desecrating the Sabbath,
and malicious gossip.[93]   But to colonial parishioners stimulated by
democratic   and   individualistic   values,   Edwards'   patriarchal,
authoritarian tones eventually became unacceptable and abrasive.   What
William T. Youngs, Jr., indicates generally regarding the eighteenth-
century clergy applies specifically to Edwards.   "Inevitably," says
Youngs, "the clergymen lost the central position they had occupied in
early Puritan society."[94]   The mounting challenges to ministerial
accountability and the steadily increasing egalitarian social climate
suggest that the colonists were interested in leadership which would
primarily represent them.   It is within this context of changing social
values that Edwards continues in his attempt to define the meaning and
dimensions of the office he held sacred.

The Minister's Role in Redemptive History

Edwards' 1739 sermon series on the history of redemption expressly
and repeatedly comments not only on the minister's duties relative to
****

(Footnote 92 Continued From Previous Page)
ministers. The "same informed skepticism that undermined prevailing
forms and rituals," says Harry S. Stout, "would, in the final analysis
turn on Scripture itself" and the guardians of Scripture. "Puritanism
Considered as a Profane Movement," Christian Scholars Review, 10,
(1980), p. 19.

[93]See The Justice of God in the Damnation of Sinners, Works
(Hickman), I, 671, for a catalogue of what Ola Winslow calls "the
Seven Deadlies in village dress," Jonathan Edwards, p. 162.

[94]God's Messengers: Religions Leadership in Colonial New England,

the church and to society but also on the minister's official, integral
part in God's great design for the history of the world. As Edwards in
his theology of ministry persistently traces the origins of ministry
back to the biblical examples of prophets and teachers and especially
New Testament ministers, he often seems to view his own ministry as a
vocation larger and more apostolic than that of a local pastor and
keeper of souls. Already in one of his earliest "miscellanies"--#40
written in 1723--Edwards explores the ranges of ministerial power, the
extent to which official performative utterance can operate. This
miscellany is a central passage to consider in understanding Edwards'
apostolic vision and his relationship to the power of God's word:

> Without doubt, ministers are to teach men what Christ
> would have them to do and to teach them who doth these
> things and who doth them not; that is, who are Christians
> and who are not; and the people are to hear them as much in
> this as in other things; and so far forth as the people are
> obliged to hear what I teach them, so great is my pastoral,
> or ministerial, or teaching power. And this is all the dif-
> ference of power there is amongst ministers, whether
> apostles or whatever.
>
> Thus if I in a right manner am become the teacher of a
> people so far as they ought to hear what I teach them, so
> much power I have. Thus if they are obliged to hear me only
> because they themselves have chosen me to guide them, and
> therein declared that they thought me sufficiently instructed

****
(Footnote 94 Continued From Previous Page)
1700-1750 (Baltimore, 1976), p. 9. Youngs treats the tensions between
ministry's high religious ideals and its fear of popular disrespect,
the tensions between its movements to kindle spiritual renewal and its
self-interested movements to promote the ministerial profession as a
prestigious office, pp. 69, 96, and 112.

in the mind of Christ to teach them, and because I have the
other requisites of being their teacher, then I have power
as other ministers have in these days. But if it was plain
to them that I was under the infallible guidance of Christ,
then I should have more power. And if it was plain to all
the world of Christians that I was under the infallible
guidance of Christ, and I was sent forth to teach the world
the will of Christ, then I should have power in all the
world. I should have power to teach them what they ought to
do, and they would be obliged to hear me; I should have
power to teach them who were Christian and who not, and in
this likewise they would be obliged to hear me.[95]

Some critics see this entry as an early indication of a hunger for
power which would eventually erode Edwards' relations with his
Northamption parish.[96]   Some describe it as a youthful fantasy or
daydream.[97]   But primarily it is a serious consideration of the high
calling Edwards as a minister experiences, a calling from Christ
superior to that which he would receive from the people or congregation
who "have chosen me to guide them, and therein declared that they
thought me sufficiently instructed in the mind of Christ to teach them,
and because I have the other requisites of being their teacher."   In
"Miscellanies" #40 and in The History of the Work of Redemption Edwards
seems to be saying that genuine power to minister in the apostolic age
or any age is that power which occurs when a minister submits himself
wholly to Christ's call and authority.   Thus the most profound
ministerial challenge is to be so obedient and susceptible a vehicle in
****

[95] Philosophy of Jonathan Edwards, ed. Townsend, p. 200.

[96] Patricia Tracy, Jonathan Edwards, Pastor, p. 65.

[97] Wilson Kimnach, "The Literary Techniques of Jonathan Edwards,"
p. 26.

God's work of redemption that the self is entirely under "the
infallible guidance of Christ." Then God's word in the mouth of a
minister becomes, as it was in the mouths of the Old Testament prophets
and the New Testament apostles, a veritable declaration of God's mind
and will at a particular historic juncture.[98]   Then truly it is
Christ's active, living Word proclaimed with authority to the church,
the country, and the world through the voice and words of the minister,
which "they [people] should be obliged to hear." As a context for
Edwards' apostolic tendencies, Calvin's comments on ministerial offices
are relevant.   Calvin's Institutes lists the offices of apostle,
prophet, evangelist, pastor, and teacher, according to Ephesians 4:11,
adding that only pastors and teachers have "an ordinary office in the
church."[99]   The other three are "extraordinary"[100] offices which "the
Lord raised up at the beginning of his Kingdom, and now and again
revives them as the need of the times requires."[101]   Edwards'
"Miscellanies" #40 indicates that already very early in his ministry he
envisioned himself, as the need of the times might require, in the role
of a latter-day apostle. He yearned to be filled with the holiness and
power necessary to guide the eighteenth century church beleaguered by
heresy, secularism, materialism, deism, and all those other devilishly
perverse spirits darkening human understanding of "what Christ would

****

[98]We might note here that Ronald Osborne, who defines an apostle
as one "sent into the world" to "sound forth the demands of the divine
will," includes Edwards in a catalog of apostles ranging from Clement
of Alexandria, Origin, Augustine, Jerome, John of Damascus, and
Aquinas to Luther, Melanchthon, Calvin, Schleiermacher, Harnack,
Barth, Tillich, and Bonhoeffer, In Christ's Place (St. Louis, 1967),
p. 71.

[99](II), IV.iii.4.

[100]Ibid.

[101]Ibid. It should be noted how repeatedly Edwards uses the words
"extraordinary" and "extraordinarily" in his references to the New
England awakenings he urged, prayed for, and rejoiced in. In Edwards'

have them to do" and dimming their sense of "who are Christians and who
are not."

The apostolic quality of Edwards' vision certainly influenced his
ministerial activities. He traveled and preached widely beyond his
Northampton parish. He corresponded extensively with church leaders at
home and abroad. He nurtured ambitious plans to write "a body of
divinity in an entire new method, being thrown into the form of a
history."[102] He published sermons, doctrinal treatises, and Great
Awakening accounts directed far beyond a merely local readership.
There is little doubt that Edwards viewed the church, the New England
colonies, and indeed the eighteenth-century world to be in profound
need of a fearless, orthodox voice raised to speak out in the role
Calvin defined as apostolic: "No set limits are allotted to [apostles]
but the whole earth is assigned to them to bring into obedience to
Christ, in order that by spreading the gospel wherever they can among
the nations, they may raise up his Kingdom everywhere."[103] Though
Calvin considered the extraordinary ministry of the apostles generally
to have lapsed after the early Christian church was established, he did
not hesitate to say in a reference to Luther that "the Lord has
sometimes at a later period raised up apostles, . . . as has happened
in our own day."[104] In the eyes of many eighteenth-century believers
and at times in his own eyes Edwards seemed indeed to wear the mantle
of an apostle.

****
(Footnote 101 Continued From Previous Page)
The Distinguishing Marks (Boston, 1741), reprinted in The Great
Awakening, ed. C. C. Goen (New Haven, 1972), for example,
"extraordinary" appears four times in one paragraph, p. 229.

[102]Letter to the Princeton trustees, October 19, 1757, Works,
(Hickman).

[103]Institutes (II), IV.iii.4.

[104]Institutes (II), IV.ii.4. John McNeill, editor of the Institutes,
indicates that Calvin often praises Luther, in Corpus Reformatorum

Most of Edwards' contemporaries recognized in him a spiritual leadership of intellectual force and profundity practically without equal in his time.[105]   His detractors believed his views to be schismatic, "enthusiastic," or obsolete.   But his admirers during the height of the Great Awakening and afterward freely compared the "extraordinary" events of the Connecticut Valley revivals to the spiritual activities in the apostolic age.   In their Preface to the first edition of Edwards' A Faithful Narrative of Surprising Conversions (London, 1737), Rev. Isaac Watts and John Guyse praised the author and described his written acccount in glowing, superlative language: "never did we hear or read, since the first ages of Christianity, any event of this kind so surprising as the present narrative hath set before us."[106]   Subsequently, in his Preface to Edwards' Distinguishing Marks (Boston, 1741) William Cooper suggests that "the apostolic times seem to have returned upon us."   Cooper also remarks that a contemporary version of the book of Acts could appear under the direction of Edwards if "those who have been conversant in this work, in one place and another, would transmit accounts of it to

****
(Footnote 104 Continued From Previous Page)
calling him "a distinguished apostle of Christ by whose ministry the light of the gospel has shown." See Institutes (II), footnote on p. 1057.

[105]George Whitefield, James Davenport, Gilbert Tennent, and other revivalist preachers were more colorful and widely-traveled than Edwards, but Edwards was far more theologically profound than any of his contemporaries. Timothy Dwight (1752-1817), articulated the belief of many when he said that, in his opinion, Edwards' History of Redemption and his treatise on God's last end in the creation of the world contain an "intellectual sublimity" and "vast and elevated conception of truth" of which "since the days of the apostles there has been no rival," Travels in New England and New York, ed. Barbara Miller Solomon (Cambridge, 1969), IV, 230.

[106]The Great Awakening, C. C. Goen, ed., p. 130.

such a hand as the reverend author of this discourse, to be compiled.
. . . I can't but think it would be one of the most useful pieces of
church history the people of God are blessed with. Perhaps it would
come the nearest to the Acts of the Apostles of anything extant."[107]
And Sereno Edwards Dwight (1786-1850), author and compiler of The
Memoirs of Jonathan Edwards, has highest praise for Edwards as "one of
the most successful preachers since the days of the apostles."[108]
Dwight indicates: "We know of no writer, since the days of the
apostles, who has better comprehended the word of God, who has more
fully unfolded the nature and design of the revelation of [God's] mind,
which it contains."[109]

Edwards' apostolic bent and his theology of ministry give him
great confidence in the Holy Spirit's working through him, not to
reveal new doctrines or decrees but to aid him in understanding the
mind and will of God and to advance Christ's kingdom on earth. This
certitude colors his interpretations of "God's grand design" in
redemption and the minister's crucial part in it.   In History of
Redemption Edwards observes that there are "four successive great
events" in the setting up of the kingdom of Christ."[110] Each of the
first three--the apostolic times, the glorious time of Constantine, and
the destruction of Antichrist--is "a lively image, or type, of the
fourth and last event, viz. Christ's coming in the final judgment."[111]
Each of the first three, as well as the climactic fourth, is

****
[107](Hickman), II, pp. 258 and 260.

[108]Ibid., pp. 224-225.

[109]Works (Hickman), I, ccxxxii and ccxxxix.

[110]Works (Hickman), I, 584.

[111]Ibid.

accompanied by a glorious "spiritual resurrection of the church." And, as in the last judgment the angels will sound their trumpets to gather the elect, so "each of the preceding spiritual ingatherings [will be] effected by the trumpet of the gospel, sounded by the ministers of Christ."[112]

History as "the establishing of the Kingdom of Christ" is for Edwards not only linear but clearly typical and figural. Between the eventful ministry of the apostolic age and the revivals of his own age he sees notable continuity and connections. The events of his own day are rooted in and are a fulfillment of the types of the preceding ages at the same time these eighteenth-century events foreshadow the final "spiritual resurrection of Christ's church." The glorious design of holy history can only be seen as it gradually unfolds. Each age builds progressively on the knowledge God reveals to it. Until Christ came into the world, says Edwards, "the grand mystery had been kept secret from ages and generations, from men and angels from the beginning of the world."[113] But now, "in these days of the world, much more of [the history of redemption] is discovered than had been in preceding ages."[114] With these cumulative revelations come both increased receptivity and increased resistance to the work of the Holy Spirit. Conscious that there are many detractors and harsh critics of "The Late Wonderful Pouring Out of the Spirit of God,"[115] Edwards reminds the awakened saints that they must persevere against the threats of anti-christian forces until the great millennial peace is introduced and

****

[112]Ibid.

[113]Stephen Stein, editor of Edwards' *Apocalyptic Writings* (New Haven, 1977) cites this passage in a footnote on p. 51, indicating that the passage comes from Edwards' "Blank Bible" p. 478.

[114]*Apocalyptic Writings*, p. 51.

[115]The cited phrase appears in the subtitle of Edwards' *Discourse on Various Important Subjects, early Concerning the Great Affair of*

signalled by the world's extraordinary receptivity to the preaching of
gospel ministers. In fact, in a highly evocative comment Edwards notes
his belief that the current revivals may be the beginnings of the
millennial peace and the demise of the Antichrist: "We know not where
this pouring out of the Spirit shall begin, or whether in many places
at once; or whether, what hath already taken place [in the 1735
awakening in Northampton and environs], be not some forerunner and
beginning of it."[116]

     To Edwards' mind, the witness of Christ and his apostles to a
notoriously apathetic and degenerate time in Jewish history stands as a
powerful example for eighteenth-century ministers confronting an
apostate, heresy-infested church. Edwards notes that "there probably
were more souls converted in the age of the apostles, than had ever
been before from the beginning of the world till that time."[117]
Emphasizing the parallels between the early church and the eighteenth-
century church, Edwards in History of Redemption points to the
apostolic ministry as it had brought gospel light to a time of great
darkness, and then reminds his congregation that "it is now a very dark
time with respect to interest of religion, wherein there is but a
little faith, and a great prevailing of infidelity on the earth."[118]
He also remarks tellingly that "just before" the apocalyptic work of
God, "it will be a very dark time with respect to the interests of
religion in the world."[119] Further signs of the beginnings of God's

****
(Footnote 115 Continued From Previous Page)
the Soul's Eternal Salvation (Boston, 1738).

[116]History of the Work of Redemption in Works (Hickman), I, 605.

[117]Ibid., 588.

[118]Ibid., 605 (emphasis is Edwards').

[119]Ibid.

"appointed day of peace" will be that "the Spirit of God shall be gloriously poured out for the wonderful revival and propagation of religion,"[120] an outpouring which shall "soon bring multitudes to forsake that vice and wickedness which now so generally prevails; and shall cause that vital religion, . . . now so despised and laughed at in the world, to revive."[121] In 1739 Edwards was cautiously hinting that the New England revivals might be the beginning of the millennium: "We know not . . . whether what hath already taken place, be not some forerunner." By 1742, in Some Thoughts Edwards is far more direct in expressing his optimism: "'Tis not unlikely that this work of God's Spirit, that is so extraordinary and wonderful, is the dawning, or at least a prelude of that glorious work of God, so often foretold in Scripture, which in the progress and issue of it, shall renew the world of mankind."[122] Without doubt, Edwards believes God is using New England ministers to build God's kingdom much as He had used the New Testament apostles at an earlier time of profound movement in the church's redemptive history.

Lest anyone in Northampton Church listening to Edwards' interpretation of world history in the History of the Work of Redemption still be uncertain of the role and authority of ministers in the coming "appointed day" of Christ's peace on earth, Edwards insists that at the glorious time of millennial awakening "the gospel shall be preached with abundantly greater clearness and power than had heretofore been. This great work of God shall be brought to pass by the preaching of the gospel." These events will occur as "God's Spirit

****
[120]Ibid.

[121]Ibid.

[122]Some Thoughts Concerning the Revival in The Great Awakening, ed. C. C. Goen, p. 353.

shall be poured out first to raise up instruments, and then those
instruments shall be used with success."[123] To accomplish his great
redemptive design, God will fill ministers "with knowledge and wisdom,
and fervent zeal for the promoting of the kingdom of Christ, and the
salvation of souls, and propagating the gospel in the world."[124] In a
continual, incremental, and reciprocal effect, kindled preachers will
serve as a gracious means of kindling listeners whose hunger for the
gospel will further kindle preachers to rejoice in revealing the
secrets of God's will: "there shall be a glorious pouring out of the
Spirit with this clear and powerful preaching of the gospel, to make it
successful . . . for bringing vast multitudes savingly home to
Christ."[125]

Edwards' Role As A Reformer

    In his lofty view of the minister and in his intense interest in
God's providential movements revealed in Scripture and in history,
Edwards belongs to the continuing spirit of the Reformation. As with
every important theologian before him, however, Edwards thoroughly
assesses rather than uncritically accepts the tradition from which he
came. In the Preface of Freedom of the Will he acknowledges himself a
Calvinist, but adds, "I utterly disclaim a dependence on Calvin, or
believing the doctrines which I hold, because he believed and taught;
and cannot justly be charged with believing in every thing just as he
taught."[126] Likewise in the Preface to An Humble Inquiry he asserts,
****
[123]History of Redemption (Hickman), I, 605.

    [124]Ibid.

    [125]Ibid.

    [126]A Careful and Strict Inquiry into the Modern Prevailing Notions
of that Freedom of Will, Works (Hickman), I, 2.

as his grandfather Stoddard before him had "asserted this scriptural and protestant maxim, that we ought to call no man on earth master, or make the authority of the greatest and holiest of mere men the ground of our belief of any doctrine in religion."[127]

Calling no man master, Edwards pursues a course of study which primarily and carefully seeks the Spirit's guidance in developing a continuing dialectic between the Old and New Testaments. Perceiving the gospel minister to be a discoverer of spiritual mysteries, Edwards recommends and clearly exercises an approach to biblical truths and secrets which might well be considered his paradoxical hermeneutic method: the Bible is both plainspoken and mysterious; only when one grasps the meaning of the Old Testament types, figures, and events can one fully comprehend the New Testament, but only through the New Testament Word can one penetrate the shadowy significations of the Old. Viewing the Old and New Testaments in their symbiotic relationships clarifies and magnifies the beauty of God's "grand design and glorious scheme of providence from the beginning of the world." This in turn glorifies Christ by intensifying the believer's awe of "how great a person then must He be, for whose coming the great God of heaven and earth, and Governor of all things, spent four thousand years in preparing the way."[128]

This historic, dialectic method of understanding the word of God requires the minister's diligent, systematic, and continuing scrutiny of the biblical text, for though "Christ and his redemption are the great subject of the whole Bible, . . . the parts of the Old Testament, which are commonly looked upon as containing the least divine

****

[127]An Humble Inquiry into the Rules of the Word of God, Concerning the Qualifications Requisite to a Complete Standing and Full Communion in the Visible Christian Church, Works (Hickman), I, 431.

[128]History of Redemption (Hickman), I, 571.

instruction, are mines and treasures of gospel knowledge; the reason why they are thought to contain so little is, because persons do but superficially read them. The treasures are not observed."[129]   Both in discovering these deep treasures of Scriptures and in revealing them plainly to his auditors, the minister practices his gifts, fulfills his vocational mandate, and exercises that part of "true faith" which the Heidelberg Catechism (Lord's Day VII, Question and Answer 21) calls "a sure knowledge, whereby I hold for truth all that God has revealed to us in His Word." As steward of God's oracles, the minister listens and studies patiently to remove the obscurities and veils especially from the Old Testament Word so that in it, along with the unveiled New Testament, believers "may see the glory of the Lord with open face."[130]

Deliberately and painstakingly, then, Edwards' sermons are efforts to reveal Christ's perfections, God's majestic sovereignty, and human limitations and dependence.   Edwards' sermonic word-deeds are unflinching attempts to "show," and to "explain," to "turn to profit," to "put in mind" God's will and ways for mankind. But, the sermons are also urgent exhortations to his hearers to learn, to "exercise," to "improve" their appropriate response to God.   While Edwards' proclamations as messages from God are bold, sinewy, and revelatory, his pastoral words prod, beseech and "woo the souls of men"[131] to profess their utter reliance on God.   In a very profound sense, the minister's words constitute his work.

****
129Ibid., 570.

130Ibid., 507.

131The Church's Marriage to Her Sons, and to Her God in Works (Dwight), III, 571.

CHAPTER II

EDWARDS' RELATION TO THE WORD OF GOD

Biographical and Critical Elements

Everything Edwards ever thought, he seems to have written down somewhere--in his interleaved Bible, on salvaged book margins, in bare spots on old grocery lists and discarded bidding prayer pages, and in his many homemade notebooks. Using whatever paper was available, he wrote insights and observations on thousands of topics ranging from dung, rotting carcasses, and maritime accidents to singing birds, rainbows, heaven's perfections, and the details of his own and others' ecstatic experiences of union with Christ. Referring to Edwards' manuscript volumes of "Miscellanies," Wallace E. Anderson estimates that "this series probably comprises one of the most complete and continuous records in existence of the intellectual history of a single person."[1] As Wilson Kimnach's meticulous study of Edwards' writings and work habits reveals, Edwards clearly valued his thoughts and words and developed a highly ingenious way of preserving, cross-referencing, and filing his great collection of notes, papers, and sermons.[2]

Edwards' diary entries, journals, minutes of meetings, accounts of noteworthy events, and numerous notebooks show he was much in the habit not only of defining and recording observations, but also of addressing himself with probing, uneasy, even painful queries. In his sermons, he dealt doggedly with such controversial or (un)popular subjects as bundling, drinking, and unruly merrymaking. In the letters he poured

****

[1] "Editor's Introduction," Jonathan Edwards' Scientific and Philosophical Writing, (New Haven, 1980), p. 28.

[2] "The Literary Techniques of Jonathan Edwards," (Unpublished Doctoral Dissertation, University of Pennsylvania, 1971).

forth to trusted friends, he freely admitted his mistaken judgments and
failures.   In his prefaces he showed a kind of quaint humility.
Certainly, Edwards as a writer is not hidden or oblique. Rather, he is
inexplicable, a remarkable fusion of exultation and sobriety, of
intense passion and brilliant logic, of radiant expression and staid
plain style.   Edwards' words being his life, modern critics should
avoid trying to detect a man hidden behind the language or coolly
detached from it.   Edwards the complex person and pastor is very much
present and active in his word as performative utterance.

Critical investigations of the impulses underlying Edwards' steady
preoccupation with words—God's and his own—have brought forth
fascinatingly divergent viewpoints. A. V. G. Allen, a late nineteenth-
century scholar and biographer, sees often in Edwards' religions
language a strength, precision, and clarity one would expect to find in
inspired writings. Allen notes the "supreme confidence" which "marks
his [Edwards'] utterance: an authoritative certainty of manner, as of
one speaking from direct insight or by divine authority."[3] Yet Perry
Miller frequently finds in Edwards' words an obliqueness, a use of
language so full of hidden meanings that the writings and sermons are
made baffling in their "cabalistic dichotomy."[4] Miller, whose works
remain an important starting point for any serious study of Edwards,
suggests that behind Edwards' oblique or guarded language is a
secretive, deeply enigmatic personality. According to Miller, the
deliberate and "deceptive simplicity [of Edwards' prose] concealed the
fact that certain immense metaphysical assumptions had been smuggled in
through the vocabulary."[5] Miller further perceives Edwards' view of

****

[3]Alexander V. G. Allen, Jonathan Edwards (Boston, 1889), p. 105.

[4]Miller, Jonathan Edwards, p. 72.

[5]Ibid., p. 48.

language and "rhetoric of sensation"[6] as deriving largely from Locke's theory that words and their meanings are not inherently related but rather that meanings are related to the sense impressions experientially associated with the words.

In his Language of Puritan Feeling, a work heavily indebted to psychoanalytic theory, David Leverenz considers Edward's writings to be the "grandest, purest, statement of the Puritan obsessive style."[7] Edwards uses language as an instrument to suppress agonizing personal rages and conflicts by carefully creating a "paternal voice" and the mask of "a public self acceptable . . . to a higher authority."[8] According to Leverenz, Edwards' professional words as they hide private anxieties become increasingly the escapist "language of logic, abstraction, and obsessive scripturalism."[9] Thus in Leverenz' estimation, Edwards' words project and insure "his sense of inward life in God's terms alone, radically disjunct from the world."[10]

Representing not escapism but a premeditated effort to "transform the audience's imagination rather than merely to convince their understanding,"[11] Edwards' language, says John Lynen, intends to create the presence of a speaker who is "submitting unreservedly to objective facts."   In doing so he is "ceasing to be himself by becoming the

****

[6]Miller, "The Rhetoric of Sensation," Errand into the Wilderness, ed. Perry Miller (New York, 1956); see also Miller's Jonathan Edwards, pp. 53–55.

[7](New Brunswick, 1980), p. 256.

[8]Ibid., p. 228.

[9]Ibid.

[10]Ibid.

[11]John Lynen, The Design of the Present (New Haven, 1969), p. 112.

truth."[12] Edwards' use of exact repetition, of chiming and revolving
phrases, of incantation is in Lynen's view evidence of a remarkable
"preternatural calm"[13] and deliberate impersonality in Edwards'
writing.

In a more theological view, Harold Simonson sees Edwards
conscientiously rejecting aesthetic creativity or literary art because
he wished to avoid the temptation of hypocrisy or falseness in such
self-conscious rhetoric. Even more important to Edwards, however, is
the idea that God's sovereignty ultimately renders human words
accidental. Edwards would agree, says Simonson, with a kind of
Kierkegaardian distinction that "art presupposes the stability [that
is, unity, coherence, and radiance] of human word[;] religion
presupposes the opposite."[14] Therefore it must be experiential
religion rather than rhetorical strategy which infuses words with any
beauty or strength that might be found in them.[15]

Finally, in contrast to Simonson, studies like those of Willis
Buckingham[16] and especially of Wilson Kimnach, who has read widely in
the unpublished sermons, attempt to demonstrate that Edwards' highly
developed sense of oracular pacing and his numerous literary and
logical devices are firm evidence of sincere and conscious artistry.
Kimnach points to the many deliberate editorial and stylistic changes

****

[12]Ibid., p. 111.

[13]Ibid.

[14]Harold Simonson, Jonathan Edwards: Theologian of the Heart
(Grand Rapids, 1974), p. 104.

[15]Ibid., p. 105.

[16]Willis J. Buckingham, "Stylistic Artistry in the Sermons of
Jonathan Edwards," Papers on Language and Literature 6, pp. 136-51.

Edwards wrought in his sermons as marks of an aesthetic and literary as well as theological integrity.[17]

On the whole, critics agree that Edwards the pastor found human vocabulary and language essentially limited. That is, Edwards, like his orthodox Christian predecessors, recognizes that human words alone cannot bring grace to souls: words have no power to convert the heart. Only the Holy Spirit in an "evidently supernatural work"[18] brings grace. Like Calvin, who once appended his remarks on grace with a statement that "words fall beneath a just explanation of the matter,"[19] Edwards understands that finite words are ultimately inadequate for the task of expressing what is transcendent, divine, and infinite. In Religious Affections Edwards humbly acknowledges that "there is a god-like, high and glorious excellency in [divine things] that does so distinguish them from the things which are of men, that the difference is ineffable."[20] This limitation and even failure of language occurs because "saints while in this world are but learning the heavenly language, and therefore speak it but imperfectly, and with a stammering tongue, and with a pronunciation that in many things" is wanting.[21]

Upholding a Calvinist tradition, Edwards believes that faithful ministers' words, though stammered or mispronounced, are nevertheless instruments of grace and evidences of the Holy Spirit vitally at work

****

[17]"The Literary Techniques of Jonathan Edwards," pp. 252-264, 269-273.

[18]"Canons of Dordt, " cited by Everett Emerson in Puritanism in America 1620-1750 (Boston, 1977), p. 29.

[19]Institutes (I), I.viii.5.

[20]Works (Yale), II, 299.

[21]Sermon on I Peter 2:9, Works (Hickman), II, 945.

in Christ's co-workers.   Ministerial utterances, being messages from
God, are a means of Christ's redemptive work.   The doctrines, biblical
truths, and exhortations which constitute the faithful preaching of the
word are essential preparation for a hearer's understanding, should the
Holy Spirit choose to convert that hearer.   Edwards indicates in one of
his "Miscellanies":

> The matter which the principle of grace acts upon is those
> notions or ideas that the mind is furnished with of the
> things of religion or of God, Christ, the future world.
> . . . If there could be a principle of grace in the heart
> without those notions or ideas there, yet it could not act
> because it could have no matter to act on.[22]

One of the most likely, propitious sources, says Edwards, from which a
hearer of the word stands to gather spiritual "notions or ideas" or
"matter" for the principle of grace to act upon is a faithful
minister's preaching.

The Voice and Word of God

Any serious investigation of Jonathan Edwards' gospel ministry
demands attention to his relation to the word—as linguistic
signification, sacred revelation, and divine Logos.   The central
position which the word—written, spoken, heard, believed, and
incarnated—occupies in Edwards' work no doubt prompted Perry Miller to
remark that New England's religious problem was, according to Edwards,
primarily a "semantic problem."[23]   As Miller demonstrates, Edwards'

****
[22]"Miscellanies" entry #539, Yale MSS, cited by Conrad Cherry in
The Theology of Jonathan Edwards, p. 49.

[23]Perry Miller, Jonathan Edwards (New York, 1949), p. 156.

relationship to the word is a crucial and exceedingly self-conscious one. Yet Edwards' connections to both the human word and the divine Word, in the light of his pastoral theology and the wealth of relevant material still untapped in his unpublished sermons, have been neglected.[24] To the studies which consider Edwards' place in the history of philosophical, scientific, psychological, and theological ideas must be added a fuller examination of Edwards' professional[25] relationship to the word as a "performative" act for speaker and listener. Studies which deal with Edwards' ministry or homiletic motives and syntax primarily in metaphysical or psychological terms, valuable as they are, may risk glossing over Edwards' principal view of himself as a divinely appointed keeper of God's oracular Word and a servant of Christ the eternal "personal Word."[26] Accordingly, Edwards'

****

[24] The unpublished sermon manuscripts, indexed and labelled, are available at the Yale Beinecke Library, for the most part, with a small collection also housed at Andover Newton Theological School. These manuscript sermons, however, remain largely unstudied. The one invaluable and extensive investigation of the sermon manuscripts is Wilson Kimnach's "The Literary Techniques of Jonathan Edwards," a study of Edwards the writer at work. Edwards' holographs are exceedingly difficult to decipher, as Thomas Schafer has documented in "Manuscript Problems in the Yale Edition of Jonathan Edwards," Early American Literature, 3 (Winter 1969), pp. 159-168. There are at present no transcripts of the sermons as there are—thanks to Professor Schafer's labors—of the "Miscellanies." Thus the sermons reveal their contents only to readers possessed of prodigious blocks of time, the strongest of eyesight, and a perverse willingness to be infected by the challenge of punctuationless sentences, erratic capitalization, minute interlineations, and a handwriting which Schafer rightly calls "exasperatingly formless." Edwards' great body of sermons is thus, like the proverbial iceberg, largely hidden from the public eye. The unpublished sermons are only a tip of a far larger bulk which is practically inaccessible for ready scrutiny or perusal.

[25] I use "professional" here in the double sense of one's vocation and one's public avowal of faith.

[26] (Hickman), II, "Notes on the Bible," 792.

philosophical and psychological avocations remain subordinated to his
primary professional identity as God's messenger and ambassador.

In Edwards' sermons his theology clearly presumes a much closer
relationship between words and things, between language and the nature
of reality, than Locke's theories or Miller's writings on Edwards
suggest. The phenomenon of Word as substance and word as shadow is the
grand design of God's creative and redemptive plan for mankind as
rational, moral, and communicative beings. For Edwards, language is
universal and inherent in the human mind rather than something largely
sensational and arbitrary as it was for Locke. Strongly shaping
Edwards' consideration of words is the all-important role of language
as an instrument by which grace is revealed and demonstrated. Indeed,
Edwards insists, "all Christians speak the same language. . . . The
Spirit of God teaches the saints the same language in their prayers;
their prayers are the breathings of the same Spirit. . . . The saints
while in this world are but learning the heavenly language." While on
earth, the saints "speak it but imperfectly."[27] But gradually and
progressively they learn the "heavenly language," the language of the
Spirit, as they hear God's voice and are sanctified by the Word.

From his early years in the ministry until his final years of
pastoring in Stockbridge, Edwards emphasized the great power of God's
voice and the great duty of men, women, and children actively to attend
to it. Repeatedly in his ministry, Edwards stressed that "it is our
great duty forthwith without delay to hearken to God's voice."[28] God's
voice comes with such strength, beauty, and majesty that no one who
fails to hear it will have excuse. Not to attend to his voice is a
most arrogant kind of disobedience. To disregard God's voice is "the

****

[27] Sermon on I Peter 2:29, Works (Hickman), II, 945.

[28] Unpublished sermon on Psalm 95:7-8, Yale Manuscript Collection.
This sermon, though undated, has the manuscript format of sermons
Edwards prepared around 1728-29 (Kimnach, "Literary Techniques,"

greatest slight to his authority . . . . What a provoking thing is it
when God himself commands, for man to delay to obey when God himself
says 'now,' for the sinner to say, 'no, not now.'" God commands that
human beings listen to his voice, to "his offers, his invitations, his
promises, and his threatenings, . . . Attend unto his voice, and act
according to it" [Psalm 95:7-8].[29] When sinners hear God's marvelously
forceful voice "not only with the ear but with the heart," they begin
to understand and themselves speak the language of the Spirit.

The voice of God is for Edwards a "four-fold voice." To the
beings God has made in his own image, he speaks with "his creating, his
providential, his verbal, and spiritual voice" [Psalm 95:7-8]. God's
"creating voice" comes to every man, woman, and child as "the voice of
God by the creatures. The whole creation of God preaches to us . . . ,
declares to us his majesty, his wisdom, and power and mercy."
Elaborating on God's creating voice, Edwards exhorts: "If we . . .
look to the heavens and the earth, and birds, beasts, and fishes, and
plains and trees, if we do but take notice, . . . they all declare to
us that we ought to worship, to fear, to love, and obey the God that
made all these things. The workmanship of God in our own bodies and
souls proclaims aloud."

In addition to God's "creating voice," his "providential voice"

****
(Footnote 28 Continued From Previous Page)
pp. 127-32). Other sermons stressing the power of God's word and voice
are the manuscript sermons on Luke 10:38-42 and I Peter 2:23; both of
these sermons were preached during Edwards' early, pre-1733 ministry
and again during 1754-55 in Stockbridge. There are, in addition to
these sermons, others too numerous to mention here—all declaring the
authority, vitality, and efficacy of God's word.

[29]All further references to unpublished sermons will be made with
brackets in the body of the text.

speaks to each passing generation through the events, experiences, and significant episodes of human life. In the progressive revelation of history, God's providential voice

> preaches aloud to us our duty and warns us of sin and danger. God so orders all his [providential] dispensations towards us that his voice may be heard in them, and . . . it behooves us to listen or hearken. There is a voice of God in his mercies which aloud calls us to love and thankfulness to God. There is also the voice of God to be heard in judgment evidently preparing and rebuking of us for our sins and misdeeds, and warning of us to flee from the wrath to come and calling us to hearken unto the Lord that he may have mercy on us and be our God that he may abundantly pardon us. [Psalm 95:7-8]

Further, there is God's "verbal voice," that is, the audible "voice of God in his word, . . . his voice to us in the Scriptures, his voice by his ministers and ambassadors." From the pages of Holy Writ and from the mouths of God's appointed preachers, sinners hear the distinctly articulated "external call" of God's word:

> There is God's thundering terrible awful voice of commands, and dreadful threatenings in his holy law, and there is a sweet gracious and compassionate voice, calling and inviting us to blessedness and most gracious benefits, making offers of his blood to cleanse us, of his righteousness to justify us, and his Spirit to sanctify us, and of his glory to glorify us. [Psalm 95:7-8]

As God's official messengers, ministers embody the full range of God's verbal communication—not only God's "thundering terrible awful voice" and his "sweet gracious" voice but also his "inviting voice," his "expostulating voice," his "warning voice," and his gentle "discerning voice, whereby he points out to us as a father to a child the best way, and the safe . . . road, and tells us how we may avoid danger, and enemies, and how we may find happiness, and this is the voice of God" [Psalm 95:7-8].

Finally, declares Edwards, there is God's "spiritual voice." This is God's "voice by his Holy Spirit. God not only calls upon us by the external call of his word, but likewise by the internal call of his Spirit." God's spiritual voice, like his creating, providential, and verbal voice, is directed to all his intelligent creatures: "As the devil is continually plying at us by his temptations, the Holy Spirit is also frequently proving upon the heart, making his gracious calls to us." And the listener is wholly responsible for the activity of listening: to ignore the Spirit's calls is to disobey God's "spiritual voice" and to "grieve the Holy Ghost by hearkening rather unto the devil than to him."

In all its profundity, richness, and variety, then, the voice and word of God is most certainly intelligible. It is persistent, lively, and explicit, for "all those abundant instructions which are contained in the Scriptures," asserts Edwards, "were written that they might be understood."[30] The problems related to comprehending the gospel are not the fault of the word but stem from the hearer's sinful nature.[31] The divine word's power, truth, and beauty are an extensive demonstration—to those who hear and see it rightly—of God's redemptive work being accomplished in Christ. The inscripturated words as well as the personal Word is performative, revealing the nature of reality with a transcendent vigor and authority which obligates the hearer or reader to reckon with it:

****

[30] (Hickman), II, 160.

[31] Solomon Stoddard in his sermon A Plea for Fervent Preaching said of those who are not moved by God's word, "There is a great fault in Hearers, they are not studious of the mind of God; they are Enemies of

God gives mankind his work in a large book, consisting of
a vast variety of parts, many books, histories, prophecies,
prayers, songs, parables, proverbs, doctrines, promises,
sermons, epistles, and discourses of many kinds, all
connected together, all united in one grand drift and
design, . . . so as to become one great work of God.[32]

For all people, but for ministers especially, this "great work of God"
serves as a fundamental, infallible textbook and inerrant
"professional" guide.[33]

Edwards' enormous manuscript collection of notebooks and sermons
reveals that the great burden of his ministry is to discern, declare,
and "improve" (turn to the profit of souls) the Scripture's
instructions through the obedient instrument of his own written and
then spoken words in collaboration with the word and voice of God.
Through God's messengers God's people learn God's mind and will. And
if Edwards' verbal intensity or vigor rankled his listeners, he
confidently pointed to the Scriptures as the source of his authority:
"What I have now said, it is enough for you to whom I have spoken it,
that I have demonstrated that what I have delivered is the mind of God;
and also (if there be any truth in [God's] word) that what I have
recommended is . . . for your own both temporal and spiritual

****
(Footnote 31 Continued From Previous Page)
the gospel: And when Christ Himself Preached among them, many did not
Profit by it," The Great Awakening, ed. William Bushman, (New York,
1970), p. 15.

32
   Exhortation to Gain Christian Knowledge, Works (Hickman), II, 160.

33This "great work of God" is also the touchstone and measure by
which the fidelity and integrity of the minister's word as deed will
be examined before the divine Judge in the final day of accounting
when "the book of Scripture will be opened, and the works of men will
be tried," The Final Judgment, Works (Hickman), II, 160.

interest."[34]   Particularly   when   Edwards'   sermons   attacked   his
parishioners' pet sins, he was likely to exhort irritated listeners "to
suffer their ears to be open to what I have to say to them upon this
point, as I am the messenger of the Lord of Hosts to them."[35]

The intensity evident in Edwards' activities directed to preaching
God's word plainfully, forcefully, and effectively is wedded to his
understanding that ministers, like Old Testament kings and prophets and
New Testament apostles, are indeed lively types "of the Son of God, the
eternal personal Word."[36]   In his definition of "types," Edwards notes
that types stand as "mystical and symbolical representatives of things
of a higher and more divine nature."[37]   Relating types to ministry, he
explains that because "the external word of God came" to God's
appointed prophets and apostles, "they were rendered types and images
of the Son of God, the internal word of God (emphasis Edwards')."[38]
Ministers as God's appointed officers are also types of Christ, and
"types are a sort of words: they are a language, or signs of things
which God would reveal, point forth, and teach, as well as vocal or
written words, and they are called the word of the Lord (emphasis
Edwards')."[39] Types of Christ are doubly "the word of God." They are
"God's significations," that is, they are appointed as such by God.

****

[34]Watchman, Works (Dwight), VII, 195.

[35]Joseph's Great Temptation, (Dwight), VII, 129.

[36](Hickman), II, "Notes on the Bible," 792.

[37](Hickman), II, "Types of the Messiah," 670.

[38](Hickman), II, 792. Christ, the divine fulfillment of the Old
Testament types, declares in reference to himself: "He whom God hath
sent speaketh the words of God" (John 33:3).

[39](Hickman), II, 792.

Furthermore, "the thing signified" by the types is "the personal word of God."[40] Through the language of types, God points to the work and person of Christ, using "the instrumentality of word by calling the shadow by the name of the substance, and by declaring that he appointed the shadow that it might be for the substance."[41] The minister's office, then, is to prepare hearts for the Word and to reveal with utter integrity and clarity the vital relationships and connections between words, spoken and heard, and their ultimate meanings in the mind and will of God, who is both creative and redemptive Word.

Ministerial Words

Edwards stands firmly in the evangelical tradition of Paul, Augustine, and Calvin, in holding that preaching as a means of conversion and grace is a collaboration of the "word of God" and the Word of God. The Holy Spirit directs the minister to "signify" and then uses these spoken words to touch the hearts of the listener. Augustine was profoundly moved by the preaching of Ambrose. John Cotton was shaken by the impressive power of William Perkins' ministry. Seventeenth-century Thomas Shepard was deeply stirred by the authoritative preaching of John Preston. In describing his conversion experience, Shepard relates, "The Lord so bored my ears as that I understood what [Preston] spake and the secrets of my soul were laid open before me—the hypocrisy of all my good things I thought I had in me—as if one had told him of all that ever I did . . . I thought he was the most searching preacher in the world."[42]

****

[40] Ibid.

[41] Ibid., 670.

[42] Thomas Shepard, God's Pilot: The Paradoxes of Puritan Piety, Being the Autobiography and Journal of Thomas Shepard, ed. Michael

Like Shepard and other orthodox Christian church fathers, Edwards conceives of the preacher's words as works performed in God's behalf. Sermons are means of understanding and grace for hearers: "God hath appointed a particular and lively application of his Word, to men, in the preaching of it, as a fit means to affect sinners, with the importance of the things of religion" (emphasis added).[43] Accordingly, Edwards' sermons—especially the sermons related to the Word and word— are painstaking efforts to avoid obscurity, ambiguity, or hiddenness. These sermons stand as emphatic, sturdily clear, plain utterances on the ultimate nature and beauty of God's word—God's primal word by which everything is created and upheld, God's word made flesh in the Son, the infallible written Word of God, and the "word of God" brought in the person and language of God's messengers.

Each expression of God's "four-fold voice," each kind of word becomes an essential part of God's incarnational work. God's creation is "but a kind of voice or language of God to instruct intelligent beings in things pertaining to Himself."[44] Through the God-breathed words recorded by the writers of the Scriptures, God communicates to the eyes and ears and souls, giving a holy, certain, and "sure rule of faith . . . that we might prize and improve."[45] Benevolently considering that human nature is both physical and spiritual, God came to the world in the person of Christ the God-man, Christ the Logos, so that people could see and hear God as they see and hear "one another,

(Footnote 42 Continued From Previous Page)
McGiffert (Amherst, 1972), p. 41.

[43]Religious Affections (Yale) p. 115.

[44]Images or Shadows, p. 61.

[45]"Miscellanies" entry #72, Schafer transcript at Beinecke Library.

which shall not only be spiritually but outwardly."[46]   So too in the
person and work of the gospel minister--who represents Christ the
personal Word and declares the written Word--God manifests himself
incarnationally to his creatures' reason and affections, to their
insights and emotions, to their hearts and their minds. Conceiving of
the gospel minister thus as a kind of incarnate word, Edwards could
unhesitatingly describe his own activity and that of other ministers
during the Great Awakening as an important and impressive part of God's
"call" to sinners:

> There is at this day amongst us the loudest call, and the
> greatest encouragement, and the widest door open to sinners,
> to escape out of a state of sin and condemnation, that
> perhaps God ever granted in New England . . . . You are
> invited on all hands . . . God the Father invites you . . .
> and he sends forth his servants, the ministers of the
> gospel, . . . and the Son himself invites you. And God's
> ministers invite you.[47]

Throughout his ministry Edwards remains convinced of the primacy
of preaching: "The preaching of the Gospel is the principal means of
glorifying God" [II Cor. 2:15-16]. But, for Edwards there is often an
intermediate stage between "hearing" the written Word and speaking the
ministerial word to an auditory. As he indicates in a letter to the
trustees of Princeton College, writing is for him a deeply exploratory
stage: "My method of study, from my first beginning the work of the
ministry, has been very much by writing; applying myself, in this way,
to prove every important hint; pursuing the clue to my utmost, when

---

****

[46]"Miscellanies" entry #460, Schafer transcript at Beinecke Library.

[47](Hickman), I, 667.

anything in reading . . . has been suggested to my mind, that seemed to promise light, in any weighty point."[48] As he reaches and gropes for certainties, Edwards' writing attempts to "incarnate" and externalize what comes to his mind upon hearing the Word of God, so that the thought as experience can be improved, held fast, retrieved, or reexperienced.

Edwards' written efforts reflect not only a longing for clarity and concreteness, a profound yearning to respond personally to the glorious things contained in God's word, but also an intensely pastoral desire to listen to God, as it were, and then paraphrase, interpolate, organize, collate, exegete, and repeat His words in forms, phrases, and cadences an eighteenth-century congregation could hear and keep in their minds and hearts. This vigorous kind of exploration enables Edwards to declare confidently to his congregations—as he directs their attentions to a passage of scripture: "I would speak from these words: 1. By shewing what is meant by . . . these words. 2. By shewing how they were true of those [New Testament] days . . . . 3. By shewing how they are applicable to those days, and 4. By giving agreeable exhortations unto those that are in this congregation" [Acts 17:30].

"How great an honor is it," says Edwards in his unpublished sermon on II Cor. 4:7, "that God should make his word in the mouths of men to be a means of [His] work." The integrity or performative force, therefore, of the minister's word is not that it is speech about God, but that it is speech by and from God through a human agent. In Religious Affections, Edwards remarks that "impressing divine things on the hearts and affections of men, is evidently one . . . main end for which God has ordained, that his Word delivered in the Holy Scriptures

****
[48]Works (Hickman), I, ccxvi. The letter is dated October 19, 1757.

should be opened, applied, and set home upon men, in preaching"
(emphasis added).[49] To reject or ignore the preached or written Word
is to reject or ignore the Incarnate Word, who is "on the sabbath day,
especially set forth as the bread of his church in the preaching of the
word."[50] It is appropriate that Edwards evokes the biblical metaphor
of Christ the Bread of Life in his defense of preaching, for Edwards
speaks thus with the certainty that in the performative language and
acts of ministry as well as in the sacraments, the atoning work of God
is embodied—to borrow a phrase Augustine used in reference to the
Eucharist—in a "visible word."[51] Edwards elsewhere uses the phrase "a
visible word of God" to refer to those things which signify or
typically represent the mind of God.[52]

Through the medium of spoken and written language God sets his
aims for mankind in view, even though human words are inherently feeble
as an instrument to convey exactly the fullness of God's grace and
infinite perfection. Human words, like the scriptural types and the
material creation, are only shadows or images of the transcendently
grand, spiritual realities they represent. But God, for the time
being, does not shun human words as an earnest means of reaching people
or as a way of being addressed, indeed, glorified by his creatures. In
dealing with the fallen human race, the infinite Creator does "not see
it meet that our way of intercourse with God should be left to
ourselves, but God hath given us his ordinances [scripture, preaching,

****

[49](Yale), p. 115.

[50](Hickman), II, 726.

[51]Cited by Robert Jenson in Visible Words: The Interpretation and
Practice of Christian Sacraments (Philadelphia, 1978), p. 2.

[52]Works (Dwight), I, 574.

prayer, communal worship, the sacraments] as ways and means of conversing with him."[53]   These ordinances are primarily verbal, and, most important, God himself in the person of Christ the Word of promise, deliverance, and restoration stands as the prototype of significant language.   It is not strange, then, suggests Edwards, that the words of the New Testament would be heavily influenced by Christ's speech; in frequently using such a saying as "new birth" or "born again," the apostle John had "doubtless learned his language from his Master" whose words "left the deepest impression on his mind."[54]

Such a comment also reminds us how deep an impression Christ's words leave on Edwards' mind. Edwards' attention to verbal clarity and to words that leave impressions on the mind is an essential part of his view that the Bible is intelligible and impressive and the minister's task is to "improve" its revelation for the profit of souls. All that is required for human salvation is told in the written Word of God: its revelation is "most intelligible wherever it is most necessary for us to understand it in order to our guidance and direction in the way to our happiness."[55]   Further, when the minister as devout student searches the Holy Word for guidance in preaching divine truths, God's Spirit graciously "assists and engages the attention of the mind to that kind of objects, which causes it to have a clearer view of them, and more clearly to see their mutual relations."[56]   Yet as the instruction and testimony of a Being who is infinitely intelligent, lovely, sovereign, and righteous, the Word of God is spiritually

****

[53]Perpetuity and Change of the Sabbath (Hickman), II, 94.

[54]"Efficacious Grace," (Hickman), II, 554.

[55]Townsend, "Miscellanies" entry #1340, p. 219.

[56]Religious Affections (Yale), pp. 307-308.

inexhaustible. Though its single, progressive, and recurring theme is
God's redemptive plan, it contains such depths and treasures that there
will always "be room for improvement in understanding, and to find out
more and more . . . to the end of the world."[57]

The Pauline Tradition

Edwards stands in a ministerial tradition which views preaching in
the light of Paul's statement: "Faith comes by hearing, and hearing by
the word of God" (Romans 10:7). Through the centuries, both Catholic
and Protestant theologians have acknowledged the vital relationship
between hearing and faith. One discovers the content of faith, said
St. Anselm, through being told—ex auditu.[58] Seventeenth-century
Puritan Thomas Shepard, in a sermon on effectual and ineffectual
hearing of the word, asserts that true hearing goes beyond any external
hearing of "outward word, containing letters and syllables," True,
gracious hearing is hearing "not only the word spoken, but God speaking
the word."[59] Like Paul and followers of the Pauline ministerial
tradition, Edwards views church leaders and gospel ministers as persons
especially gifted to hear "God speaking the word" and especially chosen
to speak the word as an instrument of God.

A brief consideration of first-century Paul's and eighteenth-
century Edwards' views of ministerial or spiritual gifts may help in
understanding Edwards' conception of his calling. On the one hand,
Edwards' vocation is a continuation of the sacred work which Christ and

****

[57] Townsend, p. 219.

[58] See Kenneth Burke's The Rhetoric of Religion (Berkeley, Calif.,
1970), p. 12.

[59] On Ineffectual Hearing the Word, The Works of Thomas Shepard
(Boston,1853), III, 365. It is of interest to note that Edwards in
Religious Affections cites Thomas Shepard more than any other author

his apostles established in preaching the Word of God. Edwards sees himself as a manifestation—sometimes a more mature or advanced manifestation--of the spirit which so powerfully directed and guided the early apostolic efforts. On the other hand, Edwards' work differs conspicuously from the apostles' immediately inspired utterances, miracles, and extraordinary gifts.

The ministerial gifts and graces which Paul describes in Ephesians 4:11-12 and in I Corinthians 12:4 and 28 range from speaking in tongues, miraculous healings, and scriptural inspiration to faith, wisdom, knowledge, and teaching. We should note here that while Paul is not one of the original apostles known as "the twelve," he calls himself an apostle to enhance and give greater credibility to his Christ-appointed office.[60] Generally Paul does not divide or categorize gifts as "ordinary" or "extraordinary." By contrast, Edwards for the most part accepts the distinction which gradually came about in the post-apostolic church between the extraordinary gifts associated primarily with the apostolic ministry--miracles, healing, inspired writing, glossolalia--and the ordinary gifts of faith, knowledge, grace, and love given to saints in every age. Never does Edwards consider himself "apostolic" in the sense of being an eye-witness to the resurrection, receiving direct, inspired revelations from God, or possessing power which manifests itself in miracles.

****
(Footnote 59 Continued From Previous Page)
outside the Bible. John E. Smith in the "Editor's Introduction" (p. 54) to the Yale edition of Religious Affections refers to J. A. Albro's calculation that at least 75 of the 132 quotations in Affections come from Shepard's works.

[60]Baker's Dictionary of Theology, ed. Everett F. Harrison (Grand Rapids, 1960), pp. 57-58.

Nonetheless, Edwards' repeated attention in the unpublished sermons to the apostles' post-resurrection activities and spiritual successes, to their love of pure doctrine, and to their sense of mission suggests his lively emotional identity with the apostles' ministry. A note in Edwards' interleaved Bible and a passage from an unpublished ordination sermon [Luke 10:17-18] together reflect how close the identification is. The note on I Corinthians 12:28 indicates that Edwards was absolutely certain that early church leaders had a divine authority to speak "as if Jesus Christ himself spake," an authority which believing listeners recognized and confirmed.

> So far as any person had a miraculous gift by the immediate and extraordinary influence of the Spirit of Christ on their minds so far were they (as Christ, who is the head and fountain of all Church-office power, and therefore when they were in the exercise of that gift) to be submitted to by the Church as if Jesus Christ himself spake and acted. For it was not they, indeed, that spake and acted, but Christ in them.[61] (emphasis added)

Later, Edwards extends this principle of authoritative speech beyond the apostles and teachers in the early church, but notes carefully that ministers are not guided "by a command directed to them immediately from [Christ's] mouth" [Luke 10:17-18].

> The ministers of the gospel are sent forth by Jesus Christ. Tis Christ that has appointed the order of an office of the gospel ministry. The ministerial commission is from he [sic] who is the great Shepherd of the sheep. The word which they preach is his word and the ordinances they administer

****
[61] Selections from the Unpublished Writings of Jonathan Edwards, ed. Rev. Alexander Grosart (Edinburgh, 1865), p. 158.

are his ordinances and they have no authority to minister in holy things but as they receive it from him . . . and though they ben't sent as the twelve apostles and the seventy were, by a command directed to them immediately from his mouth, yet he has appointed the particular way in which they should [be] called and set apart to the work with a sufficient signification of his will, that where his words (?) are there written [and] attended, it should be looked upon as being done in his name and to be done as much by his authority as if done immediately and presently by himself. He hath left the commission with rules annexed how it should be transmitted and communicated and they are to perform all their administrations in his name and act as Christ's messengers. (emphasis added)

When we consider the above [Luke 10:17–18] passage in the light of the Greek word apostoloi (ἀπόστολοί), which means both "men sent forth" and "messengers,"[62] Edwards' own "apostolic" vision is at once differentiated from and clearly connected to that of the apostles.

Following Christ's life, death, and resurrection, the body of Christian believers grew as the gospel was preached by Christ's messengers and confirmed by converted hearers. For some time after Christ's earthly ministry, says Edwards, God continued to reveal his divine thoughts and will through the immediate, gracious influence of the Spirit of Christ upon the minds of those especially chosen to be means of grace to others. "So any one that had the word of wisdom or knowledge, or a spirit of revelation, or doctrine, or exhortation, or gift of tongues, might do the part of pastors in the exercise of these

****
[62]The Westminster Dictionary of the Bible, ed. John D. Davis (1808) revised edition (1944) (Philadelphia), p. 35.

gifts."[63] Once the revealed word of God was thoroughly inscripturated, the extraordinary and immediate revelations of the Holy Spirit were no longer necessary.[64]   The various spiritual gifts of teaching, exhorting, counseling, reproving, admonishing, and judging of offenders—all gifts requiring verbal excellence—were gradually consolidated into one office, the ordinary office of minister directed to "preaching and declaring the word of God."[65]

More important to Edwards than miracles or extraordinary gifts or revelations, however, is the honor of working as an intelligent, dynamic, verbal means of others' salvation, of serving as a human conduit between the "inspired penmen's"[66] testimonies of the Holy Spirit's life-giving work and the eighteenth-century hearers who by grace incorporate these words into their own lives. In an early sermon (1729) Edwards cites Jesus' words in John 14:12—"He that believeth in me, the works that I do shall he do also; and greater works than these shall he do"—and applies them directly to ministers.   In this

****

[63]Selections, ed. Grosart, pp. 157-58.

[64]Much of the substance of the I Corinthians 12:28 note which Grosart selected for the edition of notes from Edwards' interleaved Bible also finds its way into Edwards' August 19, 1739, unpublished sermon on Romans 23:4-8, a special sermon preached on the occasion of the ordination of the deacons in the church. In the sermon's opening, Edwards distinguishes between ordinary and extraordinary offices. The extraordinary offices of the biblical prophets, apostles, and evange- lists "depended on Extraordinary and miraculous gifts of the Holy Spirit." But, says Edwards, now "there are ordinary offices that Christ has appointed in his church and these are those [mentioned in Acts 6] viz, bishops and deacons . . . in the church of Jerusalem, from whence all other Christian churches derived and as set forth as an example to all other Christian churches."

[65]Selections, ed. Grosart, p. 158.

[66](Hickman), II, 864. Edwards states here that "the penmen of the Scriptures hath God made to be the teachers of the church universal in all ages."

unpublished sermon [II Corinthians 4:7][67] Edwards clearly values the
work of preaching—bringing souls from spiritual death to life—as an
instrumental work of greater honor and consequence than what he calls
the "occasions" of revelations or miracles.

> It was a great honour to the prophets and apostles that God
> made them the instruments or rather the occasions of working
> such miracles that were immediately beyond the strength
> . . . of men. It was a very great honour God did Moses that
> in his word such wonderous miracles should be wrought. . . .
>
> ---------------------
>
> But this work [of gospel ministers] is a far more glorious
> work than these miracles. There is more of the power . . .
> and grace and other perfections of God seen in it than in
> them. Christ declared (?) it a greater work. John 14:12
> "Verily, verily I say unto you, He that believeth on me,
> the works that I do shall he do also; and greater works
> than these shall he do; because I go unto my father." How
> should he do greater works? . . . Doubtless Christ meant
> that they should do spiritual works of wonder in bringing
> men from a state of spiritual death to life and in respect
> of this the apostles and other disciples did greater works
> than Christ himself while upon earth. Christ's speaking
> and miracles while on earth converted but few but the
> apostles turned the world up side down.
>
> ---------------------
>
> There is as glorious a work as creation in the new creation.
> How great an honour therefore is it that God should make his

****
[67]I am grateful to Thomas Schafer and Wilson Kimnach for help in
establishing the preaching date of this updated sermon.

word in the mouths of men to be a means of this work.

For Edwards, it is clear that if a minister graciously hears the word of God and speaks it, and in speaking it revealingly transmits its divine truths to the souls in his care, he performs a greater work than the apostles' miracles. God's Word attended, believed, obeyed, and communicated, Edwards explains, issues in nothing less than love, that virtue which is the greatest "grace" or fruit of holiness. And thus "it is a greater blessing to hear and keep the word of God than to be an apostle or to be endowed with any of the miraculous gifts of the early church" [Luke 11:27-28]. Edwards implies that the fuller spiritual insights and vision available to eighteenth-century Christians through the progressive revelation of God's providential voice and dispensations and the faithful preaching of the word should put colonial congregations—and especially ministers—above envying the apostles their miracles and inspirations.[68]

Yet much of Edwards' preoccupation of "declaring and preaching" rises from his unflagging determination to carry on, guided by the Spirit and the Scriptures, in the preaching and teaching tradition of the apostles conspicuously gifted in "the word of wisdom or knowledge, or a spirit of revelation, or doctrine, or exhortation."[69] Edwards

****

[68]The seventeenth century as well as the eighteenth century enjoyed "minor miracles" related to conversion and associated with preaching. One of the "miracles" is described in Increase Mather's sermon on Predestination and Human Exertions. Mather tells an anecdote: "two profane men [were] drinking together, knowing that Mr. Hooker was to Preach, one of them said to the other, Let us go hear how Hooker will bawl, yet was he converted by that very sermon, which he went to hear with a Scornful Spirit." The Puritans, ed. Perry Miller and Thomas Johnson (New York, 1938), p. 336.

[69]Selections, ed. Grosart, p. 158.

sees much about the apostles to emulate, so it is understandable that he is acutely attentive not only to the content but also to the modes and manners in which Christ and the biblical teachers address their listeners. This interest prompts him to copy into a sermon notebook a commentary on John 13:3-4 from Watt's Orthodoxy and Charity: "While [John] is explaining to us these great things of the gospel, he talks in a plain, rational, argumentative method, to inform the minds of men, and give them the clearest knowledge of the truth."[70] Edwards also observes that Christ and the apostles use analogies and similitudes because these are not only effective but superbly vivid and efficient: "By such similitudes ['Ye are the temples of the Holy Spirit'] a vast volume is represented to our minds in three words; and things that we are not able to behold directly, are presented before us in lively pictures."[71] In "Miscellanies" #636 Edwards reminds himself of "how often have we an account in the Acts of the apostles reasoning and disputing with men to bring them to believing and of many being brought to believe through that means."[72] Because the revelation of God's work of redemption is so much fuller and clearer in the eighteenth century than it was in the types and shadows of the Old Testament or even in the time of the apostles, Edwards feels his responsibility is the greater to the souls in his charge to present a lively picture and clear knowledge of the Bible's glorious doctrines, which "alone inform us what God aims at in his works. Nothing else pretends to set [God's aims] in view" [II Corinthians 4:7].[73]

****
[70](Hickman), II, P. 554.

[71]History of Redemption (Hickman), I, p. 617.

[72]Schafer transcription, Beinecke Library.

[73]In this 1729 unpublished sermon on II Corinthians 4:7, Edwards presents an early view of the challenge of eighteenth-century gospel ministry; Edwards preaches this sermon in Northampton very shortly

Edwards would be the first to describe his own ministerial gifts as "ordinary" in comparison to the apostles' "extraordinary" gifts. Nonetheless, he was always profoundly conscious that he was chosen to convey the apostolic revelations to an eighteenth-century world and that he did indeed possess rare gifts and graces and uncommon intellectual powers and propensities to study these revelations. His diary and journal entries document his early concerns with refining, honing, purifying, and exercising these gifted elements in himself. Scripture note #348 is part articulated pleasure and part yearning that whatever the "particular gift" or the "particular or spiritual beauty . . . most conspicuous in him,"[74] it should be disciplined and committed wholly to God's glory. "Miscellanies" #40, in which Edwards envisions himself "sent forth to teach the world the will of Christ,"[75] reveals a young man with a sense of limitless abilities and powers. And as Edwards' position in the New England churches becomes more forceful, his writings assume that his own spiritual leadership and influence in eighteenth-century church renewal is crucial, perhaps even unparalleled by anyone else at that time. It is especially the egocentripetal cast or confidence of remarks in Narrative of Surprising Conversions and History of the Work of Redemption that arouses Perry Miller's judgments regarding Edwards' "sheer conceit" and the "unchastened pride of 1739."[76] Certainly Edwards' excessive use of the word "extraordinary"

****

(Footnote 73 Continued From Previous Page)
after Stoddard's death. In much the same way that Edwards' ordination sermons later would soberly exhort a congregation to pray for its newly received minister, this sermon urges the people to pray for their pastor—the pastor in this case being young Edwards himself taking up the mantle of his grandfather.

[74]"Notes on Scriptures," #348, Works (Dwight), IX, 181.

[75]Townsend, "Miscellanies" entry #40 on Ministers, p. 200.

[76]Perry Miller, Jonathan Edwards, pp. 315-316.

in describing the spiritual activity surrounding the Great Awakening and his ministry throws into question the humility in some of his other discussions on ordinary and extraordinary effects or gifts of the spirit.

Preaching "Superior Wisdom"

Whether his own gifts and graces are extraordinary, Edwards firmly asserts that his words of spiritual wisdom—and those of all God's faithful messengers—surpass the "wisdom" of natural philosophy or natural reason. Even though ministers are "earthen vessels" and speak with "a stammering tongue," they possess "the mind of Christ" (I Corinthians 2:16). God's faithful ministers speak with a "new sense" of divine things, with a reason and understanding illuminated by divine grace. In Religious Affections, Edwards describes this "new sense" thus: "The spiritual perceptions which a sanctified and spiritual person has, are . . . diverse from all that natural men have . . . . Hence the work of the Spirit of God in regeneration is often in Scripture compared to the giving of a new sense, giving eyes to see, and ears to hear, unstopping the ears of the deaf . . . . This new spiritual sense is not a new faculty of understanding, but it is a new foundation laid in the nature of the soul, for a new kind of exercises of the same faculty."[77]   Edwards calls this new foundation in a regenerate person a "new holy disposition of heart."[78]   This "new sense" is "vastly more noble and excellent than all that is in natural man."[79]

****

[77](Yale), p. 206.

[78]Ibid.

[79]Ibid., p. 207.

Repeatedly Edwards' sermons—the unpublished sermons on II
Corinthians 4:7; II Corinthians 2:15-16; Luke 10:17-18; I Corinthians
2:11-13; and Isaiah 62:4-5, to name a few—insist that a "sanctified
and spiritual" minister is impelled by the Spirit of God to speak and
teach the things of the Spirit. Edwards refers in Some Thoughts to the
"gracious and most excellent, kind assistance of the Spirit of God in
praying and preaching." In equipping and leading the gospel minister,
the Spirit "may be said, directly and mediately . . . to teach the
preacher what to say; he fills the heart, and that fills the mouth."
And this divine teaching, "this most excellent way of the Spirit of God
[in] assisting ministers in public performance . . . (considered as the
preacher's privilege) far excels inspiration."[80]   In this emphasis,
Edwards echoes Paul, who points in I Corinthians to his own preaching
with that remarkable mix of confidence and humility that also appears
often in Edwards' references to ministry: "my speech and my preaching
[are] not with enticing words of man's wisdom, but in demonstration of
the Spirit and of power" (I Corinthians 2:4).

Edwards' sermon on I Corinthians 2:11-13 declares that in much the
same way an ambassador's official words are determined by the will and
authority of the one he represents, the minister's words are informed
by the "superior wisdom" of the Spirit of Christ. The sermon doctrine
states: "Ministers are not to preach those things which their own
wisdom or reason suggests, but the things that are already dictated to
them by the superior wisdom and knowledge of God." While "great
philosophers seek after things that will be agreeable to their own
reason," faithful ministers follow the direction of the inspired
Scriptures and submit to God's revelation of the truth through grace.
Pointing to the ancient Greek thinkers, Edwards claims that "with all

****
[80]Great Awakening, ed. Goen, p. 438.

their boasted word of reason" they "could never discern the truth in the things of God." To the wise of the world "the things of the gospel seem unintelligible and absurd." Because the divine things of the "gospel revelation concerning a crucified Lord," says Edwards, "are above human reason and depend on pure revelation" and insight bestowed by the Holy Spirit, a mind unaided by grace and the means of grace "can't receive anything for truth but what it sees or thinks it sees some reason to suppose to be the truth." There is, thus, in Edwards' I Corinthians 2:11-13 sermon an acceptance of a sharp distinction between "what [natural] men would teach and what the Holy Spirit teaches." And the minister's duty is to serve as a clear, persistent "word of God,"[81] speaking courageously in contrast to the desires, tendencies, and voices of natural reason. The minister with regenerate reason hears "the voice of revelation" in God's Word, and hearing, speaks it.

If those to whom the minister speaks do not have ears opened by grace, their unregenerate reasons will not accept divine testimony. The unsanctified intelligence finds divine wisdom unreasonable. In one of his very deft uses of paradox, Edwards--speaking to a congregation of unregenerate as well as regenerate listeners--insistently reasons that divine wisdom is beyond human reason: "it is unreasonable to expect any other than that [divine wisdom] should contain mysteries . . . [and] tis unreasonable to expect any other than that . . . there should be many things . . . that should be entirely beyond our understanding and seem impossible" [I Cor. 2:11-13]. Edwards' regenerate reason here operates to persuade the listeners that it is reasonable to expect that spiritual things are unacceptable to the unregenerate reason; it is also reasonable to believe by faith those

****
[81]"Notes on the Bible" (Hickman), II, 792.

divine mysteries which lie beyond the full understanding of the
regenerate reason. Even when his sanctified but limited reason cannot
comprehend the fullness of God's wisdom, the minister must preach what
God dictates, "the preaching that He bids" [I Corinthians 2:11-13].

Word as Gracious Gift

In a marvelously intense note asserting that grace is both cause
and effect, Edwards touches on the springs of energy that propel his
words as actions:

> In efficacious grace we are not merely passive, nor yet does
> God do some, and we do the rest. But God does all, and we
> do all. God produces all, and we act all. For that is what
> he produces, viz. our own acts. God is the only proper
> author and foundation; we only are the proper actors. We
> are in different respects, wholly passive and wholly active.
> In the Scriptures the same things are represented as from
> God and from us. God is said to convert, and men are said
> to convert and turn . . . not merely because we must use the
> means in order to the effect, but the effect itself is our
> act and our duty. These things are agreeable to that text,
> God worketh in you both to will and to do.[82]

In the Lord's work, Edwards certainly does not consider himself merely
a passive means or instrument. He is no obedient puppet mouthing words
from or for God. On the contrary, Edwards' continuing verbal activity
serves to refine, clarify, and sharpen his own thoughts and words the
better to elucidate, reinforce, and express the great designs of the
Word God gave to the prophets and apostles. Edwards' professional task

****
[82]*Works*, (Hickman), II, p. 557.

is to be a performative "word of God" in order to warn souls of the wrath to come and to invite them to salvation.

Stressing the minister's word as performative even when it does not appear to be "successful," one of Edwards' sermons argues the following doctrine: "Those ministers that faithfully preach the gospel of Christ are accepted of God and are as a sweet savor to Him whether they are successful or no" [II Cor. 2:15-16]. This doctrine is true because the preaching of the gospel by God's messengers is always an act which glorifies Christ. Consequently, "the work that [ministers] do in preaching the gospel whether it be effectual or no is acceptable to God." As the sermon progresses, Edwards skillfully re-defines the word "effectual" to shift the focus from what humans consider "effectual" or "successful" to what God deems "effectual." It then becomes eminently clear that Edwards believes his preaching, as it is God's word spoken faithfully, will "take hold of all that hear it one way or another . . . . Every part of the message that God sends shall be effectual and the effect shall be great answerably to the preciousness of the word [and] the greatness of Him whose word it is." For some listeners, hearing the word will increase their personal culpability and condemnation. For others, the minister's gracious words will open the way to salvation and eternal life.

Authorized by the personal Word and enlightened by the written Word, the ministerial "word of God" acts both fervently and meticulously to reveal the mind and will of God or, in the words of Acts 20:27, to "declare the whole counsel of God." Edwards' sermons, then, especially those on ministry and preaching, can hardly be viewed as cabalistic, equivocal, or communicated in words deliberately "enigmatic."[83] In addition, since the Word of God is glorious and

****

[83]Miller, Jonathan Edwards, pp. 72, 79.

beautiful and true, Edwards believes that the faithful minister's word participates in that loveliness and glory.[84] Indeed, Edwards' use and acceptance of paradox suggests that when he is unable in terms of human rationality to explain or comprehend the mysteries of God's divine wisdom, he deliberately sets the paradoxical elements side by side to be obediently accepted by faith. The minister's work is to place such spiritual mysteries as the atonement, virgin birth, efficacious grace, and election before limited human understanding so they can be acknowledged as God's superior wisdom. In the presence of the mysteries and power of God's Word, ministers may not hedge or equivocate. They may not avoid what they do not understand: "God hasn't left it to their [ministers'] discretion what their errand shall be."[85] Ministers are faithfully to preach the doctrines Christ reveals in his word and which he himself taught in his earthly ministry. Certainly, the Scriptures' "mysterious doctrines should be taught." Otherwise, asks Edwards rhetorically, "to what purpose did [Christ] teach them?" [I Cor. 2:11-13].

In the doctrinal fabric of Puritanism the Word of God, revealed by Christ, the Scriptures, and gospel ministers, and the Holy Spirit's gift of efficacious grace are always closely interwoven. The Westminster Shorter Catechism states that "the Spirit of God maketh the reading, but especially the preaching, of the Word, an effectual means of convincing and converting sinners, and of building them up in holiness and comfort through faith unto salvation." Moreover, as God's Word and his redemptive grace are essentially linked, so are the words

****

[84] See Roland Delattre's Beauty and Sensibility in the Thought of Jonathan Edwards (New Haven, 1968) for a comprehensive study of Edwards' aesthetics.

[85] Unpublished sermon I Cor. 2:11-13.

and "gifts and graces" of God's appointed messengers. Their ministerial work of preparing souls for gracious union with Christ is possible because Christ grants special "gifts and graces" to his envoys and ambassadors.

"Gifts and graces"[86] seems, in fact, to be a kind of code phrase for the characteristics considered essential in a gospel minister. Edwards uses the phrase repeatedly. In his unpublished sermon on II Cor. 4:7 he urges the congregation at Northampton to "look to God that He would every way furnish their minister with gifts and graces . . . for their work." In Sorrows of the Bereaved, Edwards uses "gifts and graces" to describe the spiritual comeliness of the deceased Rev. Williams.[87] From a bidding prayer (#94) among Edwards' manuscripts we can deduce that the "gifts and graces" the congregation sought in behalf of missionary Gideon Hawley are zeal, self-denial, prudence, worthiness to preach God's word, and an abundance of God's Holy Spirit.[88]

The frequent verbal conjunction of "gifts" and "graces," of course, evokes Paul's epistle to the Ephesians—particularly Ephesians 2:8, 3:7, and 4:8. Paul closely relates the idea of gift and grace, considering God's grace a gift—"whereof I was made a minister according to the gift of the grace of God"—and God's gifts as graces in his messengers whose edifying words "minister grace unto hearers." Speaking to the church leaders at Corinth, Paul urges, "Forasmuch as ye are zealous of spiritual gifts, seek that ye may excel to the edifying

****

[86]Benjamin Trumbull, Complete History of Connecticut, Civil and Ecclesiastical (New London, 1898), II, 104. Trumbull notes the eminent "gifts and graces" in Edwards.

[87]Works (1843 edition), III, 618.

[88]Stephen Stein, "'For Their Spiritual Good': the Northampton Massachusetts, Prayer Bids of the 1730s and 1740s," William and Mary

of the church" (I Cor. 14:12). Edwards, likewise, is much concerned
that a minister's special gifts and graces be exercised, acknowledged,
and honored in an atmosphere of love and encouragement for the benefit
of believers at large. Appropriately then, most of Edwards' ordination
sermons exhort ministers to devote their gifts and graces unselfishly
to the people Christ has directed them to serve. His sermons also
direct congregations to love and "follow the good examples of their
pastors"[89] and to "respect, honor, and reverence"[90] the ministers
Christ has set over them.

In a 1747 installation sermon, Edwards stresses that "ministers
ought to be truly gracious and vitally united to Christ" [Zech.
4:12-14]. Edwards further states that Christ alone makes a minister a
suitable servant in the sacred work of redemption, and thus in
obedience and devotion to Christ's appointment a minister becomes an
important part of God's gift of providential grace to the souls the
minister nourishes. Edwards' Treatise on Grace describes grace as a
spiritual principle,[91] which in its exercise brings forth "Christian
virtues . . . often called by the name of grace, . . . being the
peculiar fruit of grace."[92] Ministers are most gracious when they are
a means of grace to others and when they serve as God's example and
God's gift to the church. Consequently, Edwards deems it entirely
correct on the occasion of a revered gospel minister's funeral to

****
(Footnote 88 Continued From Previous Page)
Quarterly 37 (April 1980), p. 283.

[89] The Church's Marriage, Works (Dwight), III, 579.

[90] (Hickman), II, 864.

[91] Treatise on Grace and other Posthumously Published Writings, ed.
Paul Helm (London, 1971), pp. 25, 54.

[92] (Hickman), II, 558.

comfort the family by celebrating the departed pastor's "gifts and graces." These gifts and graces in God's elect ambassadors are manifestations of Christ's loving provision for his church. They also comprise the noteworthy, typical loveliness that adorns those whose words faithfully demonstrate the beauty and vitality of the Logos, the personal Word of God.

CHAPTER III
EDWARDS ON THE WORD HEARD AND KEPT

In 1891, Yale Divinity School welcomed the Reverend James Stalker, a staunch Scotch Calvinist theologian, to its halls to give the celebrated Lyman Beecher Lectures on Preaching. Speaking on "The Preacher and His Models," Stalker's lectures eloquently presented the requirements he considered essential for vital ministry: "unless God has first spoken to a man, it is vain for a man to attempt to speak for God."[1] To underscore this fundamental theme, Stalker pointed to three of God's great Old Testament spokesmen, Moses, Isaiah, and Jeremiah, and their highly dramatic, symbolic encounter with God's Word. The encounters marked each prophet as one chosen to be a messenger to God's people. Out of a burning bush, God spoke to a reluctant Moses, saying "Go, and I will be with thy mouth, and teach thee what thou shalt say" (Exodus 4:12). In Isaiah's epiphanic experience, a temple seraphim touched the prophet's mouth with a live coal from the altar and declared, "Lo, this hath touched thy lips and thy iniquity is taken away, . . . Go, and tell" (Isaiah 6:7,9). To Jeremiah God spoke authoritatively, placing His hand to the trembling man's mouth and assuring him, "Behold, I have put my words in thy mouth" (Jeremiah 2:9).

We do not know if Stalker was conscious that he had selected the same three biblical illustrations used in a sermon preached some one-hundred and forty-six years before by one of Yale's most brilliant divinity graduates. Jonathan Edwards, whom Perry Miller describes as the American preacher in whom New England Calvinism "blazed most

****
[1]The Preacher and His Models (London, 1891), p. 50.

clearly and most fiercely,"[2] points to the examples of Moses, Isaiah,
and Jeremiah to fortify the conclusion of a 1744 ordination sermon.
Using these three figures, Edwards drives home his declaration that to
be truly excellent in bearing the "light of the knowledge of the glory
of God" gospel ministers must "hear His word, and be instructed by
Him."[3]

The Word Encountered

At a crucial stage of his young adult life, Edwards heard and saw
the word of God in a profoundly affecting way in an experience which no
doubt had permanent bearing on his fascination with religious "language
as a species of incantation."[4]   According to the testimony he gives
many years later in the Personal Narrative, God's Word—and words—
impressed and altered him deeply with their power and beauty:

> The first instance that I remember of that sort of inward
> sweet delight in God and divine things that I have lived
> much in since, was on reading those words. I Tim. 1:17.
> "Now unto the King eternal, immortal, invisible, the only
> wise God, be honor and glory for ever and ever, Amen." As
> I read the words, there came into my soul . . . a sense of
> the glory of the Divine Being; a new sense, quite different
> from any thing I ever experienced before. Never any words
> of Scripture seemed to me as these words did . . . I kept
> saying and as it were singing these words of Scripture to
> myself.[5]

****

[2]The New England Mind: The Seventeenth Century (Boston, 1939), p. 5.

[3]True Excellency, (Hickman), II, 960.

[4]Perry Miller, "Introduction" to Edwards' Images or Shadows of
Divine Things (New Haven, 1948), p. 41.

[5]Personal Narrative in Jonathan Edwards: Representative

Through the instrument of his written Word, God moved to reveal His glory to Edwards and to produce in him a gracious response. Edwards' personal note on Exodus 33:18-19 can readily be understood as a gloss on his youthful conversion or awakening experience: "The discovery of God's spiritual glory is not by immediate intuition, but the word of God is the medium by which it is discovered: it is by God's proclaiming his name."[6]   God proclaimed his name to Edwards through the words proclaimed by Paul, and Edwards' response was himself to proclaim God's name, and subsequently commit himself to proclaiming it officially as an ambassadorial "word of God." Insomuch as Edwards never doubted that "the labours of faithful ministers are the principal means God is wont to make use of for . . . conversion,"[7] his sermons are directed to proclaiming God's name and to approximating the veracity, integrity, and force of the Word of God which had so moved him.

Edwards' awakening to God's Word dramatically demonstrates his conviction that God's messengers must truly hear the Word of God in order to proclaim and do the word. It is especially by means of the verbal "labours" of faithful ministers that believers, individually and collectively, hear the Word in order to do the word and thus fulfill their great created end of expressing God's glory. A minister's verbal acts are in this respect doubly directed to expressing God's glory. The preacher's utterances are deeds performed for the glory of God.

****
(Footnote 5 Continued From Previous Page)
Selections, ed. Clarence H. Faust and Thomas H. Johnson (New York, 1962), p. 59.

    [6](Hickman), II, 726.

    [7]Cited in Gerstner, Steps to Salvation, p. 20.

The ministerial word is also consciously spoken to move hearers to the fulfillment of their purpose of being the intelligent "mouths of the creation to praise" God.[8] Edwards' conception of the ministerial word here builds upon the early Puritan belief in "the causal influence of the spoken word"[9] when that word is accompanied by the Spirit's gracious power. Donald Evans' remark on the "causal use or power of an utterance" is relevant to Edwards' view of the ministerial word: "where words have causal power there is a hearer who understands the meaning of the utterance to some extent."[10]

Though the words of those who truly hear God have no immediate or meritorious power to save speaker or listener, these words do tellingly emanate the light and beauty of God's grace. Thus the words of each person who hears the Word of God, or chooses not to hear, becomes his or her performance for good or evil. The words of reprobates ominously accumulate to damn them out of their own mouths, but the words of even the weakest of the redeemed tell God's glory.[11] And particularly the words of God's ministers—as appointed "mouths," "trumpets,"[12] and "angels of the church"--[13] demonstrate God's truth, justice, love, and beauty. Because they are both means of grace and evidences of God's

****

[8]Watchman, Works (Dwight), VII, 182.

[9]Miller, The New England Mind: The Seventeenth Century, p. 294.

[10]The Logic of Self-Involvement, p. 73.

[11]Unpublished sermon on II Cor. 4:7.

[12]The June 1741 unpublished sermon on Isaiah 27:13 declares that "the preaching of the word may fully be compared to the blowing of a trumpet."

[13]Sorrows of the Bereaved, Works (Hickman), II, 967; True Excellency (Hickman), II, 958, 959.

grace, the minister's words especially must be reckoned with. As his words are a power for salvation or for judgment, they are performative; when his words are spoken, they have an effect.

Unpublished Sermons on Hearing and Keeping the Word

Among Edwards' unpublished sermons are many which deal with the word and its important internal and external effects on hearers. Edwards' sermons on Isaiah 27:13; Hebrews 2:11; Micah 2:11; Psalm 95:7-8; I Corinthians 2:11-13; II Corinthians 4:7; and II Corinthians 2:15-16 are all forceful ministerial sermons directed to various manifestations of the word.

Unpublished Sermon on Luke 11:27-28 (1729)

An early sermon (1729)[14] on Luke 11:27-28 is especially significant because it considers at length both those who are speakers and those who are hearers of the word, and it is notable as well for its argumentation. The sermon opens with scriptural and historical examples—among them Jesus' mother Mary is a central one—of speakers or bearers of the word. These examples are deftly assembled to build a convincing case for the great privilege of revealing or bringing forth God's word. But once the case is built, Edwards shifts his emphasis to stress that ultimately "hearing and keeping the word of God renders a person more blessed than any other priviledges [sic] that ever God bestows on any of the children of men" (emphasis added). Thoroughly and deliberately, Edwards has persuaded his congregation of one

****
[14]Thomas Schafer has established 1729 to be the date of this pre-1733 manuscript.

principle--it is blessed to preach the word--only to insist that there
is a second, greater principle--"they are rather blessed that hear and
keep the word"--under which the first must be subsumed.[15]

In the early stages of developing the sermon's doctrine, Edwards
enumerates those whom God has privileged to be means of grace--
apostles, evangelists, reformers, eminent divines, the virgin Mary--to
speak or bring the Word. As we shall see, the details, vitality, and
length of this preface to the main argument suggest that while
logically Edwards is preparing to subordinate the examples of preachers
and divines to a more important focus later in the sermon, emotionally
he is identifying very strongly and energetically with them.

Accordingly, Edwards points his listeners to the great privilege
God conferred on speakers such as Abraham, Moses, David, Paul, and
John. As usual, Edwards demonstrates a lively interest in and approval
of the work of the prophets, disciples, and apostles:

> Great was the priviledge [sic] of God bestowed upon the
> apostles in choosing them to be the great instruments of
> spreading the gospel to the world and of setting up the
> Christian church. [God] made 'em . . . the foundation upon
> which the church was built next to Christ. The apostle Paul
> was in the hand of Christ a principal instrument of the
> calling the Gentiles . . . . [God] greatly priviledged the
> apostles and many others in those days by those extraordinary
> gifts of the Holy Spirit, which he bestowed upon 'em by the
> great miracles which they wrought.

But, one of the sermon's most extensive panegyrics--which I will quote
at length because it is available only in manuscript--is Edwards'
description of the blessedness of eminent preachers.

****
[15]This kind of "what is more" argument is a variation of what
Wilson Kimnach discusses as Edwards' a fortiori reasoning, "The
Literary Techniques of Jonathan Edwards," p. 366. Further examples of

They are great divines. It is as a great priviledge that
they are through God called to the work of the ministry to
be Christ's ambassadors to the souls of men, to bring the
everlasting gospel treasure committed to them, to stand in
Christ's stead, to bring his message. 'Tis a very honourable
station that such are set in the work to which they are
called and some of them are blessed with a very great and
extensive knowledge in matters of religion, are great
divines. God makes 'em instruments of doing a great deal of
good. They are instruments of the conversion of many souls
and not only are they means of a great deal of good in their
own particular flocks but many have been great lights in the
church thus by their preaching and writings, have done a
great deal toward advancing the cause of truth and piety
throughout a whole nation or in many nations, have gloriously
defended the gospel of truth against heretics . . . . Some
have   been   instruments   of   propagating   religion,   of
enlightening and instructing poor heathen and converting them
to Christianity. Some have been great reformers, have been
means of reviving the church after a long night of darkness
and time of general corruption. [Here Edwards wrote the name
'Luther' but then crossed it out, no doubt in keeping with
his   stringent   effort   in   sermons   to   avoid   direct   name
references to non-Biblical persons.]

Following this elaborate praise of Christ's spokesmen, Edwards
returns to a consideration of the virgin Mary as the object both of

****
(Footnote 15 Continued From Previous Page)
this technique appear in Edwards' unpublished Luke 10:17-18 sermon, p.
17, Beinecke, Edwards MSS Collection.

Christ's commendation and the blessing given by the well-intentioned
woman in Luke 11:27. At this point Edwards views Mary not only as a
remarkable means of grace, but also as a person who has both heard and
kept the Word. She is the woman God privileged by

> making her the mother of Jesus Christ the Son of God, a
> person that was the Creator of the world and the Savior of
> sinners and the judge of angels and men. How wonderful was
> the priviledge! . . . . Angels spoke to Mary (Luke 1:35).
> Indeed she was highly favored and blessed among women as the
> angel told her . . . . . So Christ in our text don't
> deny the woman's cry ['Blessed is the womb that bare thee,
> and the paps which thou has sucked.'] but only [intends]
> that they are rather blessed that hear the word.

In Edwards' sermon exposition, then, Mary gradually becomes a pivotal
figure. She brought forth the Word, she heard the word of God from the
angel, and she kept the word. According to Edwards, the sermon's text
can by no means be viewed as Jesus' denial of Mary's significance;
rather, the text is Christ's acknowledgement that Mary had experienced
the greatest blessing available to God's people because she both
listened and responded to the Word.

Moving to a second proposition, Edwards' sermon concludes by
remaining focused on hearing the word and keeping (that is obeying) its
commandments rather than on the ministerial means of grace which have
made--and are at the very moment making--the word audible. It is only
in hearing the Word of God with spiritually "open ears" that one can
learn of Christ's great love and sacrifice and of God's perfect rule
for life. In this sermon stressing the parishioner's relationship to
the word rather than the preacher's relationship to it, Edwards views
sincere, obedient hearing as evidence of grace; a man truly hears when
God "opens his ears to hear His word, opens his heart spiritually to

receive understanding." If one keeps the word, it takes root and brings gracious fruits of holiness. Hearing the word, like speaking it, is performative.

In conclusion, the sermon application celebrates the joys of personal, experiential religion and the benefits of saving grace and love to God. Putting aside for the moment the fundamental truth that the minister of the word is also in that very act a hearer and keeper of the word, Edwards' sermon instead speaks to the great responsibility of the listener. Underscoring for his hearers the treasures of audible and available revelation contained in God's written Word and of happiness of "knowing and loving and having God," Edwards declares the following:

> It is a greater blessing to hear and keep the word of God than to be an apostle or to be endowed with any of the miraculous gifts of the early church, than to be able to heal the sick . . . or to remove mountains.

Above all, "the hearing and keeping the word of God brings the happiness of a spiritual union and communion with God . . . and a saving intercourse with him by the influences of his spirit."

Unpublished Sermon on Hebrews 2:1 (1734)

In a February 1734 sermon which echoes many of the Luke 11:27-28 sermon arguments as well as the emphases of Thomas Shepard's sermon On Ineffectual Hearing, Edwards stresses that listeners in the presence of God's messengers are fully responsible for hearing. The sermon doctrine declares that "when we have heard the word of God we ought to give earnest heed that we don't lose what we have heard" [Heb. 2:1]. To be listless, disinterested, lazy, or insincere in hearing is to show a "wicked contempt" to the "infinitely great God when he in a solemn manner directs himself to us and gives us his holy counsels and instructions." Much of the sermon's vigor comes from imperative verbs which recommend the proper attitude and activity of attentive listening. As you listen to the word and carry it away in your thoughts, says Edwards, act upon it--"resolve," "labor," "recollect," "remember," "endeavor." Do not allow the word to fade. "Keep [the word] in your memory and keep it alive in your affections."

Edwards' strategies and arguments attempt variously to arouse the congregation to more devout, responsive listening. He reminds listeners of their mortality: "we don't know whether we shall ever hear the word of God preached to us any more," and "we don't know whether ever we shall live to hear another sermon." He pleads: don't engage in distracting thoughts during worship, for "the word of God that is preached . . . is an unspeakable treasure, . . . more precious than gold and all earthly treasure." Edwards also threatens dire consequences for "those that come to the house of God and sit and hear the word preached as though it were a thing of no importance, . . . hear it only as they hear any other noise that happens to be made within their hearing, as the whistling of the wind or the roaring of the water or the lowing of cattle." The word of God spoken by God's ambassadors is never mere "noise." It is God's eternal intelligible message of salvation or judgment.

This sermon expresses profound concern for the many souls, both young and old, who are Edwards' charge. Edwards gives clear evidence that as a pastor he is struggling with the "most obvious symptom of social decay"--as Patricia Tracy terms it--"the disrespect for authority shown by [Northampton's] young people."[16] In the development of his Hebrew 2:1 sermon doctrine, Edwards asserts his sacred, official

****
[16] Jonathan Edwards, Pastor. p. 72.

authority to chasten, warn, and direct: God "has appointed an order of
men . . . to preach his word to men and inculcate the great things of
it in their minds." Much of the sermon stresses the importance of
regular sabbath worship, faithfulness in attending lecture day
teaching, respect and response to the weighty words of God's ministers.

Toward the end of the sermon come the clues as to why Edwards
deemed this sermon necessary for the Northampton congregation. He
urges the church elders and heads of families to instruct the youth of
the church that "the design of lecture days" is "not to be as a play
day or day of drinking and company keeping." Edwards decries "the
degeneracy of young people" who seem to have no interest in the word,
who go "to taverns after lecture," and engage in practices that hinder
concentrating upon and responding to the word. The sermon application
is heavily freighted with appeals to parents to "restrain the children"
and prevent them from "making sabbath evening and lecture days
especially to be times of diversion and mirth." Edwards is here not
simply railing against youthful evils in his day. As generations come
and go, Edwards wishes to insure a climate conducive to continuity of
hearing God's word. Thus he soberly urges both the parents and
children not to "allow of those things that directly tend to frustrate
the most faithful labours and endeavors of a minister."

Unpublished Sermons on Preaching and Teaching the Word

The theme of faithfully preaching and teaching the word—the
correlative to obediently hearing and doing the word—informs two
unpublished ministerial sermons important for their treatment of
sinful, irresponsible tendencies which ministers must confront not only
in their listeners but also in themselves. Micah 2:11 is a youthful
(November 1733) sermon with an arrestingly-argued doctrine: "If the

business of ministers were the further gratification of men's lust they would be much better received." I Corinthians 2:11-13 is a May 7, 1740, ordination sermon which declares, "Ministers are not to preach things which their own wisdom or reason dictates." Both sermons, as we shall observe, stress that if the people are to hear God, the preacher must preach God's Word and no other. Faithfully teaching and preaching the word is, for the minister, hearing and keeping it.

Unpublished Sermon on Micah 2:11 (1733)

The Micah 2:11 sermon stands as a beautifully firm example of the Puritan three-part sermon form of text, doctrine, and application. Though the language is simple and direct, the examples are rich and lively, and the argument at times is highly dramatic. The sermon remains remarkably unified as it makes its impression economically, using a single theme, hammering it home persistently, and allowing almost no digressionary comments. Edwards uses a minimum of points and subpoints, with each element woven tightly into the sermon fabric. The sermon's outline is an excellent brief overview of the content I will be treating, and it demonstrates the Puritan sermon format in a most compact way.

Text: "If a man walking in the spirit of falsehood do lie, saying, I will prophesy unto thee of wine and strong drink; he shall even be the prophet of this people" (Micah 2:11).

Doctrine: If the business of ministers were to further the gratification of men's lusts, they would be much better received by many than they are now.

1. If ministers were sent to tell the people that they might gratify their lusts without

dangers . . .

2. If ministers were sent to offer men a Savior that countenanced and encouraged men's lusts . . .

3. If ministers were sent to direct men how they might fulfill their lusts . . .

4. Some would like ministers better if they would countenance their scandalous indulgences of their lusts . . .

5. If ministers were sent to offer men a carnal and sensual heaven . . .

Application:

1. Use of Self-examination

    1. Enquire how is it you receive ministers with the message they do bring to you in the name of the Lord.

    2. How it has been with you when you have been hearing other things that tended to gratify your carnal inclinations.

2. Use of Reproof

    1. Consider what horrid contempt you call on God and on heaven . . .

    2. Consider how foolishly (?) and unreasonably you act in thus preferring and in gratification of your lust . . .

    3. Consider how [?] it may be . . . that you never should get any good by the word preached . . .

    4. How grievous it may [?] be to any faithful minister of Christ when men no more regard the message they bring . . .

This sermon on Micah 2:11, in contrast to the heavily theological thrust of I Corinthians 2:11-13, relates to its hearer in an earthy, colloquial manner, even as it stresses that preaching the whole counsel of God requires firm exhortation, warning, and reproof. The sermon's greatest impact is derived from homely examples and cumulative arguments wielded as weapons to make God's and the true minister's opponents look utterly puny and absurd. Dramatically, Edwards imagines the damnable consequences of ministerial words which would flatter or thoroughly please self-indulgent sinners. Already in this youthful sermon, Edwards is demonstrating his skills, later employed so effectively in his imprecatory sermons, of bringing an argument or description to an extreme state and leaving the listener painfully suspended in horror of the inexorable consequences.

Marshalling examples of evil found in the very best of persons, Edwards creates an extensive procession of sins, prefacing each description or account with some variation of an obviously ludicrous conjecture--"if ministers were sent to preach sin." Edwards' parade of sins, which only a false prophet would approve, include heavy drinking, pandering to base lusts, love of luxury, dreams of "carnal delights," greedy concerns "about the market, about land and cattle, and bargains that have been made," and the gossip-monger's pleasures "when you sit and hear such and such persons reproached and run down and ridiculed and you are entertained, and don't the time pass every man pleasantly." The stinging ridicule of Edwards' remarks in this sermon is heightened by his frequent use of an ironically agreeable tone.

Clearly, Edwards is saying in this sermon, human nature left to its own desires takes the path that is ultimately most injurious and damnable. This tendency is as true for negligent or unredeemed ministers—the worst kind of hypocrite--as it is for the laity. In fact, ministers must consciously and constantly resist the temptation to gain their listeners' approval by preaching what is contrary to God's message. To make this point, Edwards' imagination cleverly--one could almost say perversely--operates to create a fictional pulpit in which ministers preach sin, offer rewards for evil, promise freedom from punishment for willful sins, and encourage their parishioners to drink, game, and lust. And again each hedonistic description incorporates some incredible condition--"ministers were sent from God to tell people how they might lay in [material gain]"--obviously contrary to fact.

The incongruity of Edwards' examples must at least have kept his audience awake. Certainly it would have required an effort to ignore a minister who presented the admittedly ridiculous spectre of a Christ who "was desirous that they should have more liberty to enjoy their carnal pleasures," a Christ who "came into the world for that end to lay down his life to purchase for men a dispensation for sinning and an indulgence that they might gratify their strong . . . carnal appetites with impunity and that God would not be angry with them for so doing nor punish them for it." Such a Savior or such a minister preaching such a Savior the world

> would receive . . . gladly. If sin could be encouraged and evil be mocked, ministers [would] need not stand calling and inviting sinners to come to Christ so long in vain. There would be multitudes flocking to such a Christ as this. They could embrace such a Savior as this with all their hearts. Where there is one now that comes to Christ, there would be a hundred . . . . They would not need to have the minister to spend so much breath to set forth the beauty and excellency of Christ . . . urging and entreating men to close with Christ, no, they would fall at the first word.

Knowing full well that sinners do not come to Christ at the minister's "first word," Edwards nonetheless believes that if the

minister is faithful to the gospel, the breath he spends and the words
he speaks, even if they are rejected, ignored, or ridiculed, are an
irrevocable part of God's revelation. Acting as God's instrument,
perhaps in this sermon a "two-edged sword," Edwards intently makes his
sermon application a two-fold approach to the natural human tendency to
ignore the personal Word and the pastoral word of God. The application
moves first into a very probing exercise in self-examination and then
into an exercise in reproof--Edwards reproving the guilty and, if he is
successful, the guilty reproving themselves.

     In the exercise of self-examination Edwards shifts from third to
second person, soberly urging each listener to ask "how it is you
receive ministers with the message that they do bring to men in the
name of the Lord. How do you attend to them in their delivering their
message?" More particularly, each hearer is pressed to answer whether
he or she is "guilty of a careless manner" in listening to the word; or
"little regarding what is said"; or having "no conscience of keeping
your heart intent on what is preached"; or "thinking of other things
that have no relation to the minister's discourse"; or "sleeping while
the minister is preaching the word of God."[17]   Pushing even further
into the secrets of the listeners' hearts, Edwards asks, "How is it
when you hear an impure thing?"; "Do you find it more interesting than
the word of God?"; and "Ben't you more in your element when you sit
talking of [carnal] things, than when you are hearing of God and Christ
and heaven and the glorious benefits of the gospel?"

     Even in a most devout group, the judgmental thrust of these
carefully wielded questions would be powerful. Thus the exercise of
reproof is applicable to each person inasmuch as "you are one of the
persons" who has not been entirely attentive to all of God's words.

****
[17]Here Edwards echoes the words of Increase Mather, whose lengthy
sermon exhortation illustrates "woefully corrupted" and depraved human
nature by giving examples of those who "sleep when the precious Truths

Edwards reminds each hearer "what horrid contempt you call on God and Christ and heaven in that you should prefer the gratification of your evil lusts before them." But the callous, indifferent listener not only pours contempt on God; he or she heaps contempt on God's ambassador; he or she is heavily accountable for the great grief brought to the heart of "any faithful minister of Christ when men no more regard the message they bring to them." Looking at the positive side only briefly, Edwards reminds his congregation "what an encouragement would it be to a minister that labours to speak acceptable words, and does what an horn[18] does to speak so as to influence and affect its hearers, to see them attentive and willing to hear and learn, accepting of what he declared."

Finally, Edwards indicates to those who have despised, ignored, ridiculed, or slept through the preaching of the word, that God does not judge a minister's faithfulness by whether the word has been heard, but by whether it has been preached faithfully as God's message which condemns sin and glorifies Christ. In the great day of reckoning, hearers will be held accountable as to whether they encouraged their pastor in a faithful gospel ministry and whether they indeed heard the Christ whose word is preached. The eschatological element in Edwards' theology appears here pointedly, as it inevitably does in his sermons.

****
(Footnote 17 Continued From Previous Page)
of God are dispensed in his Name." Mather even suggests that many persons "are more apt to sleep then, than at another time," even "when soul-awakened Sermons are preached, enough to make rocks to rend and bleed; when the word falls down from Heaven like thunder, the voice of the Lord therein being very Powerful and full of majesty . . . yet some will . . . sleep under it." Miller and Johnson, The Puritans, p. 348.

[18]This anticipates the unpublished sermon on Isaiah 27:13, an entire exposition on preaching as the blowing of a trumpet.

Neglected or disheartened ministers do not give their final words in their earthly pulpits. Rather, Edwards ominously warns his hearers in the sermon's peroration, "ministers that have been . . . treated [disrespectfully] rise up in the day of judgment before their master that sent them and set them to work, declaring what orders they took and how they laboured to their utmost to speak so as to influence and affect their people and yet how regardless [their people] were of the message they delivered." God is the final judge of a minister's weaknesses or strengths. At worst a minister preaches what self-indulgent, sinful people desire. At best, the minister's word will contain some of the glory, mystery, and power of the personal Word, and so it will at times be subject to the same kind of mockery and rejection which the Word experienced when He dwelt on earth and walked among men and women.

The sermon on Micah 2:11, written and preached fairly early in Edwards' ministerial career, seems a strong example of his experiments with the degree to which the ministerial "horn" or "trumpet" bringing God's message may be allowed its own tone, timbre, or brightness. It is a sermon containing much dramatic irony and pungency, even as its message consistently asserts that a minister may say only what God approves. Edwards' consideration seems, thus, to be that so long as a sermon is thoroughly informed by Christ's redemptive message, the formal elements of style, artistry, and argumentation will admit—as does God's "verbal voice" in the Scriptures—a wide range of colors and tones.

Unpublished Sermon on I Corinthians 2:11-13 (1740)

As we have noted, Micah 2:11 particularly addresses the impediments a minister confronts in self-indulgent listeners. But not

all hearers of the word are overtly carnal, lusty, or hedonistic.
Edwards' May 7, 1740, sermon on I Corinthians 2:11-13 is most
significant in recognizing that some listeners are sophisticated
philosophers, deists, rationalists, or logical purists. To such the
minister's messages from God may sound foolish, unreasonable, even
absurd. Against these charges, Edwards' sermon on I Corinthinas
2:11-13 defends the gospel and the faithful gospel minister. Edwards
particularly addresses pastors as the official keepers and revealers of
the word. He urges them to resist all forces or persons—including
their own natural tendencies—tempting them to place human reason above
God's wisdom. In focusing upon the conceit and arrogance inherent in
fallen human nature, this sermon pointedly warns against the
presumptuous, self-serving uses of reason rather than asserting, as
does The Peace Which Christ Gives, that a sanctified reason can be the
saint's "great friend" and guide in viewing "things with truth and
exactness."[19]

As Edwards' sermon on I Corinthians 2:11-13 argues the superiority
of God's wisdom, a kind of familial hierarchy emerges in his view of
the church. As God is grandfather of the church, the minister is wise
father or head of the congregational church family. His relation to
the souls in his charge is parental. In the church, the minister whose
words and wisdom graciously embody the "superior wisdom and knowledge
of God" is superior to the souls in his charge, whom he regards
paternally as his offspring "begotten" through the gospel.
Simultaneously, however, Edwards is democratic, even egalitarian, in
stressing that the Bible as the Word of God is a treasure available for
all God's people, not only for ministers. All the laity—men, women,

****
[19] Jonathan Edwards, Representative Selections, eds. Faust and
Johnson, p. 139.

and children—no less than their spiritual fathers, must hear, read, study, and ponder the Word and be held fully accountable for their response to it. Yet the preacher, the honorably appointed steward of the word, is especially delegated to communicate authoritatively, plainly, and fully the redemptive Word's beauty and mystery.

As part of his sacred duty to God and to hearers, a minister is obligated to withhold nothing in his preaching from the perfect revelation of God's Holy Word. A minister must scrupulously eschew insubordination to Christ; he must shun judging any parts of the Scripture presumptuously by saying "these are fit for me to preach and these are not fit. This part of my errand is fit to be done and this not. God don't need to be told by his messengers which message is fit to declare to those to whom he sends them." God's message to his messengers is clear, says Edwards: "Ministers are not to teach those things that their own reason teaches . . . . God hasn't left it to their discretion what their errand shall be; they are to preach the preaching that He bids." Thus preachers are unconditionally responsible to declare God's Word, not "their reason." A preacher's words stand before God as faithful or unfaithful deeds, active demonstrations of the power of good or evil in the speaker's life.

Accordingly, Edwards censures the "absurd" notion that preachers or listeners can "make the dictates of [their] own reason the highest rule in judging of the things of God." For ministers to choose from God's word only what their limited understanding perceives to be consistent, logical, useful, or reasonable is to fly arrogantly in the face of God's infinite knowledge. To select on the basis of flawed, finite, human reason—the minister's or the hearer's reason—is to impose upon God's words the distorted, inadequate criteria of philosophers, rationalists, humanists, and pragmatists. Edwards' sermon application is a strong warning that ministers must unconditionally guard against Arminians and the like in their "unjust and fallacious practice . . . so much insisted upon by many of late viz. to determine by our own reason what is agreeable to the moral perfection of God and then interpret the scriptures by this."[20]

The impressive hold on Edwards of the I Corinthians 2:11-13 doctrine extolling God's superior wisdom is dramatically visible in the sermon manuscript. Its revisions and corrections demonstrate Edwards' painstaking and repeated struggles to set forth written words that are imbued with an authenticity, precision, and clarity commensurate with the beauty and power of the message God bids him deliver. The sermon's subject is the minister's duty respecting the glorious realities of God's mind and will which appear foolish to man's reason. The enormous burden or challenge this seems to place upon Edwards' expressive capacity actually causes him to "stammer."

To explain the implications of the sermon's doctrine, Edwards begins the first point under his Proposition II, judges it unsatisfactory, crosses it out with a large X, begins again, and falls into an abstruse, tangled philosophical discussion—which the very emphasis of his message would dictate that he avoid. He then draws a line through the entire second effort, makes a third start, this time achieving a more firm, succinct, and particularized, yet still exceedingly complex statement. The material is dense and complicated stuff for a sermon. It is the essence of paradox—how to be reasonable and plain-spoken in dealing with spiritual conceptions whose heights and depths transcend human reason and language. We see upon the manuscript page the evidence of an intellectual, spiritual, and rhetorical struggle for "acceptable words" with which to make God manifest and with which to influence the hearer. These manuscript

****
[20] One wonders if Edwards would have found any humor in the face-
tious observation Benjamin Franklin made about what a "convenient
thing it is to be a reasonable Creature, since it enables one to find

efforts, so revelatory of Edwards' determination to present God's mind and will accurately, are extremely significant:

II.   To speak particularly to several things implied in the doctrine as belonging to the duty incumbent on gospel ministers.

1.   'Tis their duty not to reject any doctrines that by comparing one scripture with another appears truly to be held forth by the voice of revelation tho their own reason don't teach it.

1.   'Tis their duty not to reject any doctrine that is taught by divine revelation tho men's reason don't teach it.   If men are to receive no doctrine of revelation that are above reason or none that are taught by revelation but what their reason can reach and teach 'em in the first place is to render a revelation wholly useless and indeed makes it in effect to be no revelation, for nothing is revealed by God but because it is taught by men's own reason and then there is no need of its being revealed in order to its being revealed.   If no doctrine is to be received but what reason teaches them, men must first see whether their reason teaches it before they receive it.   And in (?) this rule 'tis

****
(Footnote 20 Continued From Previous Page)
or make a Reason for everything one has in mind to do."
Autobiography, cited by Sidney Mean, "The Rise of the Evangelical Conception of the Ministry in America," The Ministry in Historical Perspectives, ed. Richard Niebuhr and Daniel Williams (New York, 1956), p. 211.

impossible that God's revelation should ever really
be the ground of our receiving any one doctrine
whatsoever because no doctrine is received till we
have first consulted reason to know whether that
teaches it. So that our receiving it is always in
this way prior to our hearing the word of
revelation. So that the foundation of faith is
men's reason or word and not divine revelation, in
direct opposition to the rule of the apostle in the
fifth verse of the context.

1. 'Tis their duty not to reject any doctrine that by
    comparing one scripture with another appears truly
    to be held forth by the voice of revelation though
    it contains difficulties and seeming inconsistencies
    that their reason can't solve. We ought to receive
    doctrines that thus appear to be taught in
    scripture, though they are mysterious to us still.
    If the thing still contains what we can't comprehend
    and still have difficulties remaining in them that
    we can't solve, we are not to wait [until] they
    cease to be mysterious to us before we receive them
    for truth.

We can assume that the third attempt to articulate the
implications of an incredibly sinewy, practically incomprehensible
proposition was in Edwards' judgment the most sound. He had managed to
prune the convoluted, redundant language of the second version,
acknowledge both the divine reasonableness and the divine mystery of
God's communications, and to retain the sense of God's audible word in
his "voice of revelation." Unlike the "great philosophers [who] seek
after something that shall be agreeable to their own reason," the

messengers of God seek to hear and obey the divine "voice of revelation" and make that heard voice the foundation of all their sermon exegesis, exhortation, and application.

Edwards is greatly conscious, of course, of the "imperfection and darkness of man's reason in that fallen state which makes us stand in need of a better guide"--the guide of God's Word. The glorious and mysterious "things of the gospel seem unintelligible and absurd to the wise men of the world" because the world's wise insist on making their own reason and wisdom the test of God's reason and wisdom. Human reason is fundamentally imperfect. Therefore, Edwards states, "we must interpret the Scripture by itself and not by the dictates of our own hearts." That is, we must not "suppose that our own mean reason is a better rule or a better guide to us than God's revelation." Later, in the publication of Religious Affections Edwards elaborates much more fully on the relationship and distinctions between human reason and divine reason, claiming that it is only a view of God's glory and wisdom through grace that "sanctifies [human] reason, and causes it to be open and free" and able to see that the gospel "has its highest and most proper evidence in itself."[21] Such a view of God's glory removes "prejudices of the heart against the truth of divine things"[22] and "convince[s] the mind of their divinity."[23] The person whose reason is illuminated by supernatural grace "has his judgment thus directly

****

[21]Religious Affections (Yale, 1959), p. 307. Daniel B. Shea, Jr., in Spiritual Autobiography in Early America (Princeton, 1968), p. 190, notes that Religious Affections, though published in 1746, is based on a series of sermons given by Edwards in 1742-43, a dating which puts only one and a half or two years between the I Cor. 2:11-13 sermon and Edwards' work on Religious Affections.

[22]Religious Affections (Yale), p. 307.

[23]Ibid., p. 307.

convinced and assured of the divinity of the things of the gospel, . .
. [and] has a reasonable conviction; his belief and assurance is
altogether agreeable to reason."[24] Yet ultimately this gracious work
of the Holy Spirit is a supra-rational work, resulting in "a kind of
intuitive knowledge of the divinity of the things exhibited in the
gospel . . . . Without any long chain of arguments . . . the mind
ascends to the truth of the gospel but by one step, and that is its
divine glory."[25] In an account of this very phenomenon in Edwards' own
experience, the Personal Narrative touches on the superiority and
mystery of God's wisdom as it graciously illuminates human
understanding of divine things. The "extraordinary influence of God's
Spirit" moved Edwards to apprehend grace rather than analytical
explanation. Grace revealed to him "the justice and reasonableness" of
the doctrine of divine election, and "put an end to all those cavils
and objections"[26] his reason had previously held toward it.

Grounded upon God's superior mind and reason, Edwards can
vigorously argue in the I Corinthians 2:11-13 sermon how "unreasonable"
it is to expect the word of God to be judged by its consistency with a
human's natural or finite reason. The primary argument of the sermon,
then, is that the minister in his search for "acceptable words" can
discover and speak them only if he hears and preaches the words "which
God bids," not which fallen persons desire. Above all, God's faithful

****
[24]Ibid., p. 298.

[25]Ibid., p. 2980-99. Edwards goes so far as to say that a sight
of divine glory "not only removes the hindrances of reason, but positively helps reason. It makes the speculative notions more lively.
It assists and engages the attention of the mind to that kind of
objects . . . . The ideas themselves . . . by this means have a light
cast upon them." R.A., pp. 307-308.

[26]Representative Selections, ed. Faust and Johnson, pp. 58-59.

messengers must recognize the great truth that "divine revelation . . .
don't [sic] go begging for credit and validity by approbation . . . of
[human] understanding. On the contrary, . . . the [divine] revelations
are often given forth . . . thus: . . . 'I am the Lord,' and 'He that
hath an ear to hear, let him hear.'"

The Believer's Word as Deed

We will conclude this consideration of Edwards' relationship to
the performative word by examining his belief that hearers of the word
are to be keepers and doers of the word through their own verbal
commitments.   During the 1740's and 1750's Edwards actively urged
personal professions of faith and formal church covenants upon his
parishioners.   Much has been written on the details of the Edwards
communion controversy, and it will not serve this discussion to pursue
its complexities.   But Edwards' belief that the active, creative,
personal Word of God demands a person's clearly uttered response is a
view which informs his insistence that Christians individually and
collectively enact their assent to God's sovereign mind and will in
written or spoken testimony.[27] Not only for God and for his ministers
but also for laity, "word is deed." In The Logic of Self-Involvement,
Evans touches on this precise point when he remarks that "both the
divine Creative word of promise and the correlative human word of
acknowledgement are performative."[28]   God's Word converts; glorifying

****
[27]It is relevant at this point to note that Austin treats covenants, vows, and pledges as speech-acts which "commit the speaker to a
certain course of action." Vows and covenants are clearly a case in
which "to say something is to do something," the act being to give
one's word and declare one's intention. Austin, How To Do Things
With Words, p. 156, 157.

[28]Evans, p. 158.

God, the redeemed heart speaks words of love, obedience, and delight.
In strong terms Edwards makes this responsive performance the theme of
a November, 1744, Thanksgiving sermon: "In a right thanksgiving to
God, heart and mouth and practice all go together" [Psalm 119:108].

Those persons whose mouth and deed are a unitive performance of
the heart--the heart being a "metonym for the inner man"[29]--are called
God's "professors." As Edwards declares in the Preface[30] to his
Farewell Sermon, addressed to his parish, to New England, and the
world, the words of a professor are deeds which intelligently and
happily demonstrate that person's relationship to Christ. Professions
are to be considered essential, vital acts of consent and love to God.

Unpublished Sermon on Ezekiel 44:9 (1749)

In a 1749 unpublished sermon on Ezekiel 44:9 which Edwards
preached in defense of his position in the Northampton communion
controversy, he argues intently that believers must publicly profess
their faith. This profession must precede participation in the
sacrament of holy communion because public profession is an essential
demonstrative act in the believer's spiritual, covenantal relationship
with God:

> The very design of a profession of religion is to profess to
> be on Christ's side, on the side of his friends and not his
> enemies. Christ came into the world to proclaim war with
> sin and Satan and all the world is on one side or the other
> in this war. Now the reason whereby Christ has appointed

****
[29]Norman Pettit, The Heart Prepared: Grace and Conversion in
Puritan Spiritual Life (New Haven, 1966), p. 1.

[30](Hickman), I, ccxli.

a public profession of religion is this is fit and
reasonable that those that would be received into the
company of his friends should openly declare on whose side
they be ([Ezekiel 44:9], pp. 23-24, pagination Edwards).
In order to adult persons coming to sacrament they must
covenant with God by their own act . . . . We are now
speaking of adult persons that are capable of acting for
themselves. Doubtless such as are capable to act for
themselves ought to act for themselves in order to their
admission to the seals of the covenant . . . . It is evident
that any adult person that comes to these seals of the
covenant of grace must by his own act own the covenant of
grace, by his own actual profession enter into covenant
with God by this covenant. But no man can do this without
professing saving faith, 'tis that and that only is the
condition of the covenant of grace. There are two parties
in this covenant, Christ and the believer, and if a man
professes to enter into that covenant then he professes to
become one party in the covenant but he can't profess to
become a party in the covenant of grace unless he professes
to be a believer. Christ and believers are the two parties
within that covenant. For a man to own the covenant is to
own one's part in the covenant. Man's part in the covenant
is faith and Christ's part is salvation. He that don't
profess nor pretend to own and comply with this part of the
covenant . . . don't own the covenant. ([Ezekiel 44:9],
pp. 26-27, pagination Edwards)

If public professions deliberately avoid the essential, affective, and
personal elements of the Christian faith, or if they are merely
superficial statements or mouthed sounds, they are not true espousals

to Christ. Instead, they are lukewarm, deceitful, and hypocritical deeds against God.[31]

When a person makes a public profession of faith, whether the profession be sincere or insincere, it is not merely a saying something; it is a unified act of one's heart, soul, body, and mind, the verbal expression of the person's inward attitude or disposition. Furthermore, says Edwards, this public profession is not simply a requirement arbitrarily imposed by some human jurisdiction or authority. God himself demands it. God himself in his holy word requires it and accordingly appoints ministers to act "not as a private person" but as public officers of Christ's church to teach his word and will to believers and to hear their professions. Edwards presses these points repeatedly in his unpublished sermon on Ezekiel 44:9:

> When the prophet foretells that in the days of the gospel that the priests and ministers of the gospel should admit none into the temple but those that are visibly circumcised in heart, the meaning must be that they should admit none but such as in profession and visibility are anointed . . . . By circumcision of heart is here meant conversion of heart and not moral sincerity. (pp. 6-7)
>
> Ministers are expressly forbidden to admit those which are not visibly such [that is, circumcised of heart] into the sanctuary which Ezekiel had a vision of which is evidently the church of God in the gospel day. (p. 8)
>
> When I say communicants ought to be in the eyes of a reasonable judgment godly persons I mean not a private but a public judgment. 'Tis properly a visibility of godliness to the eye of a public charity and not a private judgment

[31]Evans also indicates that profession is a necessary act of faith, for "in the biblical context, religious knowledge is a sort of doing. When a man 'knows' God, he acknowledges God . . . . To know

that gives a person a right to be received as a visible Christian by the public saints. The minister in this affair is to act as a public officer in behalf of the church and not as a private person in his own name and so in this matter he must not be determined by any skill he may think he has to discern and search men's hearts. And therefore he must accept the serious profession the person makes of godliness if there be an agreeable conversation. But only it belongs to him as a public officer to instruct the person and to see to it that he has a good degree of doctrinal knowledge and that he will understand that he professes and that he don't use the words of his profession by rote and merely as a parrot. But when a minister has diligently instructed and directed a person in his soul's concerns and is satisfied of his good doctrinal understanding of things of this nature and that when he professes, he professes understandingly and his outward conversation be agreeable he [the minister] must take his [the professor's] sincere profession of religion as what properly recommends him to a public charity as a true Christian believer. (pp. 9-10)

'Tis most manifest by the Scriptures and what none denies or disputes that none ought to be admitted into the Christian church but professing Christians. But they that make no profession of godliness do not profess themselves to be Christians. They are not professors of the Christian

****
(Footnote 31 Continued From Previous Page)
God is to acknowledge Him . . . to carry out this performative act without Infelicities," Evans, p. 197, p. 198.

religion in a scriptural sense. The Christian religion is the religion of Christ or the religion that Jesus Christ came to teach. But the religion that Christ taught consisted in true piety of heart and life. Indeed the custom of the present day has called something else the religion of Christ, considering (?) that 'tis customary to call the doctrines of Christianity the Christian religion. But that is nothing to the purpose. The question is what the Scripture represents is the Christian religion, what the Bible informs us is the religion Jesus Christ taught. The Scripture teaches that the religion of Jesus Christ is a heart religion, a spiritual religion. The worship that Christ came to teach was a worshipping in spirit and in truth. Now in order to man's professing the religion of Jesus Christ man must profess that which is the religion of Jesus Christ. But if men profess only the doctrine of religion . . . and leave out what is scriptural, the thing that they profess is not the religion of Jesus Christ because the most essential things that belong to his religion are left out. To profess a very small part of Christianity only is not to profess Christianity. Tis unconscionable to say a man professes Christianity if the whole essence of Christianity is what he don't profess . . . . . So if a man professes to be a healthy man, it implies something more than a professing that his extreme parts are sound . . . . He that professes only that his hands and feet are well and don't pretend but that his head is sick can't be said to profess to be a healthy man . . . . The religion [which] professes externals is no more the religion of Christ than the hands and feet only are a man.

If to love God with all our heart and soul and our might as
our selves be in effect the sum total of the Christian
religion as the Scripture teaches, then those professors
that don't profess these things in effect become one of
those professors who in effect professes nothing.

Individual and Collective Covenants with God

Seldom at a loss to express the believer's relationship to God,
Edwards himself drew up a number of drafts or samples of what he called
"a public profession of religion"[32] to present to his church council,
as model statements for hopeful professors.   The form of a profession
was generally very brief:

I hope I do truly find a heart to give up myself wholly to
God, according to the tenor of that covenant of grace which
was sealed in my baptism; and to walk in a way of that
obedience to all the commandments of God, which the
covenant of grace requires, as long as I live.[33]

Edwards does urge however, that, if possible, persons should freely
speak their own words before the assembled church so as not "to be tied
up to any form of words, but to have liberty to vary the experience of
a public profession, the more exactly to suit the sentiment and
experience of the professor, that it might be a more just and free
expression of what each one finds in his heart."[34] Likewise, in his
1749 sermon on Ezekiel 44:9, Edwards urges that a professor "don't use

****

[32]Preface to Farewell Sermon, Works (Hickman), I, ccxli.

[33]Ibid.

[34]Ibid.

the words of his pastor by rote and merely as a parrot." Genuine professions stand as a demonstration of faith inasmuch as persons "must profess espousals to Christ" and "must covenant with God by their own act" [Ezekiel 44:9].

Persons professing without sincerity stand charged with a negative performance; they are in danger of damning themselves out of their own mouths. Empty, deceitful words are in no case mere sounds, ornament, or habit. Professors may not say one thing and mean another. Nor may they say words without meaning them. "I can conceive of no such virtue," says Edwards, "in a certain set of words, that it is proper, merely on the making of these sounds, to admit persons to Christian sacraments."[35] That is, true professions are words spoken genuinely from a heart-knowledge of God.[36]

For Edwards, not only individual profession but also collective church covenants are important performative utterances. A notable incident in the history of Northampton church clearly signals Edwards' enormous respect for the visible word of covenant—in this case a thoroughly premeditated, public, and collective covenant—as deed which irrevocably commits the covenanters to continuing the efforts their words embody.

****
[35] (Hickman), I, ccxli.

[36] Edwards' dismissal from Northampton was precipitated in part by his insistence that a person's religious profession—as verbal deed— must be graciously consonant with the living Word. As he states in his Farewell Sermon, "The great thing which I have scrupled in the established method of this church's proceeding, and which I dare no longer go on in, is their publicly assenting to the form of words rehearsed on occasion of their admission to the communion, without pretending thereby to mean any such thing as a hearty consent to the terms of the gospel-covenant, or to mean any such faith or repentance as belong to the covenant of grace, and are the grand conditions of that covenant. It being, at the same time that the words are used, their known and established principle which they openly profess and proceed upon, that men may and ought to use these words and mean no

In a long letter dated December, 1743[37] Edwards relates to a
Boston minister some details of the action surrounding the Northampton
church covenant of 1742. The letter's narrative indicates that Edwards
initiated and proposed the idea of covenanting, drew up the "solemn
public covenant with God," circulated it throughout the community for
consideration, and invited people to "subscribe the covenant with their
hands." He then planned for and preached on a "day of fasting and
prayer" in which the subscribers "altogether presented themselves
before the Lord in his house, stood up, and solemnly manifested their
consent to it, as their vow to God."

This Northampton church covenant of March 16, 1742, stands at an
important point in the Great Awakening events. It comes at the end of
a ten-year span during which the entire older generation of Connecticut
Valley divines had passed on, thus leaving Edwards to take up the
mantle of revival leadership. Edwards' call for a church covenant
follows his very successful visits to other communities, including the
famous visit to Enfield in July 1741 and the overwhelming response
there to Sinners in the Hands of an Angry God. Perhaps most
significantly, it follows several weeks in February, 1742, during which
time Mr. Buell preached in Northampton during Edwards' absence and
powerfully stirred the people into "a great and continual commotion,
day and night . . . indeed a very great revival of religion."[38] In the
context of all these events, Edwards' presentation of an elaborate
church covenant seems an overt attempt to channel his awakened
parishioners' spiritual energies into a public, communal commitment.

****
(Footnote 36 Continued From Previous Page)
such thing, but something else of a nature far inferior." Works
(Hickman), I, ccxli.

[37] (Hickman), I, xclx.

[38] (Hickman), I, cl.

This 1742 covenant is by its own definition a vow "owned before God," a pledge, and a "solemn act of public worship." Together its professors promise to eschew all manner of sins—from backbiting to worldly gains, from unchristian bitterness to fraud, from lasciviousness to sloth. Above all, they verbally commit themselves to achieve visible sainthood. Each covenanter seeks God's help in avoiding any "wicked dissembling in these our solemn vows." All ask God's ever-present help in their efforts to be measuring or "trying" themselves by this covenant and "to be often strictly examining ourselves by these promises."

A very revealing sequel to the 1742 covenant appears documented in an Edwards manuscript sermon prepared for an August, 1747, quarterly lecture on Joshua 24:21-22. The degree of binding power which Edwards considered the 1742 promises to have upon the covenanters can be plainly noted here in Edwards' words five years later. The Great Awakening, which had seemed to Edwards the dawning or at least a prelude to the millennium, had lost its momentum in a thicket of controversies. Many of his parishioners were again thoroughly apathetic or disillusioned with religion. In his 1747 lecture sermon Edwards points back to the professors' "covenant with God in a day of fasting in the year 1742 which was done in a very solemn manner,"[39] underscoring the performative nature of the word, as well as acts, they expressed at that time.

In Edwards' forceful handling of the text, the 1747 sermon on Joshua 24:21-23 becomes a remarkable exercise in bringing the word of God in the mouth of his messenger to stand against the words of careless professors. The sermon's theme is a negative one: "They that don't take heed to keep their vows wherein they have promised to serve

****

[39]The 1742 fast day sermon was quite likely on Joshua 24:15-17, the passage which includes Joshua's public vow, "As for me and my house, we will serve the Lord."

God, what they have said and done in covenanting with God will be brought as a witness against them to render 'em inexcusable and to condemn 'em out of their own mouths." As Joshua had reproved the Israelites, Edwards faces his congregation in a "trial whether they would regard their vows or no." Thus the minister's pulpit becomes a somber tribunal anticipating God's day of judgment, that "future time when they [the covenanters] should be called to account" for their words. In the sermon's extensive use of self-examination, Edwards exhorts the hearers to consider "how many things you will have to witness against you" when the time comes to stand before God's throne. To spur their soul-searching and aid them in imagining the sober implications of that last judgment, Edwards obliges with a catalogue of witnesses capable of testifying against covenant-breakers; the witnesses include God himself, God's saints, holy angels, the "workings of providence," "your special obligations to God's great mercy," God's ministers, the "many ill consequences of your wickedness," and of course "your own words." Thus Edwards moves the consequences of a pastor's performative utterances and those of the congregation's beyond time to eternity.

The Efficacious Word

The immediate power of God's Word, Edwards reminds his listeners [II Cor. 4:7], can destroy or save. Certainly, God does not need to use vehicles or means—written, spoken, or visible—of grace. God "could with perfect ease, without any external means at all influence, awaken, or convert men." Likewise, God could also "if he so pleased" destroy the wicked "by a word, speaking." But it pleases God, instead, to convey his divine mind and will through the voice of his messengers. And it also pleases God to hear his name professed by all those who believe in Him. In this way, Edwards reminds himself in his note on efficacious grace, "we are not merely passsive, nor yet does God do some, and we do the rest. But God does all, and we do all. God produces all, and we act all. For that is what he produces, viz our own acts."[40]

As God's collaborator, actively speaking with the authority of a divine officer, Edwards believes that his word—even in the imprecatory sermons—breathes with the same spirit of performative force that God's glorious word breathes: Ministers "speak and act wholly under Christ, as taught of him, as holding forth his word, and by light and strength communicated from him."[41] God's word proclaimed by ministers is positively performative, even as it warns, threatens, judges, and condemns, for God's word is a word of holy, perfect justice, condemning the wicked so that God's name may be more abundantly glorified. One of Edwards' scriptural notes comments on the two-fold effect of gospel ministry: "Christ that is a shepherd to his people, their protection and comfort, is destructive to unbelievers . . . . His salvation is poison to them through their rejection of it." So also, says Edwards in the same note, the "word of God by Moses" was "a means of the salvation of Israel," and at the same time "a sword to destroy the Egyptians."[42] And the faithful word, qua faithful word, of God's ministers is likewise positively forceful: "Every part of the message that God sends shall be effectual and the effect shall be great answerably to the preciousness of the word" [II Corinthians 4:7].

Here is the central paradox of Puritan preaching. The minister's pressing desire is that the souls under his care be touched, awakened,

****
[40] (Hickman), II, 557.

[41] Ibid., 963.

[42] Ibid., 719.

and nourished by the gospel he preaches. He strives continually to find acceptable words. He devotes his particular gifts and graces to bring God's message perspicuously, completely, and stirringly. Yet he also realizes that "even if ministers knew perfectly the circumstances of every soul, knew all his thoughts and the workings of his heart and so knew how to suit the word exactly to his case, if he could set forth the gospel in the most powerful, moving, and convincing manner that the nature of words will allow of, yet if the matter be left there and God does nothing, nothing will be done. The soul will remain as before" [II Corinthians 4:7]. Conversion, like creation and resurrection, is a miracle of which the Holy Spirit alone is capable: "Conversion is the peculiar work of God." In a very special sense, "The conversion of the soul . . . is both a creation and a resurrection" [II Corinthians 4:7]. Conversion is the Spirit's restoration of the image of God in fallen man or woman; it is the elevation of a person's heart and understanding by a divine and supernatural power.

Though the minister cannot change or convert a single soul, he prepares the way for the moving of the affections. When the Holy Spirit acts to convert, [it acts to convert] it acts upon the matter that the preaching of the word has furnished to the understanding of the hearer. The minister firmly believes that through grace his preaching demonstrates God's counsels, reveals God's mind, and shows forth God's glory. Thus Edwards' concluding words in the unpublished sermon on Micah 5:7 evoke images of the hearer's day of accounting before God's judgment seat even as his words insist that God does not wait until the last day to reveal Himself plainly and intelligibly. God sends his ministers throughout the world to speak for Him as His messengers, as His trumpeting heralds. Confronted with these messengers, listeners can in no way be passive:

Whether you will regard what has been said, I know not, but

whether you hear or whether you forebear, these things will
one day appear important considerations to you. And
remember that agreeable to what you have heard under these
doctrines, this sermon will have its effect one way or the
other. As it stands, it is one of the means of grace that
you have enjoyed. (emphasis added)

Edwards' peroration is a significant juxtaposition of his pastoral
reminder that the ministerial word is an inevitable power for good or
for evil to the hearer and an affirmation that preaching as a means of
grace demonstrates God's temporal and spiritual provision for His
beloved church.

CHAPTER IV

EDWARDS' ORDINATION AND INSTALLATION SERMONS--1736-1747

Throughout his ministry, Edwards was enormously conscious of
ecclesiastical status and professional identity. Particularly in the
official installment and ordination-related sermons he delivered
between 1736 and 1756, Edwards demonstrates his continuing fascination
with the exploration of the "nature and design of that office to which
[ministers] are . . . , in the name of Christ, to be solemnly set
apart."[1] Edwards' awe before the ministerial office prompted him in
his first ordination sermon to tell his listeners that gospel ministry
brings to its laborers a "distinguished and peculiar honor and joy."[2]

Edwards' deep consciousness of his own official status also
appears unmistakably in several small but richly symbolic events
related to his early years of ministry at Northampton. Initially,
Edwards served the Northampton church as an assistant to his
grandfather Solomon Stoddard. After Stoddard's death in 1729, Edwards
took on the full ministerial responsibility for the congregation's
spiritual welfare. When Edwards first joined the Northampton church in
1727, Stoddard placed the name "Jonathan Edwards" on the membership
role. To this day, the name stands inscribed in the aged Stoddard's
handwriting. But sometime in 1729, soon after young Edwards became
chief officer of the Northampton congregation, he returned to the
membership list where his name had been recorded by his grandfather,
and with a strong, steady hand affixed to it the word "Pastor."
Patricia Tracy remarks of this incident: "Edwards was only twenty-five
when he received his new title, his hand was vigorous and assertive,

****
[1](Hickman), II, 959.

[2]Unpublished ordination sermon on Luke 10:17-18, at Lambston,
May 17, 1736.

and the word he wrote represented all that he hoped to be."[3]

Without doubt, Edwards' self-identifying gesture is emblematic of his constant efforts to define, describe, and establish himself faithfully as one bearing the honorable office of gospel minister. In using the term "pastor"--or "shepherd" in the Latin—Edwards acknowledged himself as one appointed not only to guard and protect but also to nurture and feed the souls in his charge. In registering his title by means of a personal word-deed enacted in the church's records, Edwards committed himself to ecclesiastical servanthood under a divine Master, and he articulated how thoroughly his personal and professional identity would be fused. It is notable, too, that Edwards not only initiated his ministry in Northampton with a quietly firm declaration of his pastoral identity; he concluded it with a similar but more nuanced assertion when he placed a letter to the Northampton people as an appendix to Truth Vindicated (1752) and poignantly signed it with "I am, Dear Brethren, He who was once (as I hope through grace) Your faithful pastor, devoted servant for Christ's sake, Jonathan Edwards."[4]

For over twenty-three years Edwards labored in Northampton, attempting to be worthy of the name "Jonathan Edwards, Pastor." His ministry was shaped by his efforts to take the place of his grandfather, who was an ecclesiastical legend in his own time and was often called "Pope Stoddard" by the Connecticut Valley people. Upon attending Stoddard's funeral, Edwards heard his eminent predecessor eulogized as one of those outstanding pastors to "whom it pleases God to impart so much of His wisdom and grace that under God they are accounted as shields of the earth, the strength and glory of the places

****

[3]Jonathan Edwards, Pastor, p. 3.

[4]From Edwards' "Appendix" to Misrepresentations Corrected and Truth Vindicated in a Reply to the Rev. Solomon Williams' Book, (Hickman), I, 531.

where they be."[5] Many years later, Edwards would observe of this
"shield of the earth"

> I had the happiness to be settled . . . two years with the
> venerable Stoddard; and was then acquainted with a number
> who, during that season, were wrought upon under his
> ministry. I have been intimately acquainted with the
> experiences of many others who were wrought upon under his
> ministry, before that period.[6]

Edwards' reiterated use of the words "were wrought upon" evokes
the traditional view of ministers as God's instruments and tools, a
view which Edwards, standing in the orthodox ministerial heritage,
cherished. Calvin also understood ministers to be God's vehicles; God
"uses the ministry of men . . . not by transferring to them his right
and honor, but only that through their mouths he may do his own work."[7]
Other Reformed ministers likewise perceived their task as the
indispensable one of delivering messages to soften and touch the hearts
of their hearers in readiness for the Spirit's gift of efficacious
grace. "A powerful ministery," said the eminent Thomas Hooker, "is the
only ordinary means which God hath appointed soundly to prepare the
heart of a poor sinner for the receiving of the Lord Jesus."[8] Solomon
Stoddard, in one of his last printed sermons, preached in 1723 and
published in 1724, vividly described ministers as God's impressive
"sons of thunder" and persons who labor to pull men "as Brands out of

****

[5]William Williams, Death of a Prophet Lamented and Improved
(Boston, 1729). Cited by Tracy, Jonathan Edwards, p. 14.

[6]Distinguishing Marks (Hickman), II, 271.

[7]Commentaries on the Epistle of Paul the Apostle to the
Corinthians, trans. John Pringle (Edinburgh, 1842-49), II, 172.

[8]Cited by Perry Miller in The New England Mind, p. 299.

the burning."[9] Following Stoddard, Edwards also referred to ministers
as "sons of thunder" and emphasized that a preacher's message should
prod and awaken men's consciences.[10]

Like Stoddard and other Puritan preachers, Edwards frequently
employed militant language and references to various vocations,
physical activities, and objects to aid in imaging the ministerial task
of representing Christ in the care and protection of souls. Stoddard
compares the work of ministry to that of an archer shooting the
conscience-pricking "arrows" of God's word into the hearts of
listeners.[11] William Williams called Stoddard, and by extension all
faithful ministers, the protecting "shields of the earth."[12] Edwards
likens a minister's voice to "the roaring of heaven's cannon"[13] and
declares that the sword of God's word "ought not to be sheathed by its
ministers."[14] In addition to pugilistic metaphors, Puritan sermons—
elaborating upon cues taken from the Scriptures—represented the role
and task of minister through a host of other analogs and comparisons.
Edwards explains this phenomenon and its rationale at length in Some
Thoughts:

> 'Tis the duty of ministers especially to exercise . . .
> discretion: in things wherein they are not determined by an

---

****

[9]Defects of Preachers Reproved in The Great Awakening:
Documents on the Revival of Religion, 1740-1745, ed., Richard L.
Bushman (New York, 1970), p. 13.

[10]Some Thoughts (Hickman), I, 401.

[11]Bushman, Great Awakening, p. 13.

[12]Cited in Tracy, Jonathan Edwards, p. 14.

[13]Future Punishment of the Wicked, (Hickman), II, 82.

[14]Some Thoughts, (Hickman), I, 401.

absolute rule, and that are not enjoined them by a wisdom
superior to their own, Christ has left them to their own
discretion, with that general rule that that, which upon the
best view of the consequences of things they can get, will
tend most to the advancement of his kingdom . . . . The
Scriptures always represent the work of a Gospel minister by
those employments that do especially require foresight of,
and provision for, future events and consequences. So it is
compared to the business of a steward, that is a business
that in an eminent manner requires forecast, and a wise
laying in of provision for the supply of the needs of the
family, according to its future necessities: and a good
minister is   called a wise steward. So 'tis compared to
the business of an husbandman . . . . So the work of the
ministry is compared to that of a wise builder or
architect, who has a long reach and comprehensive view . . .
. So also it is compared to the business of a trader or
merchant . . . . So 'tis represented by the business of a
fisherman . . . . 'Tis also compared to the business of a
soldier . . . . [15] (emphases added)

The more one explores Edwards' ministerial sermons, especially the
unpublished ordination sermon manuscripts, the more clear it is that
Edwards' preaching graphically celebrates the office and the "gifts and
graces" of the gospel minister. These pointedly "ministerial" sermons
provide abundant evidence of his attempts to communicate and project
the role of ministry by imaging it—making it visible. These sermons
are also highly significant as part of an eighteenth-century preaching
pattern in which colonial ministers were, as Youngs carefully

****
[15]Ibid., 407.

documents, "increasingly . . . preaching sermons about themselves." In
fact, characteristics and metaphors—such as the "light on a
hill"--"that had [previously] been applied to the whole body of
Christians in New England"[16] were now being applied by ministers
specifically to ministers as shining lights held faithfully against the
powers of darkness around them. Ministers were "preaching themselves,"
claims Young, to assert their waning ecclesiastical authority and the
decline of their official status in a society increasingly distracted
by secular, political, and materialistic interests.[17] Along with many
of his ministerial contemporaries, Edwards at times found the religious
climate chilly enough to complain, "How much is the gospel-ministry
grown into contempt! and the work of the ministry, in many respects,
laid under common difficulties, and even in danger of sinking among
us!"[18]

Office and Office Bearer

Although Edwards is part of a strong movement to uphold the status
and work of gospel ministry, his concommitant efforts to affirm the
apostle Paul's self-abnegating motto--"we preach not ourselves, but
Christ Jesus the Lord" (I Cor. 4:5)--appear in his frequent attempts
to distinguish between the greatness of the office and the lowliness of
its office bearers. In Some Thoughts Edwards warns that Christ's
officers are not to succumb to the temptation of arrogance or pride
because they hold so honorable an office; ministers are never to
aggrandize themselves, "assuming, or taking too much upon them, and

****
[16]Youngs, p. 88.

[17]Ibid.

[18]A Call to Extraordinary Prayer (Hickman), II, 293.

appearing as though they supposed that they were the person to whom it especially belonged to dictate, direct, and determine."[19]   Edwards' view of ministry is emphatically christological. Christ invests the office of gospel ministry with authority, dignity, and awesome responsibility, but, Edwards insists, those who fill that office must comport themselves with humility and proper self-denial.   Self magnification has no place in the minister's life: "The nature and design of the gospel is to abase men, and to ascribe all the glory of our salvation to Christ the Redeemer."[20]

Samuel Willard in Decline of Piety (1700) had also noted of ministry that "it is true, there is a difference to be acknowledged between the work itself, and the persons that are employed in it." But immediately he adds that there is little likelihood that "men should profit by their [ministers'] ministration, while they despise their persons, or entertain a low and a base esteem for them."[21]   Willard then continues his sermon by pleading that both office and officer be heartily respected. The issue of proper respect for both minister and ministry constitutes a continuing ecclesiastical and social problem in Edwards' time. The problem's prevalence is indicated by the question and answer considered at the 1731 organizational meeting of the Hampshire Association, a group of ministers who formed a fellowship to deal with common difficulties:

> What is the Duty of ministers, when any Under their Jurisdiction and Government refuse to come to them when sent for upon account of Misbehaviors?
>
> Ans. They ought to look upon them as Guilty of condemning

****

[19](Hickman) I, p. 387.

[20]Justification By Faith (Hickman), I, 635.

[21]Bushman, Great Awakening, p. 8.

Christ's authority, and to deal with them accordingly.[22]

Representing Christ's authority with both courage and humility thus becomes a major ministerial motif in Edwards' work. An early expression of this theme appears in the sermon on II Corinthians 4:7 which Edwards preached very shortly after Stoddard's death.[23] In his first weeks as the chief ecclesiastical officer of Northampton he emphasized to his hearers that "the instruments that God makes use of to do his work on the souls of men are of themselves utterly unable to do it." Consequently, "minister should take heed when their labours are succeeded (?) not to glory in it as if it was because they are better and more able than others." With all humility, ministers as "earthen vessels" must perform their official labors "with great seriousness (?) and consideration of the vast importance of the work, how great a thing it is to have the care of precious souls committed to them." And with all courage ministers must "give themselves wholly to these things and with all their might . . . seek the advancement of Christ's kingdom."

As Edwards articulates his views of ministry, however, his own words occasionally demonstrate the great difficulty he faces in making sharp distinctions between honorable office and humble office bearer. In Some Thoughts, Edwards may not have intended to elevate the office bearer. But when three times in one paragraph he points to ministers "above all others," the ambiguity of his language and syntax reveals how hard it is sometimes for an office bearer to avoid all appearance

****
[22]Winslow, Jonathan Edwards, p. 227.

[23]Thomas Schafer's dating determinations indicate that this unpublished sermon was written at several different times, the earlier part perhaps in 1727 or 1728. It was completed and preached in 1729. I am endebted to Schafer as well as Wilson Kimnach for sharing this information with me.

of pride.[24] Further, Some Thoughts contains an interesting ambivalence bordering on contradiction in its discussion of humility adorning the redeemed; they appear "clothed with lowliness, mildness, meekness, gentleness of spirit and behavior." But when he describes humility in minsters, he urges that in handling the word of God ministers "ought not to be mild and gentle."[25] Moreover, there is a kind of inevitable hierarchy of persons in Edwards' view that Christ, possessing God's spirit without measure,[26] graciously gives his spirit to all the saints, but pours forth "a double portion of that Spirit" upon ministers.[27] Thus, in Edwards' conception, pastors do stand apart from the laity, are measured by special standards, are enabled in their work by special "gifts and graces," and are officially appointed "above all others" to be Christ's ministers.

Ministerial Onlooks

The complexity and tension in Edwards' conceptions of his vocational task and role inform and are in turn informed by the images and metaphors he uses in his ministerial sermons. Edwards' images of ministry are not merely rhetorical devices. His comment in Images or Shadows of Divine Things on biblical types is readily applicable to his ministerial analogies and images: they are intended to be evidences of a divine truth, and as such are "something further than meer [sic] illustration."[28] In a very tangible way the ministerial images expose

****

24 (Hickman), I, p. 387.

25 Ibid., p. 401.

26 "Miscellanies," #764, Beinecke Manuscript Library.

27 The Sorrows of the Bereaved Spread Before Jesus, Works (Worchester), III, 622. See also Edwards' unpublished sermon on II Corinthians 4:7.

28 Images or Shadows of Divine Things, p. 98. See also Images, p. 49, #26.

the great spiritual and vocational concerns which absorb Edwards; the images demonstrate concretely his official relationship to the human souls in his care and his relationship to the being who appoints, equips, and directs him in his office.

In their complexity, these metaphorical images reveal both how Edwards looks on himself as a minister and also how Edwards perceives God looks on him as a minister. The term "religious onlooks," coined by Donald Evans, is an apt one for Edwards' ministerial images because these images derive from and embody, as do religious onlooks, the conviction that there exists a hidden being who has an authoritative onlook "to which one's own onlooks must conform."[29] In fact, the term "onlook" is utterly consistent with Edwards' evident belief that a minister's view of himself (his onlook) must thoroughly correspond with the biblical view of ministry (God's onlook), for, as Edwards states it, "above all others, is God's eye upon the ministers of the gospel, as expecting of them that they should arise, acknowledge, and honor him."[30]

In the most profound sense, Edwards' religious onlooks commit him "to a way of behaving and thinking, a mode of life."[31] Essentially they are affirmative reponses to God's power, authority, and glory. It is certainly true for Edwards that his religious onlooks have integrity as God enables him "to act in accordance"[32] with them and thus with God. Most important, that Edwards goes to the infallible Scriptures for his ministerial images accords with Evan's assertion that the "true

****
[29]Evan's Logic of Self-Involvement, p. 225.

[30]Some Thoughts (Hickman), I, 387.

[31]Evans, p. 251.

[32]Ibid., pp. 255-256.

onlook is true because it is God's."[33]

Edwards certainly grasped the grave personal implications and challenges embodied in the biblical images of ministry. His onlooks make clear how fully he was intrigued and impressed with the concept of analogy or types. As Perry Miller has said in the introduction of Edwards' Images or Shadows of Divine Things, Edwards' notes on images and shadows are full of his delight in discovering the ways in which "natural things were ordered for types of spiritual things."[34] He enjoys articulating the relationships between substance (the true thing or idea in God's mind) and shadow (the natural or physcial representation of the ideal thing). Between natural activities or corporeal objects and God's eternal ideas, Edwards uncovers many a "great and remarkable analogy," "lively emblem," "wonderfull [sic] analogy," "remarkable type," and innumerable "lively images."[35] Edwards' use of images, analogies, and types builds upon an epistemological framework which recognizes that God's will and mind is revealed in the natural, physical world of things, processes, and activities. Viewing the ministerial images in Edwards' sermons as religious onlooks reveals his more personal, self-involving application of his conception of vocational type or analogy and helps to illuminate his exercise and practice of ministry.

In his treatise on Freedom of the Will Edwards remarks that "of all kinds of knowledge that we can ever obtain, the knowledge of God and the knowledge of ourselves, are most important."[36] An exposition

****

[33] Ibid., p. 256.

[34] Images or Shadows, image #45, p. 56.

[35] Ibid., pp. 44, 70, 75, 50, and 64.

[36] Author's Preface, Freedom of the Will, ed. Paul Ramsey (New Haven, 1957), p. 133.

of Edwards' ministerial sermons and religious onlooks reveals his zealous attempts to apprehend the knowledge of God and of self, especially the self that is appointed to be office bearer and spiritual counselor to souls. Particularly in the ordination and installment sermons, Edwards' preaching is animated with a high consciousness that he is ministering to ministers, bringing a message to God's messengers, and visibly embodying the images and ministerial onlooks he articulates. Especially during the Great Awakening, Edwards became a center of ministerial attention as "numerous ministers" came to him, says Sereno E. Dwight, "from various parts of the country. . . to gain from his counsel and his measures, more just conceptions of the best manner of discharging the highest and most sacred duties of their office."[37] Indeed, there are, as we shall see in this chapter and the next, notable shifts in mood, imagery, and style in Edwards' sermons on ministry. There is the warmth and exuberant joy in early ministerial sermons; the confidence and matured religious onlooks during the Great Awakening years; the heavily reiterative, defensive sermons during the painfully contentious years in Northampton; and finally, the last ordination sermons, which set aside metaphors and look directly at Christ as the perfect image of suffering ministry and obedience to the will of God. Edwards' fundamental intent, however, in all his years of preaching is to represent faithful ministry by declaring the mind and will of God.

David Hall makes the important observation that Calvin envisioned the preacher's work and style as "a fusion of two modes, the pastoral and prophetic."[38] Successive generations of ecclesiastical leaders following Calvin then developed variations on the "double character" of

****
[37]"Memoirs of Jonathan Edwards" (Hickman), I, lxxxvi.

[38]The Faithful Shepherd, p. 269.

ministry, says Hall.[39] Like his Calvinist and Reformed predecessors, Edwards continued to examine the ministerial office for ways to combine and fuse qualities of self-abnegation and confidence, serenity and zeal, shepherding and evangelism, sober warnings and peace-loving gentleness, gracious intelligence and faithful love. In trying to balance these elements, Edwards held to the ideal that the most eminent ministers and saints are those with the greatest humility, those "who think meanly of their attainments in religion, as compared with the attainments of others, and particulary of their attainments in humility."[40]

If ministerial humility is to be genuine, Edwards observes, then pastors must diligently emulate the selfless love and faithfulness of "the man Christ Jesus that is the Head of all creatures [yet] is the most humble of all creatures."[41] As Edwards' "Miscellanies" entry further considers humility and ministry, it presents one of the most idealized, beatific, and paradoxical models of ministers to be found in Edwards' writings. It envisions ministers to be among "the highest" inhabitants of heaven, but in humility "below" all others, happily employing "their superior excellency" in service to the "lowest" in heaven:

> in heaven will be a kind of ministers in that society teachers ministers to their knowledge & love & helpers of their joy as ministers of the gospel are here. Hence we may learn . . . how far those that are lowest will be from envying those that are highest or the highest from despising the lowest. For the highest shall be made ministers to the

****

[39]Ibid., pp. 19 and 49.

[40]Religious Affections (New Haven), p. 336.

[41]"Miscellanies" #681, Beinecke. In using this passage I am indebted to Thomas Schafer's typescript copy retaining Edwards' ampersands and omitted punctuations.

happiness of the lowest, & shall be even below them in humility. & the lowest shall have the greatest love to the
highest for their superior excellency & the greater benefit
which they shall receive from their ministrations, as tis the
disposition of the saints to love & honour their faithful
ministers here in this world.[42]

Edwards' ministerial vision is shaped by an intense awareness of
ministerial responsibility and authority and also by a firm belief that
ministers who are humbly faithful in representing Christ are marked
with a "superior excellency," an excellency and faithfulness which
elicits and in a sense renders them deserving of the "love and honor"
of the saints "here in the world." Edwards' conception, then, of the
minister as elevated servant and humble leader and his distinctions
between "highest" and "lowest" are a sociological as well as a
spiritual paradox.

To gain a deeper, more substantial view of this "superior
excellency" fundamental to right ministry, it is necessary to turn to
Edwards' published and unpublished official sermons preached over a
span of thirty-five years. In one of his best-known published
ordination sermons, True Excellency of a Ministry of the Gospel, the
theme of "superior excellency" becomes central. Many of Edwards'
unpublished sermons corroborate the ministerial views in his published
sermons as well as provide additional insights into his vocational
onlooks and conceptions of ministerial excellency.

****
[42]Ibid, see above footnote.

MINISTERIAL SERMONS

Unpublished Ordination Sermon on Luke 10:17-18 (November 17, 1736)

During 1736, many religious awakenings occurred under Edwards' ministerial leadership in the Northampton Church. As these "extraordinary" events were attracting much attention throughout the colonies, on November 6, 1736, Edwards completed A Faithful Narrative of Surprising Conversions in its initial form as a letter to Benjamin Colman. A week and a half later, Edwards went to Lambston (a small settlement in Massachusetts) to deliver his first ordination sermon. The sermon, based on Luke 10:17-18, formulates its message into a single doctrine: "When those ministers of the gospel that have been faithful and successful come to give an account of their success to their Lord that hath sent them, Christ and they will rejoice together." Following the traditional Puritan form, the sermon moves through opening, doctrine, and application. In addition Edwards responds to the occasion of ordination by using the application to address pointed remarks first to all ministers, then to the minister about to be ordained, and finally to the people whose souls are about to be placed under his care. This distinctive three-part application becomes a common element in almost all of Edwards' ordination and installation sermons.

One of the most notable facts about his first ordination message is its joyous celebration of the minister as trusted, stewardly servant uniquely accountable to God: "They that Christ appointed as stewards in his house must give an account of their stewardship. They must give an account to their great master how they have done the work that he had appointed." Here Edwards expresses a nascent form of the stewardly servant onlook which he develops more elaborately in later sermons such as the unpublished sermon on Romans 12:4-8 (1739), Concern of the Watchman for Souls (1743), True Excellency of a Gospel Minister

(1744), and the Northampton _Farewell Sermon_ (1750). The 1736 ordination sermon compares the spiritual relationship between God and his ministers to the relationship between a great lord and the faithful manager of his estate. Ministers, like stewards, are honorably prepared and entrusted by their master to care for his household, his business, and his most treasured possessions. Ministers, like stewards, are delegated to their employment and are fully accountable for the success and faithfulness of their work. Ministers, says Edwards in the sermon on Luke 10:17-18, are "called and set apart to the work with a sufficient signification of [Christ's] will that when his orders are thus attended, it shall be looked upon as being done in his name." As a faithful steward's greatest happiness is in the joy and satisfaction of his master, so the success of a gospel minister will be "greatly to the glory of Jesus Christ." And Christ's honor and glory are a minister's greatest reward.

This sermon's key words and phrases--"joy," "rejoice," "joyful," "rejoicing," "happiness," "successful," "faithful ministers," "successful ministers," "an account of their successes"--mark it as preaching which projects an optimistic, almost exuberant spirit. Edwards portrays stewardly ministers as a significant part of the divine economy of salvation. Ministers in their preaching and management of Christ's kingdom on earth happily anticipate the reward of their master's approval and glory. Ultimately Christ and the minister will rejoice not only as Lord and servant, but as intimate friends. The faithful minister, having accomplished his appointed labors in an orderly, judicious, and productive manner—"bringing home souls to [Christ] and building them up in holiness"--will find himself a beloved, honored member of his master's household.

With its strong emphasis on success and accountability, Edwards' sermon seems something of an attempt to give the work of ministry a quantitativeness or measurability. Yet this sermon, for all of its lively joy and spirited exaltation, remains somewhat vague and redundant, lacking the concreteness with which his later ordination sermons treat the details, circumstances, and difficulties of the minister's task. The descriptions of the actual work of ministry are hardly more than generalized reiterations. The labor is awesomely great." The Master is infinitely "great." The minister's success is "great." The rejoicing is "great." And the minister's vocation greatly surpasses all other earthly vocations:

> There is no employment that the children of men are employed in wherein they have such opportunity to lay a foundation for their own blessedness. Faithfulness in serving God in any calling will be crowned with glorious rewards, but there seems to be promises of distinguished and peculiar honor and joy in a faithfulness in this work [of gospel ministry]. This employment may well be looked on as a yet more excellent and honorable employment on the account of the joy that the success of it occasions to Christ. The very business of those that are called to this employment is to do that in which Christ exceedingly rejoices. Surely that must be great and excellent indeed that the Lord of angels and men takes such notice of and so rejoices in.

Clearly, the intent of the sermon is not so much to detail the rigors and complexities of gospel ministry as it is to present a richly impressive, eschatological view of the rejoicing and crowning rewards waiting for ministers who render both a faithful and successful account to their lord. In a main point of the sermon application, Edwards specifically encourages ministers to consider their ultimate goal and reward:

> Let us who are employed in or about to be employed in this work consider how blessed a day that day will [be] to us when we return to our Lord to give an account, if we have

been faithful and successful . . .

> And when we shall be admitted unto fellowship and intimate conversation with our Lord and relate to him our labours and self-denial through his grace and the blessed success we had . . . we have reason to conclude from the word of God that they [ministers] shall be admitted as friends to converse freely with him, no less freely than the disciples on earth did.

As Edwards moves through the three propositions, he extrapolates from his doctrinal statement--ministers are sent forth by Christ, must return again to Christ, and will rejoice with Christ if they have been faithful and successful. He then refers to various biblical texts, anecdotes, and parables, drawing his listeners' attention to the Luke 15 story of the good shepherd, the Matthew 25 parable of the unfaithful servant, and the lesson of the prodigal son. Each of these he relates directly to gospel ministry. Edwards also alludes to the mystical passage of Canticles 3:11, and in so doing, briefly anticipates and explores the metaphors of espousal and marriage which become the primary informers of his 1746 ordination sermon, The Church's Marriage to Her Sons. The following words from the 1736 sermon as it depicts the minister's task and goal reverberate with spousal, parental, and natal imagery. Ministers are

> employed in setting the crown of joy upon Christ's head in that they are the Instruments of bringing to pass the work of conversion which is the marriage between Christ and his spouse. The day of [a soul's] conversion is the day of Christ's espousal and the day of his exceeding gladness of his heart.
>
> It is thought to have been a custom among the Israelites that in the wedding day the mother of the bridegroom put a crown upon his head to be a crown and joy

and rejoicing which is mystically applied to Christ in
Canticles 3:11.   By king Solomon is probably meant Christ.
And by his mother and his bride, by both is meant the
church, but by his mother seems especially to be meant the
church as holding forth the word of Christ and administering
his ordinances whereby souls are converted and as it were
brought forth and brought to a spiritual marriage with
Christ and therefore the ministers of the gospel seem
especially to be intended by his mother for they travaill
[sic] with souls 'till Christ be formed in them.   Galatians
4:19.   Christ said of his disciples, they are my brethren
and sister and mother.   These therefore when they are the
instruments of converting souls and their espousal to
Christ, they do as it were put a crown of gladness on
Christ's head.

And what an honor is that upon . . . faithful ministers as
the instruments of the conversion of . . . persons, that
brings a soul to espousal with Christ and occasions gladness
in his heart and adds a jewel to his crown of rejoicing.

And hereafter when they [ministers] come to give their
[account] of their success, they shall then behold the crown
of joy which they have set on Christ's head, and Christ will
at the same time give the same souls to them to be their own
crown of rejoicing and thus they shall have communion in the
same crown of joy which shows (?) the exceeding blessedness
of that work.[43]

One of the few dark passages in this sermon has an eschatological
emphasis.   Following the Puritan logic of exclusive disjunction,
Edwards believes that for ministers and for the souls in their care,

****
[43]In this passage, the celebrative application Edwards makes here
of "travaill" in the birth of souls is a remarkable contrast to his
use of the same metaphor in Watchman where he moves from travail to an

there is ultimately no middle ground.   One is either faithful or
unfaithful.   One receives either commendation or condemnation.
Eternity will be either glorious or miserable.   Edwards reminds the
ministers among his listeners "how dreadful will our case be when we
come to give an account to our Lord if we have been unfaithful" in so
"honourable a work" as the "care of the precious souls of men."
Edwards then holds up the spectre of the horrendous humiliation and
eternal judgment certainly awaiting ministers who neglect their
minsterial labors in order to pursue "worldly concerns" or to "hoard up
for prosperity." Including himself through the use of the first person
pronoun, Edwards warns that the shame will be unspeakably great "when
we shall see those precious souls that were committed to our love, lost
through our neglect and standing at the left hand of the judge . . .
and they shall rise up in judgement against us . . . . The misery will
be eternal. As faithful ministers shall be distinguished in glory, so
perhaps none shall be so distinguished in misery as unfaithful
ministers." With the exception of these doleful words, however, this
sermon stands as a lively celebration of the joys and honors of gospel
ministry, delivered by the man whom the world was fast coming to
recognize as "the charismatic leader"[44] of a wide-spread American
revival.

Unpublished Ordination Sermon on Romans 12:4-8 for Deacons (1739)

       Among Edwards' hundreds of sermons there is only one commemorating
the ordination of deacons.   The diaconal office in the orthodox

****
(Footnote 43 Continued From Previous Page)
elaborate description of Christ's painful crucifixion and death for
the eternal life of souls.

      [44]C. C. Goen, editor's Preface to The Great Awakening (New Haven,
1972), p. 32.

Christian tradition does not stand as a "teaching or ruling office" equal in rank with the pastoral office. Nonetheless, in a discussion on Edwards' views of ministry, this sermon on Romans 12:4-8 deserves attention for its extensive treatment of ecclesiastical offices. The sermon's doctrine--"The offices that Christ has appointed in his church do respect either the souls or bodies of men"--is developed through a set of reasons asserting an ecclesiastical hierarchy in which ministers attend to the needs of people's souls while deacons in their supporting office assist the minister by caring for the church members' physical needs.

The sermon on Romans 12:4-8 was delivered in the Northampton church and is dated August 19, 1739. The rather plodding opening section seems not to have benefited from the care Edwards usually gave to sermons he prepared for ministerial ordinations and other occasions at which he anticipated the presence of visiting clergy. Unpolished and repetitious, the first pages serve Edwards primarily as a rhetorical warm-up, an opportunity to draft the themes and issues to be handled at length in the Doctrine and Application of the sermon.

The sermon's beginning does demonstrate Edwards' preliminary concerns to develop a firm working vocabulary for the rest of the sermon and to define terms clearly, especially the term "ministering," which in this sermon and biblical context has a narrower-than-usual, diaconal meaning to distinguish it from exhorting, teaching, or prophesying. Here follows the first several pages of the opening including the peculiar paragraphing, lines, and markings Edwards used:

> Romans 12:4.5.6.7.8. "for as we have many members in one body, and all the members have not the same office"
>
> --------------------
>
> In the words we may observe three things.
>
> 1. We observe what is the theme of the apostle's discourse in these verses viz. the different offices there are in the

church of Christ as in the 1st of these verses.

-----So in the following verses he speaks of the different gifts that are exercised in the church in those different offices.

----

2.   Here is an account of the business belonging to those several offices delineated in a variety of expressions, prophecying, teaching, exhorting, ruling, ministering, giving, showing mercy.

Concerning these businesses that the apostle speaks of in this place as belonging to the different offices that are in the church, we may observe two things: 1. That they all concern the welfare of the church as it is in that to which the apostle compares it viz. the natural body. Different members of the body have different offices but the office of every member in some way subserves to the benefit of the body.   So it is in the body of Christ. The different offices that are in it respect the benefit of the body as of the church. The business that belongs to each office in the society is to do good to the society. The business of one office is to do good to that society in one respect and another in another.

Thus to prophecy, to teach, to exhort, and to rule is to do good to those that are [?] exhorted and ruled. So to minister, give, and shew mercy is given as another way to do good to the members of the body.

----

2.   It may be observed that all those businesses or offices in the church that are here mentioned are of two sorts.

Some of them respect the souls of men and some their bodies. They are all to do good to the members of the society in which they are officers but these are two ways of doing good to the society, one is to do good to their souls and another is to do good to their bodies.

And tis observable that all the businesses here mentioned are one or the other of these—prophecying, teaching, exhorting, and ruling all refresh the souls of men. They are so many different waies [sic] of offices, doing good to the souls of the society. But the other thing mentioned, ministering, giving, and shewing mercy especially respect the good of their bodies.

So here are two sorts of work of a different kind that the apostle mentions when he reckons up the kinds of work that belong to the different offices in the church. One is to do good to the souls and the other is to do good to the bodies of men.

And tis observable that all these businesses here mentioned that concern men's souls belong to the office of elders or bishops, prophecying, teaching, and exhorting and ruling. The other therefore, viz ministering, giving, shewing mercy that concerns the bodies of men belong to some other offices Christ has appointed in his church. All these expressions—ministering, giving and shewing mercy are only a diverse expressing the same thing. By ministering, as the word used in the New Testament, is most commonly meant giving or communicating of our goods to others. So the apostle Paul when he was going to Jerusalem to carry the contributions of other Christians to the poor saints, then he says, Rm. 15:25 "But now I go to Jerusalem to minister to the saints." So also in 2 Cor. 8:4 speaking of the same contributions he says, "Praying us with much intreaty that we would receive the gift and take upon us the fellowship of ministering to the saints." So when he explains the same contribution [to the Corinthians], he says 9 chap. 1 v. "For as touching the ministering to the saints, it is superfluous for me to write to you." So when the apostle commends the Christian Hebrews for their charity to the saints he says, Heb. 6:10 "For God is not unrighteous to forget your work and labour of love which ye have shewed toward his name in that ye have ministered to his saints" and so in innumerable other places that might be mentioned.

And therefore Mr. Henry in his annotations says that when the apostles say in the text "ministering," "let us wait in our ministering," that he has respect to the office of deacons as that is the general opinion of expositors and divines.

The word that is here cited "deacons" is in the original "diaconoi." The significance of the word is "they that minister." The name is taken from that business which is to minister to the saints. This is the business spoken of here as ministry. Let us wait on our ministering. The word "ministering" in the text in the original is diaconia or deaconship, whence Mr. Henry argues that the office of a deacon is meant in the text. What that ministering is is plainly expressed in the following expressions of giving and shewing mercy.

3. This is observable in the words of the context the apostle gives to the different offices of the church.[45]

Moving beyond the opening of the text to an exposition of the sermon's doctrine, Edwards distinguishes carefully between the extraordinary offices—which appeared for a time in the post-resurrection church and "depended upon extra and miraculous gifts of the holy spirit"--and the ordinary offices of Christ's church, the offices of bishop and deacon which "continue to this day and must continue to the end of the world."

We also find in the sermon exposition an elaboration of the minister-as-steward metaphor implicit in Edwards' earliest ordination sermon, the November 17, 1736, sermon on Luke 10:17-18. In the sermon on Romans 12:4-8, Edwards states vigorously that both bishops and deacons have a stewardly role in overseeing Christ's family. Edwards stresses the caretaking, nurturing aspects of both offices:

They are both stewards in the house of God. The business of both alike are that they are stewards to bake and to supply the meals of Christ's family. The business of both is to feed God's people. The business of both is to see to it that everyone has his portion of meat in due season.

And while there are similarities between the stewardly offices of bishop and deacon, says Edwards, there are also marked contrasts:

'Tis with regard to the substance [that] they [the offices] differ . . . . Bishops are to have a watchfull [sic] eye on the state of the whole flock to observe the consequences of their souls that he may adapt spiritual supplies to their particular needs.

So deacons are to have a watchfull eye on the state of the

****
[45]The allusions to Matthew Henry, a renowned English expositor, are a deviation from Edwards' usual pattern in sermons of avoiding direct references to theologians or ecclesiastical leaders. When he

whole flock also, to take notice of the circumstances of
their bodies to observe who are in straits and in necessity,
that their necessities may be supplied.

Bishops are stewards of the household, that every man may
have his portion of meat in due season in spiritual respects.
So deacons are stewards in the same household, that everyone
that is in necessity and is a proper object of charity may
be relieved and may have his portion of meat in due season.

The broad affirmative aim of the sermon is to celebrate Christ's
gracious response both to the physical and to the spiritual needs of
his people. As one who healed bodies as well as souls in his ministry
on earth, Christ continues this care for his beloved household, says
Edwards, through the appointed offices of bishop and deacon which are
"both perpetual and constantly to be respected in the church to the end
of the world." To emphasize Christ's attentive, providential care,
Edwards gives five doctrinal "reasons" why Christ has appointed two
sorts of officers in the church. Each reason points to the duality of
human nature, but does so in a way which interrelates rather than
dichotomizes body and soul; thus, the church needs deacons as well as
bishops for the following reasons:

>   1. . . . man's nature is both spiritual and material, of
> which Christ is Savior . . . . When man fell, he wounded

****
(Footnote 45 Continued From Previous Page)
wished to bolster a point or argue a position with authority beyond
his own, he typically gathered, often in a cataloguing fashion, evidence or texts from Scripture. In the hundreds of Edwards' sermons I
have read, I have found the names of very few persons outside the
realm of biblical history. In a 1729 sermon on Luke 11:27-28, for
example, Edwards followed a general reference to the great reformers
with the name of "Luther," but then crossed it out, no doubt to avoid
such a specific reference to a non-biblical person.

both body and soul, and Christ is the redeemer of both and has taken both under his care . . . .

2. This is agreeable to the two sorts of needs of his people, ... They ben't only needs of soul but also of body . . . .

3. Herein the stated stewards of God's house are agreeable to the two sorts of commands that he has given to his people in the commands of the first and second table, . . . one sort more immediately respecting our duty to God and the other more immediately respecting our duty to man. So God has appointed two sorts of services to be attended in his house . . . .

4. This is agreeable to the two sorts of works that Christ did when he was personally present with his church on earth, which was to instruct the souls and shew mercy to the bodies of men . . . .

5. This is agreeable to the two sorts of promises of the covenant of grace, viz. the things of this life and that which is to come . . . .

Theologically, this sermon is a thorough exegesis of the text from Romans 12. It reveals very little, however, about the practical needs and diaconal administration in the Northampton church, or the actual relationship between its minister and deacons. Some comments in the sermon seem to be Edwards' pastoral plea for more diaconal assistance. Were the deacons not carrying out their responsibilities faithfully? Were the deacons not cooperating with Edwards' vision for their ministry as he had presented it two months earlier in a June, 1739, unpublished sermon with a doctrine stressing "that the main business of a deacon by Christ's appointment is to take care of the distribution of the church's charity for the outward supply of those in need"?[46] We

****

[46]Unpublished sermon on Acts 6:1-3.

can only wonder what exactly prompted Edwards in his sermon on Romans
12:4-8 to add to one of his doctrinal "reasons" a reminder that deacons
must supply the "table of the Lord and of their pastors" as well as the
poor of the" church's flock":

> There are many things they [deacons] may occasionally do
> whereby the ministers may be much helped and that office
> supported and encouraged that their [the ministers'] main
> support don't come through their hands as formerly it did.
> Tis the end of committing the church's flock into the hands
> of the deacons, most especially the supply of the poor as
> necessity is plain. Yet as they had the whole flock in their
> hands, doubtless they dispersed of it to all those uses for
> which the church had need of it and so we may argue that they
> supplied the table of the Lord and of their pastors.

Finally, as Edwards moves to this sermon's application, he returns
to the metaphor of the church as Christ's body and rejoices in the
beauty and suitableness of Christ's design for the harmonious
interrelationship and health of the body's parts. Clearly, Edwards in
his office of gospel minister is inspired by God's administrative
provision for the church and by "the nature of his redemption which
refreshes body and soul." And as usual, Edwards attempts to arouse his
listeners to an understanding of and consent to God's mind and will for
his people who are his "mystical body" in its parts and its whole.
Says Edwards,

> Hence we may see the excellence of Christ in the constitution
> [of Christ's body] in all the parts of it, the more shall we
> see cause to admire that wonderful agreement and harmony
> there is between one part and another of it, and offices and
> officers, and all agree together as the several parts of a
> skillful frame in which every part of it fitly joins together
> and cooperates as one. They beautifully [embrace?] one

another.[47]

Of particular interest in this sermon's application is the way in which Edwards uses the biblical metaphor of the church as Christ's body to compare specific ecclesiastical offices to specific body parts:

> In the body of Christ, the office of minister fitly answers to the office of the eye that guides and directs the body. The office of deacon seems well to answer the office of the hand in the natural body that feeds it and helps its suffering members.

In light of the grave controversies which gradually developed between Edwards and his church members in the decades following this sermon, the comparison of minister to eye is an arresting one. History reveals that the Northampton people, unable to live harmoniously with the spiritual leader they had called to guide and direct them, eventually deposed Edwards; finding its ecclesiastical eye offensive, the Northampton church plucked it out.

Unpublished Ordination Sermon on I Cor. 2:11-13 (1740)

On May 7, 1740, using I Corinthians 2:11-13 as his text, Edwards preached on the ordination of Edward Billing into the pastorate of the Congregational Church of Cold Springs, New York. The onlook inherent in this sermon is that of the minister as God's messenger. It is as God's spokesman, and especially on this occasion a messenger to God's messenger, that Edwards speaks "earnestly and humbly." Edwards declares emphatically to Billing, "I would . . . recommend to you that Holy Book which God is about to commit unto your hand, as containing the messages which you are to deliver to these people in his name."

The doctrine formulated from I Corinthians 2:11-13 includes a warning and a mandate: "Ministers are not to preach those things which

****

[47]We have here an example of Edward's life-long fascination with unity in diversity and harmony in complexity. This description from

their own wisdom or reason suggests, but the things that are already
dictated to them by the superior wisdom and knowledge of God."
Intensely polemical, the sermon wrestles with the troubling issue of
Arminian rationalism.   This sermon is outstanding among Edwards'
ordination sermons primarily as an apologia of divine revelation as the
rule of faith and religion. Focusing on God's infinite perfection and
man's depravity and unworthiness, the sermon presents a direct
challenge to the presumptions of Arminian thinking which invite "the
finite to accept itself with all its deficiencies as adequate."[48] In
treating the "vast disproportion" between human reason and divine
wisdom, Edwards' preaching in this sermon becomes at times an abstract
metaphysical analysis, at times an anti-rationalist harangue, and at
other times a theological disputation quite in contrast to the
celebrative, honorific tones traditionally used in ordinations.

     The historic context and important theological publications
preceding the I Corinthians ordination sermon provide vital clues to
its aggressively argumentative thrust.   During the years 1734-36
Edwards' battle against Arminianism intensified and became increasingly
public. More and more, Edwards accepted an apostlic role as authorized
representative of God's mind, select messenger of God's words, and
dauntless defender of the orthodox faith.   In the events surrounding
the suspected heresy of Robert Breck of Springfield and William Rand of
Sunderland Edwards took a public position as ministerial spokesman for

---

****
(Footnote 47 Continued From Previous Page)
the Romans 12:4-8 sermon has much in common, for example, with comments in Nature of True Virtue on the harmony, unity, and symmetry of
the parts of the human body as a natural analogy or "image of the consent of mind, of the different members of a society or system of
intelligent beings, sweetly united in a benevolent agreement of
heart." (Hickman), I, 128.

[48]Perry Miller, Jonathan Edwards, p. 124.

the Hampshire Association; he spoke out vigorously against what he viewed as creeping evidences of Arminianism in New England. In fact, says C. C. Goen, it was when Jonathan Edwards more than any one else, "called [the heterodoxy of Breck and Rand] by name and set his face against it, [that] the Great Awakening in New England was on."[49] Edwards also delivered a series of sermons (1734-1735) on justification by faith, striking hard against "the Arminian scheme of justification by our virtue," a scheme which can only be believed, says Edwards, if "we reject the Scriptures themselves as perplexed and absurd, and make ourselves wiser than God, and pretend to know his mind better than himself."[50]

When Edwards had preached his sermons on justification, many in the Old Light camp found great fault with him for "meddling with the controversy in the pulpit."[51] Later when the sermons were published (1738), Edwards' meticulous arguments against Arminianism were further criticized and ridiculed. Strongly on the side of Arminianism were Daniel Whitby and especially John Taylor, an articulate British theologian whose Scripture Doctrine of Original Sin Proposed to a Free

****
[49] The Great Awakening (New Haven), pp. 17-18.

[50] (Hickman), I, 620-621. The sermons on "justification" were consolidated into one discourse called Justification by Faith Alone and grouped with four other related sermons under the publication title Discourses on Various Important Subjects, in Boston, 1738. In Edwards' opinion, the justification sermons were "most evidently attended with a very remarkable blessing of heaven to the souls of those that heard them, and served as an important element in the latter part of December [1734]" in which "the Spirit of God began extraordinarily to set in, and wonderfully to work amongst us," A Faithful Narrative of Surprising Conversions (1736) reprinted in The Great Awakening, ed. Goen, p. 149.

[51] Faithful Narrative in Great Awakening, ed., C. C. Goen, p. 149.

and Candid Examination appeared in 1738.[52] In Edwards' estimation,
Whitby's and Taylor's statements were dangerous because they posed
fundamental theological questions in such a way that the issues became
stumbling blocks to orthodoxy. Both Whitby and Taylor emphasized the
unacceptability of the standard Calvinist mysteries and paradoxes in
religion. Summarizing Whitby and Taylor, Perry Miller sets forth the
problem as they saw it:

> . . . if men are irresistibly predestined, how can you ask
> them to be good? You cannot exhort them to perform what you
> and they know cannot be accomplished. If God has an
> antecedent purpose to withhold the aid by which alone they
> can succeed, all their pleas are repugnant to the will of
> God . . . . There seemed only one way out: to grant that
> God proposes rational persuasions because men, in themselves
> and by themselves, being causes of their own effects, have
> ability to accede or refuse, and that heaven or hell depends
> on their own decision.[53]

The liberal theological views of Whitby and Taylor provided the
foundation for Charles Chauncey's and Jonathan Mayhew's rationalistic,
enlightenment formulations in the colonies during the 1730's and
1740's. These men had great reverence for natural human intelligence
and educated understanding. In 1739 Chauncey published an essay
asserting unequivocally, "As Men are rational, free Agents, they can't
be religious but with the free Consent of their Wills; and this can be
gain'd in no Way, but that of Reason and Persuasion."[54] Faced with the

****

[52]Edwards' Great Christian Doctrine of Original Sin Defended is a
direct response to and refutation of Taylor's work.

[53]Jonathan Edwards, p. 110.

[54]Cited by Perry Miller in Jonathan Edwards, p. 165.

increase of Arminianism among liberal ministers and the serious declension of piety following the mid-1730's revivals, Edwards stepped up his preaching on the inherent limitations of human reason and the total depravity of fallen human nature. Fighting heresy and praying for another spiritual awakening, Edwards wrote George Whitefield on February 12, 1740, inviting him to Northampton and confessing sadly, "We who have dwelt in a land that has been distinguished with Light, and have long enjoyed the Gospel, . . . are I fear more hardened than most of those places where you have preached hitherto."[55]   Edwards profoundly hoped that if orthodox ministers joined together to resist the powers of Satan, God would use them as means to another awakening. We are not certain whether Edwards read Rev. William Cooper's April, 1740, published tract before preparing the May ordination sermon on God's superior wisdom, But if he did read it, he most certainly would have rejoiced in Cooper's remarks on conversion and faith as the result of God's work of grace and not of man's reason "excited by those rational arguments that have been set before them."[56]

Cooper's tract, Edwards' Discourses, and his May 7, 1740, ordination sermon are all motivated by the same high purpose—a defense of the orthodox mysteries of a crucified God, justification by faith, and the infallibility of Scripture.   Christians must own the great Protestant doctrines, says Edwards in the Preface to Discourses, "to be a matter of pure revelation, above the light of natural reason, and that [they are] what the infinite wisdom of God revealed in the gospel."[57]   God's superior wisdom as found in his Holy Word is a revelation of "such a way of reconciliation of which neither man nor

****

[55]Cited by Patricia Tracy in Jonathan Edwards, Pastor, p. 135.

[56]Cited by Miller, in Jonathan Edwards, p. 165.

[57](Hickman) I, 621.

angels could have thought."[58] Accordingly, the 1740 ordination sermon
stresses that the "duty incumbent on gospel ministers" is absolute
submission to God's will and word.   "The great imperfection and
darkness of man's reason in the fallen state," says Edwards, "makes us
to stand in need of a better [a holy and infallible] guide." Thus, in
this sermon Edwards often makes his point by an exhortation negatively
phrased:

> Ministers ought not to preach those things which their own
> wisdom and reason suggest, but the things that are already
> dictated by the Spirit of God . . . . They are not to preach
> those things that would seem right to their understanding if
> left alone and acted independently of an testimony or
> teaching or some understanding of any other Being . . . .
> Their preaching ought to rely on what [is] revealed and
> discovered to their minds by an understanding infinitely
> superior to others.

God's messengers are not to reject doctrines which seem to contain
"difficulties and seeming inconsistencies that their reason can't
solve."   The great truths of the gospel "are above our natural
faculties and our knowledge of 'em depends purely on the Revelation
made by the Spirit of God."

Under attack in this sermon are all who question God's sovereign
will and mind as seeming inconsistent with human reason;   Edwards
disputes all who suggest that salvation comes to people primarily
through reason or an inherent ability to comprehend or discover God.
Again and again Edwards rings variations on the theme that many things
in the Scriptures are "entirely beyond our understanding, and seem
impossible," yet God's revelation is the "very truth concerning his own

****
[58]Ibid.

nature and acts, counsels and ways, and of the spiritual and invisible world."

Although this sermon persistently asserts that God's revealed word is the infinitely superior light to which human reason must submit, it is notable that once the sermon text is set forth, Edwards' manuscript of 37 pages makes very little use of Scripture texts for proof or reference. Instead, he uses his reason--sanctified by the light of faith--as a "great friend"[59] to reinforce his assertions that "it is unreasonable to expect any other in a divine revelation than that it should contain mysteries." Edwards points extensively to the history of ideas and to developments in human culture as proof that persons have often been baffled by natural and philosophical mysteries, not to speak of religious ones:

> When was there ever a time when if there had been a revelation from heaven of the very truth of philosophical matters and concerning the nature of created things which must be supposed to lie more level with our understanding than divine things, but that there would have been things in such a revelation that would have appeared not only to the vulgar but also to the learned men of that age absurd and unacceptable. If many of those positions in philosophy which are now received by the learned world as understood truths had been revealed from heaven to be truths in past ages, they would have been looked upon as mysterious and difficult and would seem as impossible as the most mysterious Christian doctrines do now. And is it now reasonable to be questioned but that even now, after all the progress that is made in philosophy, if there should

****
[59]The Peace Which Christ Gives, in Jonathan Edwards Selections, eds. Hill and Wang, p. 139.

come a revelation from heaven of what is the very truth in
those matters without deviating at all from strict (?) truth
to accommodate its doctrine to our reasoned notions and
principles, there would be many things in it that to our
reason would seem to be absurd and self-inconsistent.

As he argues further on behalf of God's superior wisdom and the
mysteries of faith, he appeals directly to the listener's personal
experiences: "No doubt . . . there are learned men here present that
do now receive principles in philosophy" which at an earlier time in
their lives "they would have looked upon as difficult as any mystery
that is commonly supposed to be in the Bible." Edwards also uses an
analogy based on the rationality of numerical principles; he reminds
the congregation of "mathematical theorems that relate to Quantity and
and nature," which adults understand but "yet if told to children
appear very absurd and seem to imply great and evident contradictions."
At this point in the sermon Edwards incorporates a remark which echoes
the more coherently-phrased conclusion of his "Miscellanies" #652 which
he entitled "Mysteries in Religion." In the sermon manuscript he
writes, "The best of us are but children of God. There is vastly a
greater proportion between the understanding of the oldest philosopher
or mathematician than between his and that of the smallest child." But
the "Miscellanies" entry first presents an anecdote about a thirteen-
year-old boy confounded by a mathematical problem[60] (one wonders
whether Edwards' sermon may have allowed him the flexibility to add the
same anecdote or illustration extemporaneously) and then concludes by
musing, "Why should we not suppose that there may be some things that
are true, that may be as much above our understanding and as difficult
to them [mathematicians and philosophers], as this truth was to this
boy? Doubtless there is a vastly greater distance between our

****

[60]The anecdote which I include here is taken from Miscellaneous
Observations in Works (Hickman), II, 466, where it stands as #41. In
Schafer's typescripts of the "Miscellanies," it is listed as #652 and

understanding and God's than between this boy's and that of the greatest philosopher or mathematician." Clearly in using the example of the child Edwards is reinforcing the ancient and experiential pattern of "faith seeking understanding."

Suggesting that it is not orthodox Christians but enlightenment rationalists who are guilty of absurdities, Edwards declares, "Certainly those with whom difficulty and seeming inconsistencies are a weighty objection against doctrines of revelation don't make suitable allowances for the vast disproportion there is between God's understanding and ours." God's revelation is given "for all ages," and

****
(Footnote 60 Continued From Previous Page)
has the conclusions which John Erskine deleted as editor of the 1793 publication of Miscellaneous Observations on Important Theological Subjects: "I once told a boy of about thirteen years of age, that a piece of any matter two inches square, was eight times as large as one of but one inch square; or that it might be cut into eight pieces, all of them as big as that of but one inch square. He seemed at first not to think me in earnest, and to suspect that I only meant to make game of him. But when I had taken considerable pains to convince him that I was in earnest, and that I knew what I said to be true, he seemed to be astonished at my positiveness; and exclaimed about the impossibi- lity and absurdity of it; and would argue, how was it possible for two inches to be eight inches? and all that I could say, did not prevail upon him, to make him believe it. I suppose it seemed to him as great a contradiction, that what was but just twice so long, and twice so broad, and twice one should make eight, as any other absurdity what- soever. And when I afterwards showed him the truth of it, by cutting out two cubes, one an inch, and another two inches square; and let him examine the measures, and see that the measures were exact, and that there was no deceit; and cut the two inch cube into eight equal parts, and he counted the parts over and over, and took the parts one by one and compared them with the one inch cube, and spent some time in counting and comparing; he seemed to be astonished, as though there were some witchcraft in the case; and hardly to believe it after all. For he did not yet at all see the reason of it. I believe it was a much more difficult mystery to him, than the Trinity ordinarily is to men: and seemed to him more evidently a contradiction, than any mystery of religion to a Socian or deist."

it "becomes us," says Edwards, "to receive what God reveals to be truth
and to look upon his word as pure and sufficient whether what he
reveals squares with our notions or not." In his word, God declares
the "truth as it is without accommodating himself to men's notions or
principles, which would indeed be impossible, for those things which
are revealed notions in one ages are contrary to what are so in
another."

Looking ahead to a time when fallen human nature will be perfectly
recreated and restored, Edwards believes that the many things which now
appear "exceedingly difficult and incomprehensible while our faculties
are in the present low state" will "all be unfolded and seem easy in
some future time of an higher elevation of our faculties." To make
this spiritual principle concrete, Edwards turns to a vivid example
from daily life:

> If one looks for any thing in the dark by so low a faculty
> as the sense of feeling or by seeing with a dim light,
> sometimes we cannot find it and it will seem impossible that
> it should be there, but yet when a clear light comes to
> shine into the place and we discern by a better faculty or
> by the same faculty under a better advantage, the thing that
> before was irrefrangible appears very plain to us.[61]

As the sermon progresses, Edwards concentrates on exposing the
hypocrisy and treachery of those who seem to embrace the Scripture but
instead compromise and manipulate God's word by using specious,
pragmatic reasoning to suit their proud and stubborn hearts.
Facetiously, Edwards simulates the excuses of rationalist, Arminian
preachers "who say . . . these and these mysterious doctrines that are
taught in the Holy Scriptures . . . are attended with great
difficulties and are hard to understand [and] have puzzled the heads of

****
[61]Again here is evidence that Edwards has his notebooks close at
hand to stimulate, reinforce, or augment the flow of ideas while
constructing a sermon. The above passage roughly parallels

the most learned divines, and therefore 'tis impudent for ministers to meddle with them in their preaching. There are plain, practical truths enough for us to insist on. 'Tis not best for ministers to trouble their people's heads of such nice speculation." The sharpness of Edwards' remarks suggests he is still smarting from "the very open abuse"[62] given him by critics who "reproached"[63] him for preaching "speculative niceties and subtle distinctions of Christian doctrines"[64] in the pulpit.

Because for Edwards this sermon functions primarily as a polemical defense of orthodoxy and the sanctity of God's divine revelation, he leaves very little time for the traditional application and address to the participants and congregation. In his brief application and concluding remarks, he once again attempts to distinguish between the limits of human reason and the infinite mystery of God's mind and will: though our reason might tell us "that there is a God . . . and the Scriptures are his word, . . . modesty and humility and reverence to God requires that we allow that God is better able to declare to us

****
(Footnote 61 Continued From Previous Page)
"Miscellanies," #765. I give it here as it is transcribed by Thomas Schafer in his typescripts at Beinecke Manuscript Library. "If one seeks for any thing in the dark, by so low a faculty of discerning as the sense of feeling or by the sense of seeing with a dim light, sometimes we cannot find it, tho it be there, it seems to us to be impossible that it should be there, but yet when a Clear light comes to shine into the Place, and we discern by a better faculty, viz of sight, or the same faculty in a Clearer manner, the thing appears very plain to us. So doubtless many truths will hereafter appear Plain, when we come to look on them by the bright Light of Heaven, that now are involved in mystery and darkness."

[62]Preface to Five Discourses (Hickman), I, p. 620.

[63](Hickman), I, 620.

[64]Ibid., 621.

what is agreeable to His perfection than we are to declare to Him in
our Selves." The application also echoes the sermon's earlier
references to human childishness, reminding the listeners that in God's
eyes they are all children, and "the supreme legislative authority of a
nation don't ask children what laws are just for them to make or what
rules are just for them to proceed by, nor do they wait for the
judgment and deliberation of every subject in order to oblige them to
satisfaction. Much less does the infinitely great and wise Judge of
Heaven and Earth." Similarly, a minister speaking as God's messenger
does not ask his listeners which doctrines or truths they wish to hear.
The minister faithfully declares the Word of God the Father in a
message both powerfully and lovingly parental.

Speaking specifically to Edward Billing, Edwards urges him to be
faithful to the task as one of God's ordained messengers. To
underscore "the sacred work of the ministry," Edwards reminds Billing
that God's spokesmen must submit themselves wholeheartedly to the power
and authority of God's word. God's messengers must declare God's word
as God himself declares it. Edwards emphasizes this declaratory tone
in God's voice as it appears in the very "style in which [God's]
revelations are often given forth . . . 'Thus saith the Lord,' 'I am
the Lord' and "He that hath an ear to hear, let him hear' and "Who art
thou, O man, that repliest against God.'" And Edwards does not
hesitate to warn Billing that the time may come, if he is an obedient
messenger of God's word, "that you should be reproached for so doing
with such kind of reproaches as are in these days commonly used on such
as earnestly preach the mysterious doctrines of revelation, and you
should be called a bigotted zealot, one whose zeal runs before your
knowledge." Here too there is little doubt that Edwards is still
feeling the pain of being "greatly reproached"[65] and verbally abused

****
[65] (Hickman), I, 620.

for his own zeal and strict orthodoxy. Yet in all of this, he says to the young man about to be ordained, "your Lord and Master that commanded you to preach will defend you."

In his remarks to the people of Cold Springs, Edwards' words press once more the theme of God's superior wisdom and human's limited reason: "For you to oppose your reason to God's word is the way for you to go backward." Edwards follows warning with encouragement, urging the congregation to believe God's word and doctrines with "an implicit faith" and so demonstrate that you are "willing to become fools for Christ's sake." Edwards' exhortations to the lay listeners affirm one of the great mysteries of faith. Paraphrasing a paradox which had also fascinated the apostle Paul, Edwards declares: "He that would be wise must become a fool that he may be wise and glory in that which [the worldly] call your foolishness . . . [which you] have by God's instruction."

As in most of Edwards' ordination sermons, the final words--in this case addressed to both "pastor and people"--are an incantatory weaving of images of light and beauty contemplating the glorious state of God's redeemed saints in eternal union with the Redeemer. For those who adhere to "the word of God rather than [their] own minds," Edwards holds forth the promise that they shall hereafter "shine forth as the sun in the kingdom of your Father and shall appear to be some of those truly wise that shall shine as the brightness of the firmament." Through grace, ministers are God's "truly wise" messengers who "above all men" are not only to accept the Scriptures as God's instruction but are also delegated to teach and preach it with undaunted trust in the perfection of God's superior will and mind.

Ordination Fast Sermon on Acts 14:23 (January, 1741)

In January, 1741, in the midst of a great burst of revival activity in the Connecticut Valley parishes, Edwards accepted the

invitation to conduct a fast preceding the ordination of a new minister
in the neighboring town of Hadley, Massachusetts. Using Acts 12:23 as
his text, Edwards formulates the following doctrine: "The solemn
setting apart one to the work and office of a gospel minister is an
affair wherein God should earnestly be sought to." In charging that
God looks on ministers as his officers, this sermon highlights the
honors and distinctions of the ministry and treats the occasion of
ordination as one "of great moment" for all who participate.   The
eternal nature of the kingdom of God is present in the temporal
relationship between a pastor and people, says Edwards, for "the office
of the ministry is an office not of any human or earthly kingdom but
'tis an office of Christ's kingdom." Though directed most particularly
to the young minister who "above all others" is concerned with the
salvific task of caring for souls in the parish of Hadley, the sermon
also pointedly addresses "the people that call him to that work and
among whom he is solemnly ordained to and settled in that work."
Further, it speaks to the "neighboring churches and especially
neighboring pastors whose proper work and business it is to solemnly
set them apart to their office." The conducting of a fast, the
gathering of "neighboring pastors," the extensive rites and celebration
surrounding ordination, the part played by fellow ministers in
solemnizing and conferring the office upon a young candidate—all these
things alluded to in the sermon are part of an elaborate effort to
reenforce "ministerial importance"[66] at a time when ministerial
authority and professional status were being questioned.

     In contrast to Edwards' 1740 sermon on I Corinthians 2:15-26, with
its keen awareness of theological division in the New England churches
and its awareness of the opposition to zealous, orthodox preachers,

****
[66]Youngs, God's Messengers, pp. 88 and 130.

this 1741 ordination-related sermon warmly endorses harmonious relations among neighboring churches. "The settlement of a minister," says Edwards, does "much concern neighboring churches" by reason of "the intercourse and mutual concerns" and by reason of "Christian charity and communion." He continues: "Necessarily . . . neighboring churches are interested in each other's welfare." And "if one flourishes and prospers, it naturally tends to the health of the rest." Edwards also believes that the devil works continuously among the saints: if one church is "corrupted it tends to disturb and infect the rest." Retrospect allows us to note the irony that in spite of Edwards' official neighborliness, the church of Hadley and its pastor sided in 1750 with the church of Northampton in its efforts to remove Jonathan Edwards as an officer whose presence they deemed divisive and contentious rather than harmonious. At any rate, in 1741 Edwards stood in the Hadley pulpit cordially reminding his listeners that "'tis difficult . . . to think of any affair that a people are ever concerned in of equal importance" than the relation between a people and a pastor who cares for their souls. The work of Christ's officer involves nothing less than the everlasting salvation or misery of a people, their children, and perhaps even future multitudes. If a people are blessed in their relationship to their minister,

> they are like to be everlastingly gainers by it the salvation of many souls, . . . bringing them to everlasting glory . . . . So then they will be happy here and forever. But if a people are not blessed in their officer, they are like to be a miserable people. The consequences are like to be the perishing of multitudes . . . their being miserable here and miserable forever.

Clearly, in Edwards' view there is a kind of eternal communality between a congregation and minister: their relationship touches "their greatest interst, even the eternal interest of the everlasting salvation of themselves."

Concern of a Watchman for Souls, Heb. 13:17 (1743)

During the 1740's, Edwards six times accepted the honored invitation to preach ordination and installation sermons.[67] Four of these ministerial sermons, those delivered between June 17, 1743, and November, 1747, are thoroughly informed by a ministerial onlook. The first of these is Concern of a Watchman for Souls, [68] which develops the onlook of minister as watchman: God looks on his ministers as the appointed watchmen in his kingdom. In his Acts 14:23 (1741) ordination fast sermon, Edwards had made a passing allusion to the minister as watchman. Now in 1743, the watchman onlook becomes the ordination sermon's shaping and organizing principle. It magnifies the dignity and honor of the work of gospel ministry and gives a solidity to the minister's official "employment" and perogatives to protect the saints, guard the church, and proclaim God's word.

That this is Edwards' first published ordination sermon suggests that his supporters and associates believed its emphasis to be vitally in need of dissemination to a wider audience. Edwards delivered the sermon for the ordination of Jonathan Judd as the minister of the newly organized church of Southampton. Patricia Tracy indicates that the church's membership included many who were "Edwards' own converted young people in 1734-35."[69] Thus the sermon doctrine on Hebrews 13:17

****

[67] May 7, 1740, on I Corinthians 2:11-13; June 8, 1743, Concern of a Watchman for Souls; August 30, 1744, True Excellency of a Gospel Minister; September 19, 1746, The Church's Marriage to Her Sons; November 11, 1747, Zechariah 4:12-14; June 29, 1749, Christ the Example.

[68] First published by this title in 1743, the sermon was later listed as The Watchman's Duty and Account in Works (New York edition, 1830). References will be made to the New York edition. See Appendix for the full sermon text.

[69] Tracy, Jonathan Edwards, Pastor, p. 155.

can be understood as a ringing assertion of Edwards' own pastoral efforts on behalf of the listeners as well as a general declaration of the great work of gospel ministry: "Ministers of the gospel have the precious and immortal souls of men committed to their care and trust by Jesus Christ."

This sermon's watchman onlook establishes the minister's sacred commitment to cherish and to attend souls in the sense of guarding and protecting them, or, as Edwards himself explains, "watch for them, which implies that they may be so taken care of that they may not be lost, but eternally saved." The word "watchman" develops an increasingly rich complexity as Edwards incorporates examples from other protective vocations such as caretaker, gate-keeper, household guardian, steward, shepherd, and ambassador.

In the first pages, Edwards meticulously works out his strategy to impress the congregation with the minister's great honor and responsibility in watching and caring for souls. First, Edwards expounds lengthily on the human soul as the crown of God's creation. To heighten and drive home the importance of the human soul, Edwards intensifies his rhetoric by employing numerous superlatives: "Indeed the soul of man is by far the greatest and most glorious piece of divine workmanship of the creatures on this lower creation"; souls are, "the chief and most noble of all, and the crown and end of all the rest" of creation; and souls "are above all other creatures which God hath made in this world, the subjects of God's care and special providence."

Human souls are God's "infinitely precious treasure." Ministers, members of that "certain order of men that are so dignified and honoured by [Christ] as to have so great a trust reposed in them," are guardians and watchmen of these precious souls. Appointed, fitted, and authorized by Christ, the minister guards the welfare of souls by holding "a continued watch" against heresy. Possessed of a great love for souls, the minister is to maintain an "incessant vigilance" against indefatigably subtle enemies. Not only does God mandate ministers to guard the wall of Zion with "a trumpet always at hand to sound, to give warning of any appearing danger" to souls. God also entrusts "the keys of his stores and treasury" to ministers and requires them to "cherish and preserve the ordinances of his house." To ministers "are committed the oracles of God and the treasures of the gospel." Thus God's watchmen are entrusted with an infinitely great "sacred depositum," the two-fold treasure of souls and the gospel.

Eschatology is seldom far away in Edwards' sermons, and this sermon is no exception. Edwards reminds ministers that in their role as the guardians and watchmen of souls, they will be called at the last judgment to give account of their work. What is remarkable in this ordination sermon is Edwards' highly imaginative use of dramatic dialogue to create a feeling for the great moment of truth when God will question his ministers and demand an account of the souls lost or saved. Edwards impresses upon the young minister, and by extension all the ministers who were attending the ordination: "You are to watch for these souls as one that must give account. If any one of these souls should be missing hereafter, having been lost under your ministry, it will be demanded of you another day, by your great Lord, 'What is become of such a soul? Here are not all the souls that I committed to you to bring home to me; there is such an one missing; what is become of it? has it perished through your neglect?'."

Drawing the rest of the congregation into the dramatic scene, Edwards bids them understand that "you must all of you hereafter meet your minister before the judgment seat of Christ." Edwards then constructs a version of what will happen to souls who have failed to listen and respond faithfully to the watchman who will ultimately say to God the Judge, "They perished not through my neglect, but through their own obstinate negligence and wickedness." In a grim statement,

Edwards insists that for those who have "so failed of the grace of God, the sight of the devil will not be so terrible to you at that day as the sight of your minister" who will "witness against you and condemn you." Deliberately contrasting this dark thought with a positive one, Edwards declares hopefully, "But how joyful will it be to you, as well as to [your watchman minister] if he renders his account with joy," and testifies happily to the faithfulness of the souls he has guarded.

Much of this sermon's force and the vividness of its ministerial vision derives from Edwards' effective use of the informing onlook of minister as watchman and from his skillfully managed dramatic episodes. Edwards' descriptive powers figure largely in this address. In extremely concrete language, he depicts Christ as the ultimate watchman, who suffers greatly in his labors for souls: "Look into the garden of Gethsemane and there behold [Christ] lying on the earth, with his body covered over with clotted blood, fallen down in lumps to the ground, . . . and look to the cross where he endured yet far more extreme agonies . . . and shed the remainder of his blood, lingeringly drained out through his tortured hands and feet, and extravated out of his broken heart into his bowels, and there turned into blood and water, through the vehement fermentation occasioned by the weight of grief and extremity of agony of soul." Although Edwards does not suggest that ministers should suffer to this degree, he reminds them through this arresting example, of Christ's tireless love for the souls which ministers are required to guard and protect.

There is one more remarkable way in which Edwards utilizes the watchman onlook to represent ministers as God's agents who deserve honor and respect. He indicates that to provide generously for God's workers is to love God; for "what is given to your pastor is given to Christ." He therefore urges that the new congregation, many formerly his own "spiritual children," must avoid envious or grudging attitudes or any "quarreling with your ministers," and must be thoughtful in

furnishing him with "comfortable and honorable support." One can only
guess the full range of motives behind these remarks, but we can be
sure that Edwards, believing it his duty as watchman ever alert to
impending dangers or temptations among God's people, felt it
appropriate to sound his ministerial trumpet in the ears of the people
about to receive the new minister "that comes on this blessed errand to
you."

True Excellency of a Gospel Minister, John 5:35 (1744)

Of the ordination sermon delivered on August 30, 1744, Wilson
Kimnach says that it is Edwards' "most completely delineated" and
"matured vision of the ideal minister."[70]   There can be little doubt
that it is one of Edwards' most radiant sermons. He formulates its
doctrine from John 5:35 to assert that "it is the excellency of a
minister of the gospel to be both a burning and a shining light." This
sermon incorporates one of Edwards' most dazzling and possibly most
beloved ministerial onlooks. In its intensity and lucidity, the sermon
provides full range for Edwards' highly cherished image—light—and
becomes a sustained, imaginative, and moving literary effort as well as
a clear doctrinal exposition of how God looks on the faithful minister,
and by extension his preaching, as serving the Redeemer and the
redeemed. Indeed, the onlook of minister as a communicating and
reflecting light is one of many expressions of Edwards' great
fascination with the sun and light as an emblem of the triune God and
his redemptive as well as providential love.[71]   In using light
extensively to represent God, grace, glory, and gospel ministry,
Edwards stands firmly on Scriptural ground and echoes a venerable

****
[70]"Literary Techniques of Jonathan Edwards" (Dissertation,
University of Pennsylvania, 1971), p. 31.

[71]Edward's light imagery appears in Religious Affections, his
Personal Narrative, Image or Shadows (#4, #50, #54, #58) and in

tradition of light imagery carried forward by orthodox church fathers such as Augustine, Luther, and Calvin.

To Job Strong, the pastor-elect of Portsmouth, and to the congregation, Edwards declares that God's ministerial messengers are light appointed "to shine with the communications of his light, and to reflect the beams of his glory on the souls of men." The onlook of minister as light beautifully illuminates and unifies the sermon. At the very outset, Edwards invokes all the key words and elements related to a minister's "true excellency"--light, warmth, brightness, holiness, zeal, piety, and diligence.   As "God's instrument of grace," ministerial light has a three-fold purpose: "to discover things, or make them manifest," "to refresh and delight the beholders," and "to direct . . . that we see where to go."   Throughout the sermon, then, Edwards elaborates on the concept that ministers are faithful to their divine calling to the degree in which they serve courageously and obediently as God's "lamps," "stars," "shining lights," or "luminaries in the spiritual world."   Ministers fulfill their purpose as "God's subordinate lights" by reflecting the perfect sun of righteousness and so illuminating and warming the recipients of their beams.

Edwards' search for "acceptable words"[72] and "most likely means to be used"[73] to convey and enact his sermon's ministerial onlook results in prose which is fervent, luminous, and hypotactic.   The following is

****
(Footnote 71 Continued From Previous Page)
countless sermons, including Divine and Supernatural Light and a very early unpublished sermon on John 8:12, "Christ the Light of the World," which Wilson Kimnach considers one of his best New York sermons.

[72]Edwards uses this phrase in Watchman's Duty (Dwight), VII, 190, and also in the Farewell Sermon (Hickman), I, ccxlvii.

[73]Watchman's Duty (Dwight), VII, 190.

part of a single sentence fusing form and content into a remarkably
fluent and incantatory expression of ministry:

> by ministers of the gospel being burning and shining lights,
> the angels of the churches will become like the angels of
> heaven, and those stars held in the right hand of Christ
> here below, will be like those morning stars above, and
> which is much more, hereby ministers will be like their
> glorious Lord and Master, who is not only the Master of
> ministers of the gospel, but is the head and Lord of the
> glorious angels, whom they adore, and who communicates to
> them the brightness in which they shine, and the flame with
> which they burn, and is the glorious luminary and sun of
> the heavenly world, from whence all the inhabitants of that
> world have their light and life, and all their glory.

Edwards' simple diction and monosyllabic directness also appear
frequently in this sermon and contribute to its strength:

> We shall be like Christ, and shall shine with his beams;
> Christ will live in us, and be seen in his life and beauty
> in our ministry . . . [and] in this way, those whom Christ
> has set to be lights in his church, and to be stars in the
> spiritual world here, shall be lights also in the church
> triumphant, and shine as stars forever.

The analogical quality of the ministerial onlook persists here: the
minister, "like Christ," shines brightly and triumphantly. Edwards'
later ordination sermons (in 1749 and 1754) stress a kind of identity
between human minister and divine Savior, but in True Excellency the
analogy of minister and the Christ-like light of grace remains the
primary focus. God the "boundless fountain of infinitely pure and
bright light" looks on his ordained servants as subordinate lights.

The Church's Marriage to Her Sons, Isaiah 62:4-5 (1746)

If True Excellency of a Gospel Minister is Edwards' most radiant ministerial sermon, The Church's Marriage to Her Sons[74] might well be both his most mystical and his most sensual ministerial sermon. Preached on September 19, 1746, this sermon celebrated the ordination of Samuel Buell at the East Hampton church. In the sermon, Edwards skillfully manages the sexual and marital images from Isaiah, Revelation, and Canticles to convey the redeemed soul's intimate union with Christ. The text Edwards selects for exposition is Isaiah 62:4-5; from it he formulates a doctrine containing two propositions: "I. The uniting of faithful ministers with Christ's people in the ministerial office, when done in a due manner, is like a young man's marrying a virgin; II. This union of ministers with the people of Christ is in order to their being brought to the blessedness of a more glorious union, in which Christ shall rejoice over them, as the bridegroom rejoiceth over the bride." To a great extent, the sermon's intensity derives from Edwards' strategic use of physical and sexual images to represent gracious, spiritual relationships. The juxtaposition of richly evocative images with the solemn portraits of the "faithful minister" produces paradoxical language which strains to bring under control an onlook that is both exciting and problematic. The onlook of minister as proxy bridegroom

> is a mystery or paradox not unlike many others held forth
> in the word of God, concerning the relation between Christ
> and his people, and their relation to him and to one
> another; such as that Christ is David's Lord and yet his

****
[74]References will be to the sermon as found in Works (New York edition, 1830), III, 559-579. See Appendix for the full sermon text.

son, and both the root and offspring of David; that Christ
is a son born and a child given, and yet the everlasting
Father; that the church is Christ's mother, . . . and yet
that she is his spouse, his sister, and his child; that
believers are Christ's mother, and his sister and brother;
and that ministers are the sons of the church, and yet that
they are her fathers . . . and also the mother . . .
travailing in birth. (560).

Edwards presumes, as did Augustine and many eminent Puritan
pastors, that all of Holy Writ—including its physical images and
figures—and all preaching, "especially when we speak to the people
from the pulpit, must be referred, not to the temporal welfare of man,
but to his eternal welfare."[75] Thus, The Church's Marriage expatiates
on the eternal connotations of young men and virgins, wooing and
winning marriage partners, brides and bridegrooms, and conjugal
intimacy and consummation. And as it claims to deal with the great
mystery of Christ and the Church as Christ's espoused wife, the sermon,
says Marc Lee, seems to be equally a "passionate expression of Edwards'
personal vision of ministry."[76] In fact, in the long tradition of
Christian orthodoxy, Edwards' treatment here of the saints' mystical
union with Christ is much more akin to Augustine's deeply-felt,
evocative, paradoxical language and sensual images than it is to
Calvin's more rigorous, strong-minded expositions of the believer's
relationship with Christ. Edwards asserts that although the church
"has but one husband" and therefore is "not an adulteress," yet there
is a profound and loving intimacy in "the church's union with her

[75]Augustine, On Christian Doctrine, trans. D. W. Robertson, Jr.
(Indianapolis, 1958), p. 143.

[76]Marc Frank Lee, "A Literary Approach to Selected Writings of
Jonathan Edwards" (Dissertation, University of Wisconsin, 1973), p. 3.

faithful pastor." Ministers are not only "set to be the instructors, guides, and fathers of God's people, but "a minister is also the church's proxy bridegroom", marrying the church "not in his own name, but in the name of his master, that he may be the instrument of bringing her into a true conjugal relation to him."

It is not the strength of a doctrinal position but the imagistic richness of the onlook of minister as proxy bridegroom which impels Edwards' expression in this ordination sermon. Theological development remains subordinate to the "mystery or paradox" of the onlook, and this phenomenon produces poetic language whose rhetoric moves, as it were, by wooing rather than by argument or logic. Ministers are "the principal appointed means" and "the instruments God makes use of" in his design for preparing souls for their union with Christ. Edwards therefore speaks of the minister's relation to the virgin bride of Christ as one of a tender lover, a "kind of spiritual husband" who is "sent to woo" Christ's beloved. It is altogether right that the church of Christ should "cleave to, and embrace the ministry of the church with endeared affection and high honor, and esteem, for Christ's sake; and . . . joyfully commit and subject themselves to them to cleanse, to honor, and help them." At one point as Edwards attempts verbally to underscore this primacy of ministry, his language becomes so intense that he refers to ministers as "instruments" nine consecutive times (pp. 571-572) in a single paragraph.

In presenting images "to excite," that is, to move ministers to absolute faithfulness, Edwards expands the proxy bridegroom onlook to persuade the clergy that they are not "mere servants" of a high master but "the special friends of the bridegroom." Referring both to his colleagues and himself, Edwards explains the duties of being a "spiritual husband" to Christ's espoused bride. We ministers, says Edwards, are appointed to spend

> our whole lives in diligent care and endeavor to provide

for, nourish, and instruct our people, as the intended
spouse of Christ . . . that we may form her mind and
behaviour, and bring her up for him, and that we may
cleanse her, as with the washing of water by the word, and
purify her as with sweet odors, and clothed in such raiment
as may become Christ's bride; that when the appointed
wedding day comes, we may have done our work as Christ's
messengers; and may then be ready to present Christ's
spouse to him, a chaste virgin, properly educated and
formed, and suitably adorned for her marriage . . . .[77]

Sometimes the proxy status of the minister is almost overshadowed by
the metaphors of married love and sexual union portraying the spiritual
love between a minister and his people: "A pastor and people are like
a young man and virgin united in marriage," and consequently the
minister "gives himself to his bride in purity . . . and she also
presents herself to him a chaste virgin."

The lyric, almost rhapsodic mood and expression in this sermon is
also related to Edwards' apocalyptic belief that "the late
extraordinary things that have appeared in the church of God" are signs
of the imminent coming of Christ. Edwards appears confident that the
splendid wedding, portrayed so majestically in Revelation, of Christ
and his bride is not far away: "that day must needs be approaching,
and we ourselves have lately seen some things that we have reason to
hope are forerunners of it." Edwards' sermon attempts to stir
ministers with the exciting prospects of their special position at the
great wedding feast of Christ and the church. Because he is both
Christ's saint and ambassadorial co-laborer, the minister will have a
special role in the marriage of the Lamb; the minister's position will
be one of "higher privilege" and "a much higher participation" than

****

[77]In his interleaved Bible (on the page facing II Corinthians 9,
10, 11) Edwards copied a paragraph of Doddridge's comments on II
Corinthians 11:2--" . . . for I have espoused you to one husband,

God's holy angels.   Indeed, loud "antiministerial"[78] voices were beginning to sound in New England; but in The Church's Marriage Edwards marshalls all the intensity of the proxy bridegroom onlook and all his gifts of rhetorical expression not only to uphold the ministerial office but to celebrate and magnify its joy as it reflects and anticipates the eschatological marriage of Christ and his pure, beautifully adorned bride.

Unpublished Installment Sermon on Zechariah 4:12-14 (1747)

In True Excellency of the Gospel Minister Edwards makes brief reference to the minister as an olive branch conveying grace from Christ to souls.   In so doing, he alludes to a ministerial onlook or metaphor inherent in Zechariah's golden candlestick vision.   Sometime in November, 1747, Edwards preached a sermon for the installment of Joseph Ashley at Sunderland.   In this sermon, Edwards exhaustively exposits the vision in Zechariah 4:12-14 of a golden lampstand directly supplied with oil by two oil-bearing olive trees--"anointed ones"--positioned on its right and left side.   Edwards' sermon in effect declares that God looks on his ministers as olive branches appointed to conduct the golden oil of God's grace and Spirit to

****
(Footnote 77 Continued From Previous Page)
that I may present you as a chaste virgin to Christ" Doddridge provides a notable historical insight: "There was an officer among the Greeks whose business it was to educate and form young women especially those of Rank and Figure (?) designed for marriage: and then to present them to those who were to be their husbands and if this officer permitted them through negligence to be corrupted between the Espousals and Consummation of the marriage great blame would naturally fall upon Him."

[78]True Excellency (Hickman), II, 959.

Christ's church, the golden candlestick. Ministers, says Edwards in
the sermon doctrine, "ought to be truly and vitally united to Christ."

The central organizing motif in the sermon is the vision in
Zechariah with its complex emblematic elements, its "five symbolical .
. . representations that need to be explained in order to a right
understanding of the text." The typical or metaphoric meanings are set
out clearly in the sermon's first eight pages. The golden candlestick
is the church of Christ. The golden oil is the Holy Spirit's love and
grace. The olive branches are God's anointed ministers, "those
officers that God makes use of as means and instruments of his church's
spiritual good." The olive root is Christ. And the golden pipes are
"God's ordinances and appointed means of grace."

Clearly Edwards feels competent to explain the rather obscure
vision; his notes and writings elsewhere reveal his personal attempts
to relate the Zechariah passage to similar biblical references. In
"Notes on the Bible," Edwards' comments on Revelation 4:5 and Zechariah
3 and 4 have an assertive edge: "The pure olive oil that fed the lamps
[in the golden candlestick] is indisputably a type of the Holy
Ghost."[79]   Further, he remarks, "The lamps were fed wholly by oil
constantly supplied from the olive tree, representing that the saints'
holiness, good fruits, and comfort, are wholly by the Spirit of God,
constantly flowing from Christ."[80] In Treatise on Grace, a posthumous
publication, Edwards discusses oil as one of the important "similitudes
and metaphors that are used about the Holy Ghost in Scripture."[81]

Once the vision's symbolical elements are clarified, Edwards is
chiefly concerned with reinforcing the dynamic relationship between

****
[79](Hickman), II, 723.

[80]Ibid., 742.

[81]Edwards, Treatise on Grace and Other Posthumously Published
Writings, ed., Paul Helm (London, 1971), p. 115.

Christ and his ministers. Christ is the great "Anointed One"; ministers appointed by Christ are called "anointed ones," a phrase, Edwards reminds his listeners, originally meaning "sons of oil." Having methodically set forth the sermon's text, Edwards proceeds with an explication considering the six qualifications essential in a minister, or "son of oil." Ministers must be vitally united to Christ, graciously anointed by Christ, wholly dependent on Christ, exemplary in walk and conversation, communicative of genuine spiritual good to the church, and faithful in using God's ordained means of grace. Especially in Edwards' exhortation to faithful preaching and pure biblical exposition, we hear echoes of the May 7, 1740, ordination sermon on submitting human reason to God's superior wisdom, and we also find manifestations of Edwards' growing reaction against the Half-Way Covenant tradition: "ministers should not preach their own word but the word of God and not be as those that . . . add to it their own notions and own imaginations . . . [and] the traditions of men."

Not until the application does Edwards disclose more directly some of the serious ecclesiastical tensions which move him in this sermon to a vigorous defense of the office of minister and the very rite of ordination wherein he is participating. Edwards here uses his authority as a prominent church leader to stress crucial points: the minister's right and duty to require from prospective church members and ministerial candidates an audible relation or expression of their conversion experience; and the need to keep the examination, licensing and ordination of clergy firmly in the hands of orthodox ministers. We have thus in this sermon one of the most articulate spokesmen for the Great Awakening struggling to curtail the damage done by revival enthusiasts and lay exhorters whose heavy emphasis on the sanctity of all believers was undermining the unique position of ministers. Edwards himself was increasingly experiencing difficulties in the area of lay versus ministerial authority. At stake in the colonial churches and in this sermon is the issue of the privileged status of clergy as a sacred order of men divinely endowed with special "gifts and graces," a rank of persons who stand in a unique, elevated relationship to Christ.

Disclaiming the anti-intellectual, anti-ministerial cries of many lay exhorters, Edwards calls for high standards among the clergy. Ministers must be educated as well as pious. They must be "men of learning and men of orthodoxy and civility"; they must also be men of whom there is "good reason" to believe "they shall justly weigh and govern"; and they must possess "a reasonable charity to induce others to believe that they are men of true piety." They must, in other words, be persons who can demonstrate their soundness, piety, and intelligence by submitting to a systematic "Inquiry" and examination regulated by orthodox clergy. Edwards is resisting a movement among laity to look for ministers who are primarily congenial, cooperative, and diplomatic; in this liberal movement Edwards sees all the earmarks of Arminianism and lax church government.

If such a serious affair as examining ministerial candidates be given over to the hands of the laity and "every individual person in a congregation . . . go to a candidate they have in probation and examine [him]," the task of maintaining ministerial integrity and doctrinal purity will be usurped by those who are "by no means sufficiently studied in the Word of God."[82] One of the fundamental duties of the clergy is "to inquire into and judge of the qualifications [of candidates] and openly to approve of candidates for the ministry." Says Edwards, "those whose business Christ has made it to liscense [sic] and ordain others" must be exceedingly careful in ascertaining whether the candidate is competent, orthodox, and above all, "vitally united to Christ."

To the above remarks Edwards hastily adds that ministers who examine a minister-elect must not act as if they have God-like powers

****

[82]These statements anticipate an unpublished June, 1748, sermon

to discern or search other persons' hearts.   Yet Edwards does assert that there is "no reason in the world why ministers in their (?) examination ought not to insist" that a ministerial candidate's preparation, doctrinal positions, and Christian faith are evident. Official, ecclesiastical examinations are exceedingly important in attempting to determine whether the golden oil of the Holy Spirit which the minister communicates to the church will be "unadulterated" and untainted and whether the "sons of oil" will demonstrate and preach the mind of Christ rather than their own peculiar notions.   Both individually and collectively, ministers are to protect believers from dubious preaching and from the appearance of heresy and heretics in their midst.

To be a genuine "son of oil" is to be born of the spirit, to convey the oil of the spirit, and like Christ to be anointed by the spirit.   To be a "son of oil," says Edwards, is an "exceedingly great honour and happiness . . . . We shall in some respects have the like honour that Christ himself has.   It was the honour of the priests and kings of old that they were anointed.   'Tis Christ's honour that he is anointed with the Holy Ghost.   Then is his name the _Mesiha_, which in Hebrew signifies 'anointed' and _Christ_ which is the Greek signifying the same thing.   As the name of Christ is the anointed, so we [ministers] shall be anointed ones."

Edwards' elevation and praise of legitimate, orthodox ministry is directly related to the problem against which Benjamin Colman of Boston had railed, the matter of lay preachers and the "many poor and miserable _Exhorters_ [who] have sprung up . . . , like _Mushrooms in the_

****
(Footnote 82 Continued From Previous Page)
doctrine on Deuteronomy 1:13-18:   "Tis the mind of God that not a mixed multitude but only select persons of distinguished ability and integrity are fit for the business of judging causes."

Night, and in the Morning tho't themselves accomplished <u>Teachers</u> and <u>called</u> of <u>God</u> to be so."[83] Edwards' ordination sermon stresses the essential differences between a rightly "anointed," authorized pastor and a falsely zealous, self-instituted one. Ministers endowed with the six "qualifications" elaborated upon earlier in the sermon are not to be confused with spurious, head-strong lay preachers burning impure oil and claiming that their separatist way is God's way.

Just as Edwards had indicated in other ministerial sermons, so he again depicts the vocation of ministry as a highly official one, "a most honorable office in this world." Ministers do not serve themselves; above all they follow the will of Christ:

> 'Tis the will of Christ to convey that golden oil, that most precious benefit that ever he bestows by ministers, whereby as Christ himself is the author of eternal salvation, so ministers become a kind of subordinate saviour. Thus the apostle speaks of his saving his hearers. Romans 11:14. I Corinthians 9:22 . . . . In the prophecy, Obadiah, verse 21, ministers are called saviors.

As Edwards continues, a conspicuous crescendo shapes the sermon's syntax:

> In this way we shall not only have this anointing that will qualify us for a most honourable office in the world, but we shall be anointed to eternal priesthood and not only so, but an eternal royalty in heaven and shall be there kings and prophets to . . . the Father.

Following this explicit celebration of ministry and ministers as "sons of oil," Edwards now addresses the lay persons in the congregation with encouragement to "approve yourself a golden candlestick, a holy and truly Christian church. And let your behavior

****
[83] A Letter from the Reverend Dr. Colman, to the Reverend Mr. [Solomon] Williams of Lebanon (Boston, 1744), p. 4, as cited by C. C. Goen in Revivalism and Separatism in New England (New Haven, 1962), p. 31.

toward your pastor be becoming such a society, receiving him and ever treating him as an anointed one, one anointed of Christ the Immanuel and God of the earth to that sacred office among you." The rhetoric of Edwards' exhortation to the parishioners intensifies further as he admonishes them to be brightly burning and shining golden candlesticks, faithfully "adhering the olive branch and constantly embibing from them the golden oil through the golden pipes of God's ordinances." The enormous importance of Edward's message to the people compels him to reiterate: "Let me repeat it and inculcate it upon you that you seek this golden oil in the way of God's ordinances, which are meant by the golden pipes in the text, and by God's ministers, regularly introduced in the way of God's institution, being . . . externally and rightly introduced . . . by the anointed ones that stand by the God of the whole earth."

Speaking in the imperative, Edwards as "a son of oil" recommends that saints are best served by attending to God's properly and genuinely anointed servants who are faithful to God's mind and will: "Seek the golden oil in this way, and not by lay teachers and exhorters, rejecting the regular ministry." Unordained preachers who lift themselves up, says Edwards, "as if they were the only pure church," and "call others anti-Christian" are not "in the way to receive the true golden oil."

Edwards' experience with impetuous, arrogant lay leaders who were stirring up great "corruption and confusion" prompts him to label them "the devil's emissaries." Earlier, in Some Thoughts (1742) Edwards had referred to the "dreadful disease" of imprudent zeal and had explained that "the reformation . . . was much hindered by . . . hasty zeal; many were for immediately rectifying all disorders by force, which was condemned by Luther, and were a great trouble to him."[84]   In his 1747

****

[84]The Great Awakening, ed. C. C. Goen, p. 450.

sermon on Zechariah 4:12-14, Edwards echoes these previous comments,
warning his listeners against a current resurgence of false preachers.
He reminds the people that several centuries before, Satan had stirred
up the church by "just such [corrupt] persons, . . . notions, and
practices, particularly . . . a little after the reformation."
Believing that Satan was now striving mightily to inhibit the
culmination of the reformation in America, Edwards urges the
congregation to hold fast to God's word and to the faithful preaching
and direction of God's anointed ones who are especially to represent
Christ and guard the church in the continuing struggle between darkness
and light, falsehood and truth.

As Edwards ends his sermon on this negative note, his final words
are strikingly unlike the jubilant, lyrical, positive conclusions of
his other ordination and installation sermons. The parting words
underscore Edwards' vision of antithetical forces, of leaders and
listeners who are either good or evil, saved or damned. The sermon's
ending is a dour warning against preachers of adulterated oil who move
listeners to be inflamed with "a false zeal" and to be "enkindled by
the fire of ~~hell~~ [here Edwards crosses out his original word choice]
the bottomless pit."

It is an irony of history that this installment sermon for the
Rev. Ashley stands as a reminder that Edwards could not always be the
most discriminating judge of a person's doctrinal propensities.
Ashley, described in this sermon as one "whom there is so great reason
to hope is a son of oil," turned against Edwards' strict view of
ministerial control over church membership and participation in the
Lord's Supper. In June, 1750, Ashley, representing the Sunderland
congregation, sided with the laity and signed the document that removed
Jonathan Edwards from his Northampton charge. Clearly in Edwards' 1747
sermon on ministry the seeds of his later controversy between pastor
and congregation were already present in his insistence that church

leadership is hierarchical and selective while the gospel of grace is democratic.

CHAPTER V
CHRIST THE PERFECT MINISTERIAL EXEMPLAR

Edwards' Pursuit of Excellence

Jonathan Edwards invested his life wholly in the pursuit of the true excellence of a saint and the true excellence of a gospel minister. At twenty, young Edwards had set his sights incomparably high, resolving that if "there never was to be but one individual in the world, at any one time, who was properly a complete christian, in all respects of a right stamp, having christianity always shining in its true lustre, and appearing excellent and lovely, for whatever part and whatever character viewed, . . to act just as I would do, if I strove with all my might to be that one, who should live in my time."[1] From then on Edwards aimed rigorously for saintliness not only in his personal life but also in his vocation as minister, one of those elect officials who "above all other men upon earth" typify and exemplify the new obedience in Christ. In a sermon on Hebrews 5:12, in which Edwards explains the Christian life to his congregation, he also expresses revealingly his own "concerns to excel."

> It doubtless concerns everyone to endeavor to excel in the knowledge of things which pertain to his profession or principal calling. If it concerns men to excel in anything, or in any wisdom or knowledge at all, it certainly concerns them to excel in the affairs of their main profession and work. But the calling and work of every Christian is to live with God. This is said to be his high calling,

---

****

[1] Jonathan Edwards, eds. Faust and Johnson, p. 44.

> Philippians 3:14. This is the business, and if I may so
> speak, the trade of a Christian, his main work, and indeed
> should be his only work. No business should be done by a
> Christian, but as it is some way or other a part of this.[2]

Edwards' pursuit of excellence in his "high calling" took many
forms. It prompted his continuing and manifold efforts to define,
describe, and discover concrete examples of that highly desirable
attribute. It throbbed in his fervent prayers to be more holy in his
relationship to Christ and the church. It shaped his diary and
personal narrative; it also directed his studies, his biblical notes,
miscellanies, and theological dissertations. Clearly, it informed the
ordination and installation sermons in which he scrutinized and
solemnized the gospel minister's excellencies as divinely appointed
steward, messenger, husbandman, light, watchman, anointed son of oil,
and spiritual father to God's people.

These metaphors exploring ministerial excellence most often
reflect the authoritative, ambassadorial side of the gospel minister's
appointed work in advancing Christ's kingdom. Somewhat less often but
just as vividly, Edwards uses images incorporating the tender, maternal
elements in the task of an excellent gospel minister. His discursive
notes on Luke 1:35,[3] for example, look upon the faithful minister as a
nurturing mother. Here, Edwards considers the virgin Mary as a "type
of the church" bringing forth Christ into the world; but most
specifically, Mary typifies ministers as the church's representatives
who labor patiently to bring Christ forth in the hearts of believers.

****

[2] Works, (Worchester, 1808), VIII, 6.

[3] Works (Dwight), IX, pp. 472-73.

"Bringing Forth Christ"

Edwards' explanation of the analogy between Christ's mother and Christ's ministers emphasizes the gently solicitous dimensions of pastoral care. Mary is, in Edwards' view, not only a type of the church but also "an eminent type of every believing soul," for Christ has been formed in every true convert as he was formed in Mary through the work of the Holy Spirit. Moreover, Edwards portrays ministers as those who participate doubly in the nurturing, maternal business of Christ's redemptive work. Not only do they labor as individual saints to bring forth Christ richly in their own lives; they labor as God's midwives to bring forth Christ in the lives of others.

The minister's faithful preaching, his gracious life, and his exemplary love for souls operate demonstrably "to promote the health and spiritual growth of believers." Conscientious ministers watch over and feed their spiritual children in much the same way as "tender mothers are want to do with their little children." Edwards' lyrical comparison of the relationship between mother and child and minister and born-again believer vibrates with domestic detail, no doubt drawn from the daily activities in the Edwards' household:

> The care that a tender mother has of her infant, is a very
> lively image of the love that a Christian ought to have of
> grace in the heart. It is a very constant care; the child
> must be continually looked after; it must be taken care of
> both day and night. When the mother wakes up in the night
> she has her child to look after and nourish at her breast,
> as it sleeps in her bosom, and it must be continually in the
> mother's bosom, or arms, there to be upheld and cherished;
> it needs its food and nourishment much oftener than adult
> persons; it must be fed both day and night; it must in
> everything be gratified and pleased; the mother must bear

the burden of it as she goes to and fro. <u>This is also a</u>
<u>lively image of the care that the church, especially the</u>
<u>ministers of the gospel, should have of the interest of</u>
<u>Christ, committed to their care.</u>(Emphasis added)

As in the family the attentive mother loves her baby, so in the
church the gospel minister heartily cherishes and feeds the offspring
of Christ's work in the believer's heart.   Just as an infant is
regularly nursed at its mother's breast, so newly-redeemed and awakened
souls need to be fortified and nourished regularly, says Edwards, by
the church and the exemplary activities and "exercises of graces in the
saints and their good works."   Such godly exercise fosters and feeds
"Christ in the heart, or the principle of grace there, and causes it to
grow."

Here, as in many of his other writings, Edwards is mindful that
saving grace is an expansive, active principle. Through the mysterious
operations of the Holy Spirit, grace begets grace.   The exercise of
grace not only invigorates the individuals in whom grace conspicuously
abounds; the manifestations of grace in exemplary individuals also
nourishes, fortifies, and encourages, by its excellence, the newer,
weaker members of Christ's family and contributes to the growth of his
body, the church: "exercises and fruits of grace that come from the
hearts of the saints, do as it were nourish Christ's interest in the
world, and cause Christ's mystical body, which is small as in infancy,
to be strengthened and increased."

Bearing Christ's Image

A saintly life expresses the beauty of spiritual conformity to
Christ. Thus, a person who genuinely and consistently exhibits God's
grace bears Christ's image—brings Christ forth in the world—visibly
for the great benefit of others. Such a saint, says Edwards, indeed

reveals "the glory of divine grace, God's own image, and that which is infinitely God's most excellent, precious, and glorious gift, and he is partaker of the divine nature, and becomes a God-like creature."[4] By grace, exemplary saints are greatly nourished and, in turn, are nourishing to others.

As one of eighteenth-century New England's most unstinting nurturers of souls, Edwards labored to arouse and encourage his hearers to Christ-likeness. His pastoral efforts to nourish led, among other things, to many pointed sermons on Christ as the crowning example of true religion, humility, and righteousness:

> The greatest example of all, that is set before us in the Scripture to imitate, is the example of Jesus Christ, which he set us in his human nature, and when in his state of humiliation.[5]

Again and again Edwards proclaimed the message that for all believers, and especially for gospel ministers, Christ the visible image of God's beauty and holiness is the exemplum exemplorum.

Though the only "perfect rule" for godliness is Christ, Edwards frequently reminds his congregation that the Scriptures also present a great number of saints "as patterns . . . to follow."[6] Moreover, these patterns are in some ways more suitable for human encouragement and nourishment than is the flawless example of Christ:

> The example of some that are fallen creatures, as we are, may in some respects be more accommodated to our circumstances, and more fitted to our instructions, than the example of Jesus Christ. . . . We need an example, that

****
[4](Hickman), II, 544.

[5](Hickman), II, 855.

[6](Hickman), II, 855.

> shall teach and direct us how to behave toward Christ our
> Lord and head. And this we may have better in some, that
> have Christ for their Lord as well as we, than in Christ
> himself.[7]

Accordingly, Edwards regularly celebrates the "many excellent examples
of religion, in its power and practice" contained in the Old and New
Testament.   These recorded examples are edifying provision for the
church of all ages. Edwards urges biblical models of righteousness—
such as Moses, Joseph, Ruth, John the Baptist, Mary, and Paul—upon his
parishioners for emulation, for "if we would have right notions of
Christianity, we should observe those in whom it is shown, . . . for
they are the examples that God himself has selected to set before us.
. . .that from thence we might form our notions of religion."[8]

     A continuing interest in examples capable of nourishing and
strengthening God's people further prompted Edwards on occasion to
endorse or memorialize contemporary persons who, in his opinion,
reflected the power and practice of genuine religion to a high degree.
Following the Awakening of 1735, Edwards described several Northampton
parishioners in great detail (four-year-old Phoebe Bartlett and Abigail
Hutchinson, a young woman who died before her story reached the world)
as he believed they illustrated the fruits and essence of genuine
religious affections and as he felt they represented exemplary patterns
of piety and spiritual excellence. Edwards included these descriptions
in his Faithful Narrative of the Surprising Work of God (1737) which,
as Patricia Tracy notes, became "a popular handbook for the second tide
of revivalism" that swept through the northern colonies in the early
1740's.[9]

****
   [7](Hickman), II, 855.

   [8](Hickman), II, 865.

   [9]Jonathan Edwards, Pastor, 109.

Several years after <u>Faithful Narrative</u>, Edwards published <u>Some Thoughts Concerning the Revival</u> (1743), including in it further contemporary examples of piety and saintliness. This time he used his wife Sarah Edwards' awakening narrative (which she wrote at his request), carefully changing the first person account to third person, and removing identifying information. At the funeral (1748) of Colonel John Stoddard, a pious and competent New England statesman, Edwards asserted that saints who are an encouragement and ministry to "God's people for good . . . are great gifts of the Most High to his people . . . and vehicles of his goodness to them; and therein are images of his own Son, the grand medium of all God's goodness to fallen mankind." 10 Edwards thus reminded his hearers that God continues to provide visible examples of godliness to edify the church and advance his kingdom, and what is more, these examples must be regarded, cherished, and imitated.

The Christ-like David Brainerd

In June 1748 while he mourned the loss of the exemplary John Stoddard, Edwards was also engaged in preparing for publication the memoirs and papers of another outstanding contemporary Christian. David Brainerd (1718-1747), an extraordinarily pious young missionary to the Indians in western Pennsylvania and the Forks of Delaware, had died in Edwards' home on October 9, 1747 at the youthful age of 29 years. On his deathbed, upon urgings from friends, Brainerd had placed his intimate writings in Edwards' custody. During the year following Brainerd's death, Edwards carefully edited and annotated Brainerd's hauntingly introspective spiritual diaries, thoroughly convinced that

****
10(Hickman), II, 38.

the young man's zealous orthodoxy would "afford instruction to Christians in general, as it shows, in many respects, the right way of practicing religion."[11]   These diaries, augmented by Edwards' biographical observations, were eventually published in 1749 as <u>An</u> <u>Account of the Life of the Late Reverend Mr. David Brainerd</u>. Some of the passages in which Edwards describes Brainerd's lively ideas of God's infinite glory and his great desires that Christ's kingdom be advanced contain what Ola Winslow judges to be "more than a suggestion that biography has become autobiography."[12]

Few acquaintances and certainly no other ministerial colleague impressed Edwards more profoundly than did David Brainerd as a pattern of ministerial excellence and conformity to Christ.   In his biographical reflections accompanying Brainerd's diary, Edwards lavishly praised Brainerd's exemplary love for God, his conformity to Christ, his humility, and his "meek and quiet spirit, resembling the lamb-like, dove-like Spirit of Jesus."[13]   Clearly Edwards considered Brainerd's "travailing in birth" for the conversion of souls a ministerial love carried on with godliness and self-denial practically unequaled in the eighteenth century.

Edwards insisted that the memory of Brainerd's ministry could serve providentially as a powerful spiritual encouragement, especially to ministers:

> How much is there, in . . . this eminent minister of Christ,
> to excite us who are called to the same great work of the
> Gospel Ministry, to earnest care and endeavors, that we may
> be in like manner faithful in our work; that we may be

****

[11](Hickman), II, 456.

[12]Winslow, p. 239.

[13](Hickman), II, 449.

filled with the same spirit, animated with the same earnest
concern to advance the kingdom and glory of our Lord and
Master, and the prosperity of Zion.[14]

On October 12, 1747, as he conducted the funeral sermon for his
youthful friend, Edwards asserted confidently that Brainerd's
evangelical efforts and "the readiness and constancy with which he
spent his strength and substance to promote the glory of his Redeemer,
are probably without a parallel in this age in these parts of the
world."[15]

Without doubt, Edwards himself was much inspired and nourished by
Brainerd's ministerial example. Certainly, memories of Brainerd appear
to inform and enrich the installment sermon which Edwards preached in
Sunderland on November 11, only one month after Brainerd's death. This
unpublished sermon on Zechariah 4:12-14 considers God's ministers as
"anointed ones." It resonates with themes from the conversations on
gospel ministry which Edwards and Brainerd had shared repeatedly during
Brainerd's final days. The biblical material upon which the sermon is
built—Zechariah's vision of the golden lampstand and his dream-like
dialogue with the Angel of the Lord—is wonderfully suggestive, even
allegorical. The text allows considerable latitude for creative
exposition. Thus, it is particularly interesting to note the
prescriptive form Edwards' interpretation takes in his first public,
official treatment of ministry following Brainerd's funeral. The
sermon carefully sets out and discusses six essential "qualifications"
for gospel ministers. These six points are strongly directive:

****

[14]Faust and Johnson, p. 184. Edwards indicates that eight neighboring pastors and at least seventeen other gentlemen of liberal education attended Brainerd's funeral. (Hickman), II, 386.

[15]Edwards, Funeral Sermon for David Brainerd, Faust and Johnson,
p. 179.

> Ministers I) . . . ought to be truly gracious and vitally
> united to Christ. . . II) . . . ought to be eminently
> gracious and near to Christ. . . III) . . . should have
> their . . . entire and uttermost dependence on Christ. . .
> IV) . . .should be strict and exemplary in their walk and
> conversation. . . V) . . . ought to be communicative of
> spiritual good. . . VI) . . . (and) in their endeavors for
> the good of their church and congregation should use the
> means of God's appointment.

It is no coincidence that all the characteristics which Edwards' sermon describes and prescribes for gospel ministers had been extraordinarily evident in David Brainerd, and that these characteristics are later highlighted in the biographical section in An Account, written by Edwards and entitled "Some Reflections and Observations on the Preceding Memoirs."[16]

Much of Edwards' commentary on Brainerd stands as a significant gloss on Edwards' own pastoral theology and doctrines of ministry; Edwards' analysis of Brainerd's piety and profession provides pertinent insights on the ministerial model Edwards endorsed and promoted at a time when he was deeply distressed by separatist criticisms of the established clergy, by increasing Arminian attacks upon religious orthodoxy, and by dissentions in his own Northampton congregation.

In Brainerd's exemplary orthodoxy and Christ-like ministry, Edwards saw not only an inspiring demonstration of the true nature of religion but also a pointed tool by which to "teach and excite to duty, [those] who are called to the work of the ministry, and all that are candidates for that great work."[17] As he reviewed Brainerd's life and

****

[16](Hickman), II, pp. 446-458.

[17](Hickman), II, 455.

prepared the memoirs for publication, Edwards tenderly rendered the abstract terms of his Religious Affections into a personal and dramatic spiritual biography that revealed the "gifts and graces" of a saint as well as the "qualifications" of an outstanding gospel minister.   For Edwards' purpose, then, Brainerd served as much more than a general case study of authentic religious piety; Brainerd stood as an exemplary messenger in Christ's great work of redemption.

In initial meetings with Brainerd in 1743, Edwards had been exceedingly impressed by the young man's humility, his "great attainment in spiritual knowledge," and his enormous dedication to promoting God's kingdom.[18]   Subsequently, as a friend and spiritual mentor, Edwards followed Brainerd's activities with great interest, endorsing his evangelizing labors among the Indians in the "howling wilderness" of New Jersey and Pennsylvania.[19]   When in 1747, the consumption-wracked Brainerd could no longer continue his ministry, he left his primitive post and went to Northampton where the Edwards family welcomed him into their home and cared for him until he died.

In his last months, Brainerd had the opportunity to share countless hours of deep conversation with Edwards, "feeding on the kernel, not the shell of religion."[20]   The relationship between these two ministers—one a veteran preacher and revivalist of international

****

[18]Brainerd met with Edwards in New Haven in 1743 to consult on procedures by which to be reinstated at Yale College; Brainerd had been dismissed some time earlier for making comments about a faculty member's lack of grace. Brainerd's apologies and petitions were rejected by the college; he then continued to study divinity under the supervision of a ministerial friend. Eventually he was licensed to preach, called to serve as missionary to the Indians, and was ordained in Newark, New Jersey on June 12, 1744.

[19](Hickman), II, 456.

[20](Hickman), II, 357.

repute, the other a pioneer missionary to native Americans—was intensely symbiotic. Their discussions together obviously informed Brainerd's final diary entries as well as Edwards' biographical observations on Brainerd. Each man reinforced the other's spiritual proclivities, theological positions, and pastoral emphases. Brainerd spoke often and fervently "of the importance of the work of the ministry"; again and again, notes Edwards, his deathbed conversations were directed to this crucial subject. Together Brainerd and Edwards prayed that God would stem the dangerous tide of liberal preaching that failed to stress salvation as an entirely supernatural work of sovereign grace.

Eagerly, Brainerd read and endorsed Edwards' 1746 treatise, Religious Affections. Frequently the two discussed the distinguishing features of genuine faith and practice, intimately sharing their various personal and professional experiences. The closer Brainerd came to death, the more he opened his heart and soul to Edwards on such subjects as conversion, "experimental religion," sanctifying grace, and the sweetness of union with Christ. And the more the dying man talked, the more he seemed to embody for the theologian that true excellency that comes from whole-hearted "conformity to God, living to God, and glorifying him."[21]

An Account of the Life of the Late Reverend Mr. David Brainerd

After his death, Brainerd's life and papers became in Edwards' hands an emphatic text to define excellence in a gospel minister. Brainerd's history as a man appointed by God, filled with his grace, and duly called and ordained to preach God's mind and will provided

****
[21] (Hickman), II, 449.

Edwards with a stinging rebuke to the separatists who were encouraging independent lay exhorters and declaring that "the standing ministry is corrupt and God has forsaken the clergy."[22]   Indeed, Edwards makes pointed assertions that Brainerd "spoke often, with abhorrence, of the spirit and practice that appears among the greater part of separatists . . . in their condemning and separating from the standing ministry and churches, their crying down learning and a learned ministry, their notion of an immediate call to the work of the ministry, and the forwardness of laymen to set up themselves as public teachers."[23]

In his biographical observations, however, Edwards moves beyond recollecting Brainerd's judgment of the separatists.   Edwards also tries to persuade readers that the "astonishing manifestations of God's power" in Brainerd's ministry are incontrovertible evidences of God's blessing upon the work of someone who thoroughly represented orthodox ministry, someone who had been "first examined and licensed to preach by such [established] ministers, and sent forth . . . by such ministers; and . . .ordained by such ministers; always directed by them, and united with them in their consistories and administrations; and . . .abhoring the practice of those who give out, that they [the established ministers] ought to be renounced, and separated from, and that teachers may be ordained by laymen."[24]

Not only were Brainerd's ecclesiastical connections orderly and strong, says Edwards, but even more important, his "history shows us the right way to success in the work of the ministry."[25]   A faithful

---

****

[22](Hickman), II, 451.

[23](Hickman), II, 381.

[24](Hickman), II, 451.

[25](Hickman), II, 455.

minister's labor is grounded in his right relationship with God, in "the new sense of his mind, the new relish and appetite given him in conversion, and thenceforward maintained and increased in his heart."[26] And Brainerd's diary, originally written for no eyes but his own, as well as Edwards' personal testimony verifies that Brainerd's union with his Lord was nourished and exercised regularly in prayers, meditations upon divine subjects, "closet devotions and solitary transactions between God and his soul."[27] Furthermore, his longings to be holy and to bring souls to a saving knowledge of Christ were not motivated by self-love, says Edwards, but by a desire to be an able minister for God's glory. As Brainerd's prayers reveal, he repeatedly besought God for grace "to imitate the life, labours, and sufferings of St. Paul among the heathen."[28]

Brainerd's preaching also, Edwards is quick to point out, reflects a thorough reliance on the power of God's spirit and word to touch the hearts of those to whom he proclaimed God's sovereignty, man's depravity, and Christ's great work of redemption. Brainerd's private notebooks provide copious evidence that he believed a minister faithful to the mind and will of God does not preach the word in his own strength. Accordingly, in preaching, teaching, exhorting, catechizing, and praying for the enlightenment and conversion of souls, says Edwards, "how sensible was [Brainerd] of his own insufficiency . . . and how great was his dependence on God's sufficiency."[29]

Numerous diary entries contain Brainerd's profound gratitude to

****
[26] (Hickman), II, 448.

[27] (Hickman), II, 449.

[28] (Hickman), II, 348.

[29] (Hickman), II, 455.

God for assistance "in feeling the truth of the text," in "being enabled in preaching to pour out my soul . . . with great freedom, fervency, and affection,"[30] in being empowered "to speak with tenderness, and yet with faithfulness. . .so that divine truths seemed to fall with weight and influence upon the hearers,"[31] and in being moved "to speak with uncommon plainness . . . and earnestness."[32] Although Brainerd frequently reports that his hearers are "sweetly melted," "all in tears," or "tenderly moved," he takes no credit for the affective powers of his preaching but says instead, "Blessed be God for any assistance granted to one so unworthy."[33]

Although Edwards does not elaborate on the details of Brainerd's ministry, he does make the sweeping claim that Brainerd demonstrates "the right way to success" in gospel ministry.[34] For Edwards, a fundamental element in that "right way" was Brainerd's selfless, disinterested love for souls, a "universal benevolence" that extended even to his opposers and enemies. This holy love, the fruit of divine grace, is the virtue which Edwards was to describe later in Nature of True Virtue as "consent to Being in general" from which flows all genuine love, including the love for souls which is indispensable to the work of ministry.

No doubt, in Edwards' estimation, another part of Brainerd's "right way" of ministry was his faithful preaching (many times during each week as well as several times each Sabbath) and his great

****

[30](Hickman), II, 365.

[31](Hickman), II, 365.

[32](Hickman), II, 341.

[33](Hickman), II, 341.

[34](Hickman), II, 449.

vigilance as a member of the "standing clergy" guarding the sanctity of the church's sacraments and ordinances. Brainerd's writings suggest that he, like Edwards, did not view the Lord's Supper as a converting ordinance but as a sacrament to be administered only to those who could give a reasonable account of God's converting work in their lives. Significantly, Brainerd did not baptize his first adult Indian converts until he had clear and "comfortable reason to hope they [were] renewed persons."[35]   Moreover, in preparing these baptized adults for the Lord's Supper, Brainerd took more than eight months to be assured that these new Christians understood the institution, nature, and purpose of the sacrament. He listened to their personal accounts of God's saving grace; he observed their lives; he catechized them at length; and he scrupulously led the Indians in a fast preparatory to communion. When the day finally arrived in which Brainerd administered the Lord's Supper to his small group of Indian Christians, he joyfully recorded the landmark occasion with the following description:

> I have abundant reason to think that those who came to the Lord's table, had a good degree of doctrinal knowledge of the nature and design of the ordinance. . . . And this competency, together with their grave and decent attendance upon the ordinance, their affectionate melting under it, and the sweet and Christian frame of mind they discovered consequent upon it, gave me great satisfaction respecting my administration of it to them. And O what a sweet and blessed season was this! God himself, I am persuaded, was in the midst of his people, attending his own ordinances. . . . The sweet union, harmony, and endearing love and tenderness subsisting among them, was,

****
[35] (Hickman), II, 394.

I thought, the most lively emblem of the heavenly world I
had ever seen."[36]

Brainerd's depiction of Indians gathered in a veritable image of
heavenly harmony brings to mind Edwards' visionary hope, expressed in
his 1739 sermon series, for a time when many "Negroes and Indians will
be divines, . . . religion shall prevail and reign, and there shall be
happy love between ministers and their people."[37]   There is indeed
solid evidence that Brainerd's ministry and church-planting among the
Indians gave lively encouragement to Edwards' apocalyptic anticipations
of a world-wide increase in gospel knowledge and light.   In a November
20, 1745, letter to a friend in Scotland, Edwards listed Brainerd's
successes with the Indians as one of several signs indicating that
Christ's church was drawing nearer to its glorious millennial state.[38]
Edwards also called public attention to Brainerd's ministry as a "very
great awakening and reformation of many Indians, in the Jerseys and
Pennsylvania, even among such as never embraced Christianity before."[39]

During the months surrounding Brainerd's final illness and death,
Brainerd and Edwards talked extensively of their common "hope that a
glorious advancement of Christ's kingdom was near at hand."[40]   Edwards
was writing a treatise urgently calling all Christians to united prayer
for the flourishing of Christ's church on earth and for a new

****

[36](Hickman), II, 414.

[37](Hickman), I, 609. "History of the Work of Redemption" was
preached originally as a sermon series and published posthumously in
1774 under the same title.

[38]Works (Yale), V, 449.

[39]An Humble Attempt to Promote Visible Union of God's People, in Works
(Yale), V, 362.

[40](Hickman), II, 384.

outpouring of the Holy Spirit across the land.   He presented this
ecumenical challenge at a time which he felt to be filled with "great
apostasy and provocations,"   a time when the "work of the ministry
[was] laid under uncommon difficulties" and many colonial churches were
suffering "fierce and violent contentions . . . among ministers and
people."[41]   Despite these problems, Edwards clung tenaciously to his
views that if Christians prayed concertedly and ministers preached
faithfully, God would send the "future promised glorious days of the
church's prosperity."[42]   One notable way in which he attempted to
encourage himself as well as others was to present Brainerd's exemplary
gospel ministry as "a forerunner of something yet more glorious and
extensive" in Christ's kingdom and to send An Account of the Life of
the Late Reverend Mr. Brainerd into the world with a prayer that it
might "prove a happy means of promoting the revival of true religion.
Amen."[43]

Developments in Edwards' Ministry

        The history of Jonathan Edwards' personal ministry and progress in
Northampton is fascinating and complex.   In his early years, Edwards'
visions of ministry were celebrative and optimistic, full of commitment
to be God's evangel, to serve in a sacred vocation as one of God's
"precious gifts from heaven."   But in his final years in Northampton
the majority of his congregation rejected his theology and care of
their souls.   Although his view of his high calling always remained
sure, his expression of it was definitely shaped by the personal

****
[41]Works (Yale), V, 362, 368.

[42](Yale), V. 340.

[43](Hickman), II, 458.

catastrophes and pain he faced within his own ministry. The degree to
which he suffered deeply from the attacks and accusations of his
parishioners can be seen in the letter he wrote on May 24, 1749, to his
friend Thomas Foxcroft of Boston: "I seem, as it were, to be casting
myself off from a precipice; and have no other way, but to go on, as it
were blindfold, i.e. shutting my eyes to everything else but the
evidence of the mind and will of God, and the path of duty ."[44]

In spite of the personal agonies, Edwards remained confident that
ministers are God's messengers. And he continued to use his highly
developed rhetorical and exegetical skills to assert this theology of
ministry. It is remarkable that Edwards' long career as the primary
pastor at Northampton is bracketed by two sermons which reflect
specifically on the meaning and consequences of a minister's departure
from a congregation, the one being a sermon he preached immediately
following the death of his grandfather in Northampton and the other
being the famous July 1, 1750, farewell sermon. These two sermons not
only demonstrate Edwards' ministerial vision but also the progression
of his powerful style, which at its best throbbed with an inexorable
certainty in the righteousness of its content.

Unpublished Sermon on Isaiah 31:1-2 (1729)

Edwards, in preparing one of the first sermons he delivered as
principal pastor in Northampton following the death of Solomon
Stoddard, intentionally directed his message to underscore the eternal
value and exemplary usefulness of God's gospel ministers. The doctrine
of this unpublished sermon on Isaiah 3:1-2 states that a community's
loss of zealous, godly leadership can indeed be a sign that God is

****
[44]Cited in Wilson Kimnach's "Literary Techniques," 91.

severely testing the community's faithfulness or punishing its
backsliding and lethargy. The doctrine thus declares: "It's a
manifestation of God's displeasure against a people when He takes away
from them many that have been useful and serviceable among them."

This sermon, delivered in 1729, is of special interest as one of
Edwards' earliest public statements on the qualifications and task of
faithful ministers. It celebrates the deceased Stoddard's fifty-seven
years as a venerable pastor of the Northampton congregation and
ecclesiastical leader in the Connecticut River Valley. But more
importantly, the sermon stresses that God's work of redemption moves
from generation to generation, accomplished through Christ's saving
grace and the faithful preaching and saintly example of gospel
messengers. Here follow several passages from this youthful
unpublished sermon on gospel ministry:

> Wise and faithful ministers of the gospel are very
> usefull [sic] men. They are usefull to a people in these
> things that concern their greatest interests, even the
> eternal salvation of their souls . . . .

> Men of good understanding, prudence and virtue, they
> may be usefull in discountenancing vice and wickedness, in
> promoting of good designs in appearing on the side of
> right . . . .

> And especially with a good understanding and much
> prudence and publick [sic] spiritedness and godliness and
> true Christian spirit and zeal for God's glory and the
> interest of religion joined together make a man eminently
> usefull . . . .

> Usefull men are some of the greatest blessings of a
> people. To have many such is more for a people's happiness
> than almost anything unless it be God's own gracious

spiritual presence amongst them.   They are precious gifts
of heaven . . . .

After making these general comments on ministers as "useful men,"
Edwards pointedly memorializes his grandfather Stoddard as a spiritual
leader whose strength and godliness had been a conspicuous power for
good:

> . . . Usefull men are as the wall of a people, and when they
> are removed the wall is broken down and destruction comes
> in . . . . God hath taken away the prophet, that eminent
> minister of the gospel that God so long continued in this
> place that you were want to hear instructions and warning
> of you from this pulpit. God has taken away him that was
> as it were the father of this people, that hath [taught]
> you through the gospel and brought up most of you from your
> cradles. It hath pleased God . . . to put out that burning
> and shining light. It will shine no more amongst us . . . .
>
> He was one that was endowed with all qualifications
> that should render a person eminently usefull amongst a
> people,   being   endowed   with   great   abilities   and
> understanding, great prudence, great experience, a great
> zeal for the public experience, a great zeal for the public
> good, expecially for the greatest good of a people, the good
> of their souls. He was a person of great piety, and he was
> in such a publick station as gave the greatest advantage to
> be usefull.

Edwards' sermon concludes with a reference to himself.   As
Northampton's new pastor, he humbly urges the congregation now in his
care to pray "that God would be with him that He hath placed here in
the work of the ministry, that He would instruct him and give him much

of His spirit and grace." Although this sermon is not particularly eloquent, it is notable as an early statement of Edwards' life-long belief that ministers are some of the most honorable and "useful" of God's servants and are "some of the greatest blessings of a people." These descriptions in 1729 of a faithful gospel minister faintly anticipate the more elaborately detailed, aesthetically rich, and stylistically mature reflections on ministry which Edwards develops in Northampton and which we see in his later official ordination and installation sermons of the 1740's and 1750's.

Northampton Farewell Sermon (July 1, 1750)

An interesting contrast -- in occasion, emphasis, and style -- to the early ministerial sermon of 1729 is Edwards' Northampton Farewell Sermon. In it he creates a masterful presentation which imaginatively brings minister and parishioners together in the judgment day when all eyes will be opened to the visible majesty of the sovereign Lord whom the minister has labored to represent. The faithful minister who has preached the word and the people who have willingly or unwillingly heard the word all stand in the last day before the living Word, "in the most immediate sensible presence of this great God, Savior, and Judge, appearing in the most plain, visible, and open manner with great glory."[45]

Considered by some to be Edwards' "greatest oration in Northampton,"[46] this sermon vividly portrays the minister's intimate relationship to God and to the souls God places in his care:

****
[45](Hickman), I, ccxliv.

[46]Miller, Jonathan Edwards, p. 225.

In this world, ministers and their people often meet
together to hear of and wait upon an unseen Lord; but at
the judgment, they shall meet in his most immediate and
visible presence.

Ministers, who now often meet their people to preach to
them the King eternal, immortal, and invisible, to convince
them that there is a God, and declare to them what manner
of being he is, and to convince them that he governs, and
will judge the world, and that there is a future state of
rewards and punishments--and to preach to them a Christ in
heaven, at the right hand of God, in an unseen world—shall
then meet their people in the most immediate sensible
presence of this great God, Saviour, and Judge, appearing
in the most plain, visible, and open manner, with great
glory, with all his holy angels, before them and the whole
world.   They shall not meet them to hear about an absent
Christ, an unseen Lord, and future Judge; but to appear
before the Judge—getting together in the presence of the
supreme Lord—in his immense glory and awful majesty, of
whom they have heard so often in their meeting together on
earth.

. . . . Ministers are [God's] messengers, sent forth by
him; and, in their office and administrations among their
people, represent his person, stand in his stead, as those
that are sent to declare his mind, to do his work, and to
speak in his name.   And therefore it is especially fit,
that they should return to him to give an account of their
work and success.[47]

****
[47](Hickman), I, ccxliv, ccxlv.

Here is a style and language which is richly impressive, moving, and incantatory. Here is a preacher standing before a people who have pointedly questioned and challenged his authority as God's messenger in their lives. And here is a clergyman who has unshakable confidence that a faithful minister is not only God's useful servant, but is God's intimate, trusted, and visible representative on earth, directed to declare God's mind and to speak boldly in God's name. Here is a pastor who, having been rejected by his people, brings all of his rhetorical gifts to bear on these last official words he speaks to his people in God's name.

Aesthetic and Stylistic Development

Edward's progress in the literary and stylistic competence of his sermons between 1729 and 1750's is undeniable. Sermons from the various stages of his ministry clearly demonstrate his development. Although many Edwards' scholars have been interested in his evolution as thinker and writer, few have examined the sermons to trace developments or changes in style. Half a century ago, Clarence Faust and Thomas Johnson studied Edwards' sermonic style and noted its vigor and clarity as well as some of its eccentricities; however, at that time they suggested that because only a fraction of Edwards' sermons had been printed and a number of the unpublished sermons—particularly the later sermons—were only sketchily written out, "it is impossible to discover developing literary style."[48] But more recently, Wilson Kimnach's extensive study of the sermon manuscripts has revealed Edwards' very conscious attempts to improve, refine, and edit. Kimnach also indicates that there are at least three discernable and important

****

[48]"Introduction" to Jonathan Edwards: Representative Selections, cx.

stages in Edwards' career as sermon writer: first, an "apprenticeship"
period from 1722 to approximately 1727; then a period of mastery from
1727 until 1742 during which time he became thoroughly established as a
pastor, ecclesiastical leader, and revivalist preacher; and finally a
period of "permutation" from about 1742 to 1758. This last period was
marked, says Kimnach, by "an increasing tendency to preach long
treatise-like sermon series in Northampton," by an "increasing desire
to publish--sermons, reports, and other materials," and by a return to
his best sermons of earlier years for repreaching in Stockbridge.[49]
Thus, as Edwards moves from young intern to mature gospel minister, we
find the rhetorical tone and style of his sermons gaining in
confidence, forcefulness, and authority.

For example, in a relatively early Northampton sermon (1729) on II
Corinthians 4:7, he preaches self-effacingly, on ministers as "earthen
vessels" which are "the meanest sort of ware and the weakest, the most
brittle." The point of the message in this unpublished sermon is that
"the instruments that God makes use of to do his work in the souls of
men are of themselves utterly unable to do it."

By contrast, in an ordination sermon fifteen years later, Edwards
eloquently and very confidently declares:

> So are ministers honored by their great Lord and Master,
> that they are set to be that to men's souls, that the lights
> of heaven are to their bodies; and that they might be the
> instruments and vehicles of God's greatest goodness, and the
> most precious fruits of his eternal love to them, and means
> of that life . . . . And hereby our ministry will be likely
> to be as beneficial as our office is honorable: we shall be
> like Christ, and shall shine with his beams; Christ will
> live in us, and be seen in his life and beauty in our

****
[49] "Literary Techniques of Jonathan Edwards," pp. 126-127, 172.
Studies such as Kimnach's have been able to build greatly upon the

ministry, and in our conversation."[50]

Throughout his preaching career, Edwards' sermons are almost without exception well-organized.[51] They are the fruits of meticulous study and laborious efforts to grasp scriptural and doctrinal complexities. But the early sermons generally do not have the great precision, the bibilical cadences, and the potently developed metaphors and images that become the hallmark of Edwards' revivalist preaching during the 1730's and 1740's.

Unpublished Sermon -- Canticles 1:3 A (1728)

An unpublished sermon on Canticles 1:3, delivered in 1728 when Edwards was an assistant pastor in Northampton, serves as an excellent demonstration of his early prose style. The sermon, probing and vigorous, focuses on the transcendently "excellent and desireable" Savior, whose being is infinitely complex and marvelous. This 1728 sermon is one of many which address Christ's excellencies. In his 1728 exegesis of Canticles 1:3, Edwards asserts:

> We may be confident that Christ's perfections reflect glory one upon another and make one another the more lovely. Thus his divine perfect wisdom makes his power the more glorious. If he were infinitely powerfull [sic] and could do what he pleased yet if he had not wisdom to direct his power he would indeed be a dreadfull [sic] being but not a

****
(Footnote 49 Continued From Previous Page)
work which Thomas Schafer did to establish dates for the sermons Edwards left undated.

[50]The True Excellency of a Gospel Minister (Hickman), II, 959.

[51]Most of the early sermons very faithfully adhere to the standard Puritan sermon progression from Scripture to Doctrine to Application.

glorious. They are not fit to have power in their hands
that haven't wisdom to manage . . . .

But he that is infinitely powerfull and has also infinite
wisdom to guide his power is one worthy of infinite honour
and glory. So on the other hand, his wisdom receives glory
from his power. For however wise he were if he were a weak
being and unable to exert his wisdom and put it into action,
he would not be so glorious as he that is wise and is able
to do whatever his wisdom directs to.

So his infinite understanding and power receives glory from
his holiness. The more powerfull and the more cunning
a wicked being is, the more hatefull [sic]. The devil is
the more hatefull for his being so powerful and so crafty.
Because his is a wicked being and he has the great
opportunity to exercise his wickedness, his wickedness is
the more mischievous.

So on the other hand Christ's holiness receives glory from
his power and wisdom to be infinitely great and wise. Being
of a holy and excellent disposition is more glorious than to
be a weak ignorant person. Holy holiness indeed is
excellent in whatsoever it be found. It is beauty and
excellency itself and makes all excellence in whomsoever it
be found. But it is more excellent when it is found with
wisdom. There are some persons that have holiness that yet
for lack of wisdom and through natural impudence don't
appear so amiable as otherwise they would do. They spoil
the beauty of their beliefs as appearing unto others through
their impudence.

. . . . But it is an amiable sight to see holiness
exercised with wisdom and discretion. Especially must it be
exceeding glorious to see infinite holiness and infinite

wisdom meeting together in one person.   Such wisdom is glorious wisdom indeed that is a holy wisdom and [?] such holiness is beautiful indeed that is an infinitely wise holiness and especially it is glorious to see both meeting in a person of infinite greatness and majesty. So the mercy and love of Christ receives a great addition of glory from the greatness and infinite happiness.   It is more wonderfull [sic] and infinite happiness.   It is more wonderfull and admirable to see one that is infinitely high and mighty and happy to be full of pity, full of love, of tender compassion, infinite in loving kindness and tender mercies.   'Tis a wonderful sight to see such an ocean of love and pity in the heart of him that sits infinitely exalted upon a throne of glory. All these receive glory from his unchangeableness for it were never so glorious, yet if he were changeable and he did not know how soon he might lose his glory he would not be so worthy that creatures should entirely set their heart upon him.

These sermonic passages on Canticles 1:3 (1728) indeed reflect the deep and subtle movement of Edwards' thoughts as he ponders the wonder of Christ's perfection.   But this sermon's use of the devil as an example risks being digressive. The reiterations seldom rise to the rhythmic, incantatory levels of his later revivalist sermons. And the prose at times falters clumsily in lines such as "Being of a holy and excellent disposition is more glorious than to be a weak ignorant person." Yet, as Edwards is moved by Christ's infinite graciousness, he points tenderly and very concretely to "the ocean of love and pity in the heart of him that sits infinitely exalted."

Unpublished Sermon -- Canticles 1:3 B (1733)

In following the stylistic development in Edwards' sermons, it is particularly telling for purposes of comparison to examine another sermon which he preached five years later (1733) on Canticles 1:3. In this second sermon on the same text, Edwards thoroughly reworks and alters the original message before presenting it as a guest lecturer to a Boston audience. The 1728 Northampton doctrine had stated that "Jesus Christ is a person transcendently excellent and desireable." In adapting the sermon for the 1733 presentation he modifies the doctrine slightly to assert that "Jesus Christ is a person transcendently excellent and lovely." The parts of this 1733 sermon are more smoothly and deftly interwoven than those of the earlier sermon. Edwards is obviously fitting his style and message to a more urbane, sophisticated group of listeners, speaking as a teacher holding before them the "excellent" Christ rather than as a pastor wishing to move a congregation to adore the "desirable" Savior. In the following passages from the 1733 unpublished sermon Edwards has wisely deleted earlier literary weaknesses--for example the extended reference to Satan--to achieve greater coherence of thought:

> Christ as a divine person is possessed of all possible excellency. And in order to conceive aright of Christ's divine excellency, we are not only to consider his several infinite perfections separately but together as illustrating and rendering each other more glorious. If there but be that any being should be infinitely powerfull and could do what he pleased without wisdom to direct his power he could scarcely be said to be the more glorious for his power. They are not fit to have power that haven't wisdom to guide them in the exercise of it. So on the other hand his power reflects glory on his wisdom. However wise he were yet if

he were weak and unable to put his wisdom in practice, the glory of his wisdom would not be manifested. So his infinite understanding and power receive glory from his holiness. The more powerfull and the more knowing and crafty a wicked being is the more hatefull. That alone is a glorious power and knowledge that is a holy power and knowledge. So infinite holiness receives justice from infinite wisdom and strength. He that is of great understanding and ability and is withall of a holy and excellent disposition is definitely more esteemed than a lower and lesser being with the same virtue of inclination and will. Indeed holiness is excellent in whatsoever subject it be found. It is beauty and excellency itself, and renders all excellent that are possessed of it. And yet more excellent when joined with great abilities as the very same qualities of gold do render the body in which they are inherent more precious and of greater value when joined with greater than when with lesser dimensions. But Christ hath each of these perfections in an infinite degree. He is infinitely powerfull wise and holy. The infinite grace mercy and love of Christ add glory to and receive glory from every other attribute. How glorious and wonderfull is it to behold infinite goodness and compassion to see him who is the great creator and [?] Lord of heaven and earth full of condescension and tender pity and mercy toward the mean and unworthy. His almighty power, infinite self-sufficiency and majesty renders his exceeding goodness to his creatures the more surprising.

One year after delivering the above 1733 sermon, Edwards, his reputation as preacher and theologian growing in New England, prepared another sermon on Christ's infinite perfection. This sermon, first

presented in 1734, was later published upon request of those who had
heard it. In print, it was titled The Excellency of Jesus Christ and
appeared with several other of Edwards' sermons in Discourses on
Various Important Subjects, Nearly Concerning the Great Affair of the
Soul's Eternal Salvation. In the Preface to Discourses, Edwards
explicitly reveals his consciousness of prose style by reminding his
readers that the sermons "appear in that very plain and unpolished
dress in which they were first prepared and delivered." He indicates
that as a "messenger from God to souls" he is not concerned about
literary ornamentation such as "politeness and modishness of style and
method" or "elegance of language." Nonetheless, The Excellency of
Jesus Christ demonstrates a masterful command of language, rich
scriptural cadences and echoes, and a growing confidence and firmness
of articulation in this "messenger from God":

> There do meet in Jesus Christ infinite highness and
> infinite condescension. Christ, as he is God, is
> infinitely great and high above all. He is higher than the
> kings of the earth: for he is King of kings and Lord of
> lords. He is higher than the heavens, and higher than the
> highest angels of heaven. So great is he, that all men,
> all kings and princes, are as worms of the dust before him;
> all nations are as the drop of the bucket, and the light
> dust of the balance; yea, and angels themselves are as
> nothing before him. He is so high, that he is infinitely
> above any need of us; above our reach, that we cannot
> comprehend him. . . . Christ is the Creator and great
> possessor of heaven and earth: he is sovereign Lord of
> all: he rules over the whole universe, and doth whatsoever
> pleaseth him: his knowledge is without bound: his wisdom
> is perfect, and what none can circumvent; his power is
> infinite, and none can resist him: his riches are immense

and inexhaustible: his majesty is infinitely awful. And
yet he is one of infinite condescension. None are so low
or inferior, but Christ's condescension is sufficient to
take a gracious notice of them. He condescends not only to
the angels, humbling himself to behold the things that are
done in heaven, but he also condescends to such poor
creatures as men. . . . Yea, which is much more, his
condescension is sufficient to take a gracious notice of
the most unworthy, sinful creatures, those that have
infinite ill deservings. Yea, so great is his
condescension, that it is not only sufficient to take some
gracious notice of such as these, but sufficient for
everything that is an act of condescension, that it is not
only sufficient for everything that is an act of
condescension. His condescension is great enough to
become their friend: it is great enough to become their
companion, to unite their souls to him in spiritual
marriage: it is great enough to take their nature upon
him, to become one of them, that he may be one with them:
yea, it is great enough to abase himself yet lower for
them, even to expose himself to shame and spitting; yea, to
yield up himself to an ignominious death for them. And
what act of condescension can be conceived of greater?[52]

Unpublished Sermon on Acts 20:28 (1754)

A sermon on Acts 20:28 written in Stockbridge in 1754 provides a
vivid example of Edwards' sermon style in his later years. This is one

****
[52]Faust and Johnson, Representative Selections, pp. 121-122.

of his last fully written-out sermons, and like the sermons on Isaiah
3:1-2 (1729), Canticles 1:3 A(1728), Canticles 1:3 B(1733), it includes
a probing examination of the infinite mystery of Christ's being and
acts. But this 1754 sermon focuses on Christ's blood; it elaborates
heavily on the infinite chasm between sinful creature and divine
savior, and upon Christ's infinitely precious sacrificial death. Here
we have the sinewy style and theological preoccupations of a man who
was spending most of his time writing lengthy treatises and volumes
defending the essential doctrines of the Christian church against
liberalism, Deism, and Arminianism. The sermon is solemn, almost
funereal. The following extensive extract from the sermon reveals
Edwards as the seasoned and penetrating systematic theologian whose awe
of Christ's beauty and sacrifice has not wavered but rather has
intensified over the years:

> Not only the nature of what was done and suffered in
> shedding blood for the souls of men should be considered
> but also whose blood it was that was shed. And we are told
> in the text that it was the blood of God shed [for] the
> church of God which he hath purchased with his own blood,
> because the person that shed the blood was God a divine
> person being not only man but God. And it being so that
> that blood was the blood of God the following things are
> here worthy to remember.
>
> 1. That it was the blood of one of infinite dignity and
> glory and it was blood that was infinitely precious and
> what was done in shedding of it for sinners was a thing
> infinitely great, infinitely greater than if the greatest
> earthly potentate had shed his blood or that of all the
> princes on earth yea and infinitely greater than the
> highest created angel yea and not only so but an infinitely

greater thing than if the whole glorious host of those pure
and glorious spirits. . . .   In that it was the blood of
God. . . .   it was the blood of him before whom all the
kings of the Earth are as grasshoppers and the blood of one
that was the great creator and king of angels. He by whom
as the apostle refers in Colossians 1:16, 17 "all things
were created that are in Heaven and that are in Earth
visible and invisible whether they be thrones or dominions
or principalities or powers by whom and for whom all things
were created and he is before all things and by whom all
things consist."

2.   In that it was God's own blood it was the blood of one
that had been from all eternity infinitely happy. As it is
a greater thing for one that is great and honourable to
suffer than for another that is miserable it is a greater
thing for one that is originally in a very happy state to be
willing to descend into a state of affliction and torment
than another.   The self-denial is all the greater in
proportion to the degree of happiness he descended from.
'Tis a harder thing for one that is perfect, is not only at
ease but in very prosperous and joyful circumstances to
comply to come down from such a state in circumstances of
extreme calamity and sorrow than for another whose original
circumstances are already not very prosperous and not at so
great a remove from the suffering which is purposed.

When Christ was on earth his human soul had communicated to
it a kind of memory or consciousness of that happiness
which his person had with God the Father before the cross
(as far as an human mind was capable of it) and he
reflected on that when he was going to shed his blood as

appears by what he says in the prayer he made the night before his crucifixion John 17:5 "and now O Father glorify." So that he had that happiness which he had with His father from eternity to compare with the extreme suffering that there was yet before him. [?] which made the self denial infinitely greater than it otherwise would have been.

In order rightly to judge the degree of Christ's self denial for the salvation of souls we must take our measure from the height of happiness he was in before to the depth of sorrow, pain, and contempt he descended to from there and this will show it to be humiliation incomprehensible and truly great.

It is to be considered that the happiness that Christ had before the cross consisted in the enjoyment of his father's love, so that he knew by experiencing the infinite value of that Love, which made it infinitely harder to bear to have the comforts of that Love withdrawn by God departing and holding back from Him as he did on the cross, and when he [?] fulfilled the Father's will at that time when he cried out "My God, my God. . ."

3. In that it was God's own blood it was the blood of one that was infinitely above any need of us. Christ as he was God was infinitely above any need of any thing. God is self sufficient. His happiness is inherent in his being. . . .

Indeed the eternal infinite happiness of the divine being seems to be social, consisting in the infinitely blessed union and felicity of the person of the trinity so that they are happy in one another, God the Father, God the Son, are represented as rejoicing from eternity one in another. . . .

. . . as Christ's blood was the blood of God, so it was the blood of one that had not stood in need of us because he was omnipotent.

It. . . is evident that he that shed his blood for sinners needed not an salvation over sin and misery.

4.   For that it was God's blood that was shed for sinners it was the blood of one that was infinitely above all sufficiency of being regarded for shedding his blood. That also appears by what we have already observed of God's self-sufficiency and Christ's infinite happiness in the bosom of the father. That happiness that is infinite cannot be added to.

In that Christ was God it appears that he is above all, especially of being regarded immutable.

5.   In that blood that was shed for the souls of men was the blood of God it was the blood of one to whom those that it was shed for is a enemy.

Sinners are enemies to God. The very nature of sin is opposition to authority of God, opposition to his will as expressed in his law I John 3:4. Sin is an opposition to the law of God and rebellion against the law-giver. It is opposing the authority of God and a contempt of his infinite majesty. And as it is an opposition to the holy will of God so tis a contrariety and enmity against the nature of God for his will is but an expression of his holy nature which is infinitely contrary to sin. . . . And as sin is an opposition to God's nature so it implies a contrariety to all his perfections. So the nature of God and his perfections are not different. Sin being an opposition to God's perfection so it is an opposition to his life and essence and very being so the being of God and the being of his nature and perfections cant be distinguished. And as sin is in opposition to the nature of God so tis in opposition to his works in opposing the design of God in the creation of the world which is his own glory and the great eternal excellency and happiness of the creator.

Theological Developments

In examining changes and developments in Edwards' sermon style, we may well inquire whether Edwards' fundamental theology or doctrine of ministry changed over the years. To this question, the answer is no: Edwards' theology does not so much change as progressively solidify and deepen. His conception of the minister as God's messenger—appointed, called, authorized, prepared, used, honored, and blessed by God—remains constant. The sermons in which Edwards elaborates upon ministry and the care of souls do, however, contain notable shifts in concern and emphasis as he directs his attention to particular heresies, to pressures and conflicts in the church, and to situations that affected the privileged position and power of the orthodox, established clergy. The exigencies of Edwards' own life produce a gradual shift in the tone of his ordination and ministerial sermons. The sermons move chronologically from bouyant celebration and optimism to a focus on the minister's long-suffering, self-denying imitation of the sacrificial Christ.

This definite shift in the ordination sermons has received very little attention. The final stages of this development appear very clearly in Edwards' last two ordination sermons--<u>Christ the Example of</u> <u>Gospel Ministers</u> (1749) and the unpublished sermon on Acts 20:28 (delivered 1754 and again in 1756). This change in focus was no doubt influenced heavily by his very troubling experiences in the later part of the 1740's as the excitement of the Great Awakening began to die out with disturbing after-effects in the church. During his last years in Northampton, from 1748-1750, Edwards' pastoral labors became increasingly distressing and counterproductive. Controversies grew and intensified between Edwards and his congregation. The church failed to grow while he insisted upon hearing persons' "professions" of faith in Christ before they could partake of communion. Northampton showed steadily mounting opposition to their pastor's prophetic, autocratic leadership. The efforts to dismiss Edwards from the Northampton pastorate eventually became a local expression of the general, "widespread unrest between clergy and laity over the matter of authority."[53] As lay leadership and claims were on the rise--in spite of castigating sermons like Edwards' November, 1747, installation sermon which had heavily emphasized ministerial authority--the people desired a more egalitarian church government. By the end of the religiously tumultuous decade of the 1740's, the New England "pews knew their power," says Winslow, and in the case of Northampton, they "were swift and ruthless in the exercises of it."[54]

Already in April, 1749, Edwards had offered to resign from the Northampton pulpit if his forthcoming book--<u>Humble Inquiry into the</u> <u>Rules of the Word of God Concerning the Qualifications Requisite to a</u> <u>Compleat Standing and Full Communion in the Visible Christian Church</u>[55]

****
[53]Ola Winslow, <u>Edwards</u>, pp. 241-242.

[54]Winslow, p. 242.

[55]Boston, 1749.

--did not convince his people of their pastor's doctrinal correctness in the communion controversy. By the time he delivered the June 29, 1749, sermon entitled Christ the Example[56] for the ordination of Job Strong at Portsmouth, Edwards was well into the immense task of preparing An Humble Inquiry for fall publication, a treatise that firmly underscored the official position of the ministry as Christ's representative.[57]

The Last Ordination Sermons

Edward's last two ministerial sermons, prepared for June 29, 1749, and for May 28, 1754, are remarkable for several reasons. Each sermon points directly, principally, and consistently to Christ the God-man as the perfect incarnation of gospel ministry. Each sermon further stresses that ministers not only represent their Master but imitate him. And, finally, these later sermons enlarge upon the pain as well as the honor of ministry; the minister notably becomes a self-abnegating, messianic figure empowered to emulate Christ as he "exerted himself for the salvation and happiness of the souls of men [Acts 20:28]." Christ is the prototypical minister--tireless, loving, God-glorifying, obedient, and faithful in the work of redemption. And as Edwards' own experience was painfully teaching him, the work of faithful gospel ministers sometimes requires that they face cruel opposition, trials, false accusations, and mental anguish.

****

[56] This is the penultimate sermon Edwards saw into published form. His final published sermon is the Farewell Sermon delivered on June 22, 1750, and published in Boston in 1751.

[57] In Section IX of Humble Inquiry, Edwards asserts the authority and role of the minister thus:
    There is in the Lord's supper a mutual solemn profession of the

Christ the Example (1749)

Certainly in all the previous ministerial sermons there were indications and echoes of the theme that ministers "above all men" are Christ's representatives. But the June 29, 1749, sermon embodies a full vision of ministry built upon the premise that "Christ is particularly the Lord and Master of ministers" and thus it is a minister's "greatest honor to imitate Christ as he labors with Christ." Christ is the minister's great vocational example, inspiration, "inducement," and direction. In Christ as prototype and minister as mimetic, the great design of redemption is accomplished and made concrete by long-suffering, sacrificial love. As Edwards declares in this ordination sermon, "The chief trials of Christ's virtue, and so their most bright and eminent exercises, were in the abasement, labour, and suffering that he was the subject of for our salvation. Which certainly may well endear those virtues to us, and greatly engage us to imitate that example." Thus the strong identification between suffering, reviled Christ and suffering, rejected minister clearly shapes this sermon as one year later (June, 1750) it would also shape

****

(Footnote 57 Continued From Previous Page)
two parties transacting the covenant of grace, and visibly united in that covenant; the Lord Christ by his minister, on the one hand, and the communicants (who are professing believers) on the other. The administrator of the ordinance acts in the quality of Christ's minister, acts in his name, as representing him: and stands in the place where Christ himself stood at the first administration of this sacrament, and in the original institution of the ordinance. Christ, by the speeches and actions of the minister, makes a solemn profession of this part in the covenant of grace: he exhibits the sacrifice of his body broken and his blood shed; and in the minister's offering the sacramental bread and wine to the communicants, Christ presents himself to the believing communicants, as their propitiation and bread of life. (Hickman), I, 458.

Edwards' messianic words in the Farewell Sermon:

> Although I have often been troubled on every side, yet I
> have not been distressed; perplexed but not in despair;
> cast down but not destroyed. But now I have reason to
> think my work is finished which I had to do as your
> minister: you have publicly rejected me.[58]

We will recall that during the time Edwards was preparing the June
1749 ordination sermon, he was also readying David Brainerd's Life and
Diary. Each work contains passages which seem equally at home in the
other. In the 1749 ordination sermon, for example, Edwards remarks
that "the bright and glorious example of Christ that is set before us,
is chiefly. . . the devotion, heavenly mindedness, humility, patience,
meekness,   forgiveness,   self-denial   and   charity,   which   he
exercised...for the good of the souls of men." In Edwards' Preface to
Brainerd's writings, Edwards qualifies his deep respect for Brainerd's
exemplary piety with an insistence that Christ is the only reliable,
pure example of perfect holiness: Christ "exhibited to the world such
an illustrious pattern of humility, divine love, discreet zeal, self-
denial,   obedience,   patience,   resignation,   fortitude,   meekness,
forgiveness,   compassion,   benevolence,   and   universal   holiness,   as
neither men nor angels ever saw before."[59] Certainly Brainerd's
writings, which Edwards read with great personal and theological
interest, were pervaded by an intense consciousness of Christ as the
ultimate model of righteousness and ministry. So too Edwards, in
choosing the text and doctrine for Job Strong's ordination, was moved
to look directly to Christ as the pattern of gospel ministry. Because
ministry is grounded in Christ, ministers can be true ministers only if

****

[58] (Hickman), I, ccxlvi.

[59] (Hickman), I, 313.

they are transformed into the image of Christ. In this sermon, then, the minister is viewed as a Christ-like savior, prophet, and mediator.

The 1749 sermon, based on John 12:15-16, expounds on the doctrine that "ministers of the gospel ought, in the work of their ministry, to follow the example of their great Lord and Master, Jesus Christ." Perhaps more particularly than any of the previous ordination sermons, Christ the Example describes the duties and details of a minister's labors, "the chief part of it done by preaching the gospel to cleanse the souls of men even as Christ cleansed the soiled feet of his disciples." In following Christ's ministerial example, a preacher must embody faithfulness in fervent intercessory prayer, diligent daily "action and labour" for the good of souls, and a Christ-like compassion for souls.

As Christ himself adapted his discourses to extenuating circumstances, so must ministers adapt their preaching "to persons, seasons, and occasions." And like Christ, a pastor must preach the whole counsel of God "with authority, boldly, zealously, fervently." Following their divine exemplar, ministers must show gentleness to the poor and take a "gracious notice from time to time of little children." Likewise, ministers must delight in doing God's will and must patiently warn souls that God requires not only outward morality but "inward and spiritual" piety. In their office as Christ's representatives and examples,

> Ministers should be persons of the same quiet, lamb-like spirit that Christ was of, the same spirit of submission to God's will, and patience under afflictions, and meekness toward men; of the same calmness and composure of spirit under reproaches and sufferings from the malignity of evil men; of the same spirit of forgiveness of injuries; of the same spirit of charity, of fervent love and extensive benevolence. The same disposition to pity the miserable, to

weep with those that weep, to help men under their calamities
of both soul and body, to hear and grant the requests of
the needy, and relieve the afflicted; the same spirit of
condescension to the poor and mean, tenderness and
gentleness towards the weak, and great and effectual love
to enemies. They should also be of the same spirit of
zeal, diligence, and self-denial for the glory of God, and
advancement of his kingdom, and for the good of mankind;
for which things' sake Christ went through the greatest
labours, and endured the most extreme sufferings. (p. 961)
Thus in this sermon Edwards seems to have discovered that most
creaturely metaphors by their very nature fall short of the perfect
"inward and spiritual" beauty which Christ demonstrates: one must look
at Christ and try to learn from his very emblematic but utterly real
and perfect actions—his gentleness, his self-abasement, his suffering,
his prayers to his Father, and his love for souls.

Unpublished Installment and Ordination Sermon on Acts 20:28
(Preached 1754 and 1756)

The last official ministerial sermon Edwards was ever to write is
a sober, heavily theological work. Based on Acts 20:28, this
unpublished sermon, like Christ the Example, looks directly at the
ineffably perfect example of Christ's selflessness, humility, and
obedience as a pattern for all saints but especially for gospel
ministers. Edwards' personal note on the top left-hand side of the
first page indicates that it was "prepared for the [May 28, 1754]
instalment of Mr. Billing" and "preached also at No. 3 July, 1756 at
Mr. Jones' Ordination."

This sermon reflects a somber attitude toward ministry, perhaps
unwittingly revealing Edwards' loss of the bouyant, energetic spirit of

high optimism present in earlier ministerial sermons which presented a vision of ministers joyfully at work among Christ's people.[60] Edwards' own experiences of rejection and defamation seem to inform this late sermon's emphasis on the suffering, sacrifice, and painful exertions inherent in ministry. It is possible that he was depressed by nervous exhaustion and physical illness. He had passed the age of fifty, and his youthful conception of ministry must have been seriously mitigated by the pain and discouragement in his dismissal from Northampton and now from a whole set of new difficulties at the Stockbridge mission.[61]

The intent of the 1754 sermon is pointed: "My design...is to consider Christ's expending his own blood for the salvation and happiness of the souls of men, in the view both of an inducement and a direction to ministers to exert themselves for the same end." Echoing the antithetical, disjunctive patterns of light or darkness, salvation or damnation, heaven or hell, hearing or forbearing which appear in earlier sermons, this final ordination sermon plays upon extremities. Mankind's infinite lowliness and utter vileness as an enemy of Christ are dramatically set in contrast with Christ's infinite dignity, perfection, and benevolence. Edwards attempts to impress upon his listeners the enormity of Christ's sacrificial love. His rhetorical method is to push the listener step by step to an awareness that the magnitude of Christ's redemptive gifts is beyond human comprehension.

By degrees Edwards establishes ever more insistently and incrementally the infinite greatness of Christ's work. He begins by

****

[60]We recall the 1736 unpublished Ordination sermon on Luke 10:17-18: "when those ministers of the gospel that have been faithful and successful come to give an account of their success to their Lord that hath sent them, Christ and they will rejoice together." We also recall the 1746 published ordination sermon on The Church's Marriage, a sermon that glows with the joy of wedding festivities and nuptial ardor.

[61]Edwards' letters ([Hickman], I, "Memoirs," cxciii) document a time of "very great confusion" relating to dishonesty and mismanage-

explaining the Old Testament work Christ did "in the words which he
spoke," the "manifold revelations which he made of himself," and "the
miracles which he wrought of old." However, says Edwards, "Christ did
all those things without any labour, trouble, or expense." But when he

> became incarnate, he immediately began a life and labour
> with difficulty and sorrow. He went through a course (?)
> of labour for the salvation and happiness of the souls of
> men when he went about doing good,. . . preaching the
> everlasting gospel everywhere and to all sorts of people,
> not only on Sabbath Day but from day to day both day and
> night. . . in poverty, hunger,. . . in reproach and
> continual rejection of his enemies. His life was a life of
> . . . conflict with the enemies of the souls of men. . .
> and in the conclusion of those labours and those conflicts
> he suffered to the utmost extremity.

Edwards follows this passage with expressions of profound sorrow
and wonder at the extremity of Christ's crucifixion agonies. Not only
did Christ sacrifice his life; he submitted to a violent, ignominious
death, suffering "the most extreme degree of contempt and cruelty." On
the cross, "extreme were the labours he then underwent" as he expended
"of all things dearest to human nature, even his blood, his life, and
his soul" for the eternal happiness of human souls. As Edwards
considers Christ's "torments of body," his "hanging for hours on the
cross," his giving up "the blood of God" for the salvation of souls,

****
(Footnote 61 Continued Previous Page)
ment by one of the agents living at Stockbridge and "pursuing measures
very contrary to the measures of the commissioners of the [mission]
society in London." Winslow writes poignantly of Edwards' problem "of
ministering to an Indian population fatally divided against itself,
and to a small clique of whites, half of whom were his personal enemies and that half in control of the town [Stockbridge]," Jonathan
Edwards, p. 276.

Edwards' language becomes incantatory, dwelling on the infinitude of Christ's redemptive love:

> It was the blood of one of infinite dignity and glory and it was blood that was infinitely precious and what was done in shedding of it for sinners was a thing infinitely great, infinitely greater than if the greatest earthly potentate had shed his blood or that of all the princes on earth yea an infinitely greater than the highest created angel yea and not only so but an infinitely greater thing than if the whole glorious host of those pure and glorious spirits [had given up their lives].

And not only was Christ as true God infinitely great and glorious; the contempt and humiliation he experienced were the more brutal because he was "one that had been from all eternity infinitely happy." This truth makes Christ's "self-denial infinitely greater than it otherwise would have been." For knowing the perfect pleasure and "infinite value" of his Father's love, Christ found "it infinitely harder to bear to have the comforts of that love withdrawn by God departing and holding back from him as he died on the cross." And so Edwards continues to repeat "infinite" upon "infinite" to magnify and intensify Christ's ministerial love and sacrifice.

From the time Edwards left Northampton, his preaching had been directed primarily to a small group of white settlers at Stockbridge and to a group of illiterate Mohawk and Housatonic Indians for whom he preached very simple sermons from outlines or revisions of his old Northampton sermons. Yet the March, 1754, ordination sermon demonstrates that Edwards was still able to achieve the strategic use of incremental and impressive language as he had done so forcefully in his earlier revival and imprecatory sermons. His practiced sense of incantation and rhythm, amassed details, and climactic rhetoric operates inexorably in this 1754 sermon to celebrate Christ's self-denial and obedience.

As Edwards works through the six sub-points of his doctrinal statement—"the blood that was shed for the souls of men was the blood of God"—he moves from "infinite" to "infinite" in the drama of salvation:

1.   . . .it was the blood of one of infinite dignity and glory. . . .

2.   . . .it was. . .the blood of one that had been from all eternity infinitely happy. . .

3.   . . .it was the blood of one that was infinitely above any need of any thing. . . .

4.   . . .it was the blood of one. . .infinitely above all possibility (?) of being regarded (?) for shedding his blood. . . .

5.   . . .it was the blood of one to whom those that it was shed for is an enemy,. . .[the blood of one having a] holy nature which is infinitely contrary to sin. . . .

6.   . . .it was the blood. . .[of one who] perfectly saw and understood all that evil that is in sin which cannot be comprehended by any man or angel because it is infinite. . . .

In his elaboration of each sub-point, Edwards relentlessly exposes the infinite distance between God and fallen humanity. On the one hand God stands "infinitely above any need of anything. God is self-sufficient. His happiness is inherent in his being."[62] On the other hand men and women stand in opposition to the law of God and in rebellion against the law-giver; they are creatures "infinitely" in need of, yet undeserving of, redemption. The suffering Christ who mediates between holy Creator and fallen creatures is the incarnation of sacrificial

****
[62]These phrases resonate from Edwards' treatise Concerning the End for which God Created the World, which he prepared during his Stockbridge years but which was published posthumously (Boston, 1765).

love and grace.

Directing his remarks now very particularly to ministers, Edwards reiterates that Christ purchased human souls for two reasons--"that they might be his and that he might save them." Then, "to excite [ministers] to labour for their God," Edwards urges them to ponder deeply "the greatness of the infamy that [Christ] died to save [souls] from" and also "the greatness of the happiness he gave the price of his blood to purchase." The awesomeness of Christ's personal sacrifice and love should "move" ministers "to exert themselves that [souls] may be brought to this happiness."

Though Edwards here speaks of happiness, the sermon is colored predominantly by the theme of Christ's redemptive suffering. Edwards speaks darkly as he challenges his ministerial colleagues and particularly Rev. Edward Billing, whose ordination sermon he had preached on May 7, 1740, and whom he is now installing in another parish no doubt facing the heresies of Arminianism and the ecclesiastical unrest felt almost everywhere in New England.

> 'Tis undoubtedly the duty of ministers to. . .be willing to bring themselves even to the utmost as to all temporal things and even of their own death, if they should be called to it in divine providence, yea, to undergo the most tormenting and ignominious death as many of Christ's ministers have been called to it and have actually done it.

Pointing to the martyrdom of the apostles and citing Colossians 1:24, II Corinthians 4:10, and I John 3:16, Edwards, perhaps remembering his own ministerial anguish, claims that it is especially the duty of ministers "to submit willingly and cheerfully to self-denial and suffering." Alluding to II Corinthians 12:15, he urges that "ministers should be ready to give what they have and give themselves to spend and be spent." Christ's charity and benevolence, says Edwards in the sermon's application, are "an example for all the followers of Christ, but more especially an example for ministers to teach them in what they ought to behave themselves in their work."

Once again Edwards' language is heavy with superlatives as he attempts to excite his listeners to a consideration of the exemplary Christ in "the greatest test" of his love, "the highest manifestation" of his obedience, his "exercise of the fullest humility," his "most admirable kindness toward his most injurious, spiteful, and contemptuous enemies when they were in the highest exercise of their cruelty," and his suffering "the most terrible effects of [his enemies'] vile malignancy [when] they showed the most ingratitude."

Almost as if he sensed he were writing his last ministerial sermon, Edwards briefly recapitulates in the last pages of the manuscript many of the ministerial themes, metaphors, and onlooks he had employed in his long history of sermon-making. In an angular, uneven handwriting, now much less legible than his tiny but tidy round hand of younger years, Edwards jots down the key words and phrases to be woven into extemporaneous final observations. The following is page 25 (verso) and 26 (recto) as transcribed directly from the manuscript. (See facsimile pages which follow the transcription.) Each page is 4" x 4 1/4" and divided into two columns. In his manuscripts, Edwards characteristically indicates Christ with the letter X.

> 3. Ministers are not only
>   appointed to carry on
>   X's work of saving souls
>   but in shedding of
>   X's blood in every respect.
>
> Ambassadors 2 Cor. 5.20
>
> we pray you in X's stead
>
> speak in his name
>
> so in administering the sacraments

4. The relation
    of ministers to the
    church of G[od] is in many
    respects an image of that which X
    stands in

    X the good shepherd

    X is the Rep[resentative] of souls

    X is God's Great Prophet

    & teacher & the Light

    of the [world]

    ministers are regarded

    as Light

    X is the church's Head

    and Ruler

       Ministers are under X
    and are Rulers of the church
    Heb. 13.14 Obey them
    that have rule over you.

    X's Intercessors

    Christ is the spiritual husband

    Isaiah 62.5
    So shall thy sons
    marry thee

    Christ __ Angel

    X is the great Example
    Ministers are fit to be

                   ensamples I Peter
                   5. 1,2,3._____

                   _____
                   _____

                   I Tim. 4:12. Be
                   Thou an example to the
                   believers in word in
                   conversation in charity
                   in Sp[irit] in faith
                   in purity.

Having initially presented a superlative view of Christ, Edwards'
sermon subsequently moves to collapse the great gap between Christ and
ministers by underscoring the ways in which self-sacrificing, faithful
ministers not only represent but also resemble Christ: "The relation
of ministers to the church of God is in many respects an image of that
which Christ stands in."   Edwards has thus masterfully managed his
sermon at first to magnify the great abyss separating perfect Savior
and sinful creature.   But toward the sermon's conclusion, the emphasis
on the infinite span between God and fallen sinners paradoxically gives
way to an emphasis on the benevolent union between Christ and the
redeemed.   Most particularly in the gospel minister is Christ's love,
compassion, and concern for souls concretely embodied: "The work of
the ministry is the same in many respects as Christ's own work, the
work of being savior." Through the instrumental words, lives, and
persons of his ministers, says Edwards, Christ`performs his great work
of redemption.

                            Conclusion

The progression in Edwards' efforts to embody the work of the
gospel ministry can be seen across the group of ministerial and
ordination sermons as a movement from the use of biblical analogies and
secondary images of ministry--minister as steward, messenger, officer,

Facsimile Pages from Sermon on Acts 20:28

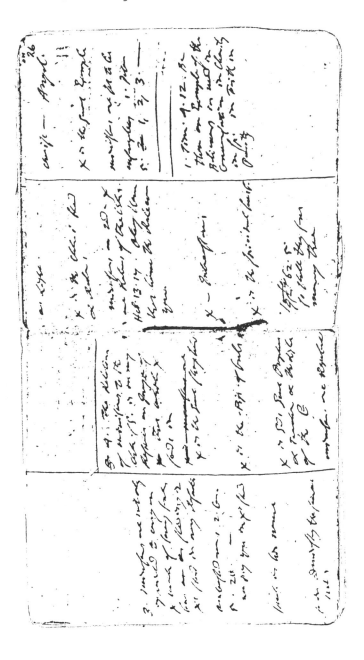

watchman, light, proxy bridegroom, olive branch—to a direct
apprehension of Christ as the incarnation of benevolence and beauty,
Christ the perfect and exemplary image not only of the believer but
especially of the gospel minister. In the last two ordination sermons
Edwards no longer attempts to use metaphor as the basis of his sermon.
Speaking directly to the ministers among his listeners and including
himself in his exhortation, Edwards declares, "We, above all others,
should imitate" clearly and faithfully "the example Christ has set"
(Christ the Example). Here Edwards subordinates the natural, material,
imperfect images of ministry to the infinitely obedient, humble, and
benevolent image of Christ the perfect minister. In one of his
epistles, the apostle Peter exhorts, "As he which hath called you is
holy, so be ye holy.... It is written, Be ye holy; for I am holy" (I
Peter 1:15-16). Paraphrasing these words, Edwards declares in his
sermon on Acts 20:28 that ministers are "to be holy even as God is
holy." The words from Scripture are a performative command. And
Edwards' ministerial utterance—as pastoral admonition and obedient
response—is a most profound form of mimesis.

To be sure, his exhortation to be Christ-like is a traditional
element in Edwards' full sermon corpus and in his many publications.[63]
But his directness in using Christ as primary pattern or image in the
last ministerial sermons during the final, deeply troubling events at
Northampton and the increasing erosion of orthodox ministry, seems to
be evidence of Edwards' desire to urge ministers to experience an
unmediated nearness to Christ in His redemptive work. Edwards invokes
a proximity to Christ that is uncomplicated or interposed by other
images or even, perhaps, by society.

Edwards' view of ministry throughout his life was informed by a
belief that ministers—transformed, appointed, authorized, fitted, and

****

[63] In Religion Affections (New Haven, 1959), pp. 258-259, for
example, Edwards presents a forceful commentary on the beauty of
Christ's incarnate holiness as it perfectly images God's holiness and

directed by Christ—embody the office of highest dignity and honor in this life and the next. But in his declining years of ministry, Edwards' encounters with ambitious laymen and with ecclesiastical and civil authorities, including some of his own vindictive, abusive kin among the Williams' clan, made it painfully clear that creaturely models of rule, direction, and administration are necessarily flawed from the outset. He came to recognize some of his own deficiencies in judgment and leadership. And especially in the Northampton debacle as he struggled to protect the position of ministerial authority and perogatives, Edwards' limitations in leading and persuading his parishioners became apparent.

Life's exigencies, then, as well as Edwards' biblical exegesis increasingly brought him to this conviction: faithful ministers best fulfill their high calling, both in ministry and saintliness, as they humbly endeavor to embody Christ's exacting mandate that "the work of ministers is in many respects like the work that Christ himself was appointed to, as the Savior of men" (Christ the Example).

Edwards never wavered in his hierarchical view of the minister's position in the church and in society. His last ministerial sermons affirm his longstanding belief that a minister's status and honor in heaven will reflect his special Christ-likeness. In his final ministerial sermon he asserts, "'Tis promised to all Christ's faithful followers. . . [to] partake with Christ in His reward. But in a special manner to the faithful ministers, those that imitate [him], as their work is greater. . . and [they] are called to greater self-

****
(Footnote 63 Continued From Previous Page)
thus makes it apparent for persons to adore, emulate, and reflect: "All the spiritual beauty of his human nature , love to God, love to men, condescension to the mean and vile, and compassion to the miserable, etc. all is summed up in his holiness. And the beauty of his divine nature of which the beauty of his human nature is the image and reflection, does also primarily consist in his holiness."

denial, so also greater rewards." Edwards adds, "The glory of heaven
is promised in a peculiar manner to them that are faithful in their
great work of turning men to righteousness."

It is significant and appropriate that in the concluding passages
of the last ministerial sermon and in the I Thessalonians 2:19 text
which ends the sermon, Edwards' emphasis is eschatological, as it had
been in the final passages of each of the other ministerial sermons.
In Edwards' view, the ministerial office does not end on earth; it
continues before the judgment seat and into eternity.

On one of the last pages of his 1754 sermon on Acts 20:28, Edwards
cites II Timothy 2:8-12 and then places three bold lines extending the
width of the manuscript column. These lines in the sermon manuscript
suggest that Edwards had this Timothy passage firmly committed to
memory and that he desired to present the II Timothy passage in full to
the congregation. II Timothy 2:8-12 carries in it kernels of all the
ministerial doctrines informing Edwards' entire ministry—the authority
of the risen Christ, the minister's role as exhorter and messenger, the
paradox of submission which becomes a superior excellency, the
unfettered power of God's performative word, the glorious work of
redemption, and the absolute faithfulness of God. Since Edwards always
believed that God's word speaks for itself through his messengers, it
is appropriate to permit the apostle Paul's words, which Edwards spoke
for the benefit of the congregation to whom he was preaching, to stand
as Edwards' final summary or manifesto of ministry:

> Remember that Jesus Christ of the seed of David was raised
> from the dead according to my gospel: Wherein I suffer
> trouble, as an evil doer, even unto bonds; but the word of
> God is not bound. Therefore I endure all things for the
> elect's sakes, that they may also obtain the salvation
> which is in Christ Jesus with eternal glory. It is a
> faithful saying: For if we be dead with him, we shall also

live with him: If we suffer, we shall also reign with him;
if we deny him, he also will deny us. (II Timothy 2:8-12)

APPENDIX

Approximately one hundred and eighteen of Edwards' nearly twelve hundred manuscript sermons have been published. Among these published sermons are four which Edwards upon invitation preached at ministerial celebrations—ordinations and installations—during the 1740's. With encouragement from friends and fellow ministers, Edwards published these special ecclesiastical sermons during the decade in his life which began with the mounting excitement of New England's Great Awakening and ended with the painful controversies and ecclesiastical proceedings which toppled him from his ministerial position in Northampton.

These four ministerial sermons were originally printed separately, and in no collection of Edwards' Works or representative selections have all four appeared together in one edition or volume.

Edwards' various nineteenth-century editors generally selected one or two or at most three of these sermons to illustrate the variety of Edwards' writings and homiletic efforts. Many of these editions are no longer readily accessible.

Included here are all four sermons. The copy of The Concern of a Watchman for Souls is taken from The Works of President Edwards (New York: G. & C. & H. Carvill, 1830) VII, pp. 178-196. The True Excellency of a Gospel Minister, The Church's Marriage to Her Sons and to Her God, and Christ the Example of Ministers are taken from The Works of President Edwards (New York: Leavitt & Allen, 1843), II, pp. 580-592, pp. 559-579, and pp. 593-603 respectively.

CHRIST THE EXAMPLE OF MINISTERS

John 13:15, 16--For I have given you an example, that ye should do as I have done to you. Verily, verily, I say unto you, the servant is not greater than his Lord, neither he that is sent, greater than he that sent him.

We have in this context, an account of one of the many very remarkable things that passed that night wherein Christ was betrayed (which was on many accounts the most remarkable night that ever was), viz., Christ's washing his disciples' feet; which action, as it was exceeding wonderful in itself, so it manifestly was symbolical, and represented something else far more important and more wonderful, even that greatest and most wonderful of all things that ever came to pass, which was accomplished the next day in his last sufferings. There were three symbolical representations given of that great event this evening; one in the passover, which Christ now partook of with his disciples; another in the Lord's supper, which he instituted at this time; and another in this remarkable action of his washing his disciples' feet. Washing the feet of guests was the office of servants, and one of their meanest offices: and therefore was fitly chosen by our Saviour to represent that great abasement which he was to be the subject to in the form of a servant, in becoming obedient unto death, even that ignominious and accursed death of the cross, that he might cleanse the souls of his disciples from their guilt and spiritual pollution.

The spiritual washing and cleansing of believers was the end for which Christ so abased himself for them. Tit. ii. 14, "Who gave himself for us, that he might redeem us from all iniquity, and purify unto himself peculiar people." Eph. v. 25, 26, "Christ loved the church, and gave himself for it, that he might sanctify and cleanse it with the washing of water." That Christ's washing his disciples' feet

----

Preached at Portsmouth, at the ordination of the Rev. Mr. Job Strong, June 28, 1749.

signified this spiritual washing of the soul, is manifest by his own words in the 8th verse of the context: Peter saith unto him, "Thou shalt never wash my feet." Jesus answered him, "If I wash thee not, thou hast no part with me." Christ, in being obedient unto death, even the death of the cross, not only did the part of a servant unto God, but in some respects also of a servant unto us. And this is not the only place where his so abasing himself for our sakes is compared to the doing of the part of a servant to guests. We have the like representation made in Luke xxii. 27: "For whether is greater, he that sitteth at meat, or he that serveth? Is not he that sitteth at meat? But I am among you as he that serveth." And wherein Christ was among the disciples as he that did serve, is explained in Matt. xx. 28, namely, in his giving his life a ransom for them.

When Christ had finished washing his disciples' feet, he solemnly requires their attention to what he had done, and commands them to follow his example therein. Verses 12-17, "So after he had washed their feet, and had taken his garments, and was set down again, he said unto them, Know ye what I have done unto you? Ye call me Master and Lord, and ye say well, for so I am. If I then, your Lord and Master, have washed your feet, ye also ought to wash one another's feet: for I have given you an example, that ye should do as I have done to you. Verily, verily, I say unto you, the servant is not greater than his Lord, neither he that is sent, greater than he that sent him. If ye know these things, happy are ye if ye do them."

When our Saviour calls on his disciples to imitate the example he had given them in what he had done, we are to understand him, not merely by the example he gave in the emblematical action, in washing his disciples' feet, in itself considered; but more especially, of that much greater act of his that was signified by it, in abasing himself so low, and suffering so much, for the spiritual cleansing and salvation of his people.

This is what is chiefly insisted on as the great example Christ has given us to follow: so it is once and again afterwards, in the discourse Christ had with his disciples, this same night, verse 34, of the chapter wherein is the text: "A new commandment I give unto you, that ye love one another; as I have loved you, that ye also love one another." Chap. xv. 12, 13, "This is my commandment, that ye love one another, as I have loved you. Greater love hath no man than this, that a man lay down his life for his friends." And so in 1 John iii. 16, "Hereby perceive we the love of God, because he laid down his life for us; and we ought to lay down our lives for the brethren."

Christ, in the words of the text, does not only intend to recommend this example of his to the disciples as Christians, or some of his professing people, but especially as his ministers. This is evident by those words he uses to enforce this counsel, "Neither he that is sent, is greater than he that sent him." In which words he manifestly has respect to that great errand on which he had sent them, when he bid them go and preach the gospel to the lost sheep of the house of Israel, Matt. x. 5, 6; and on which they were to be sent after his resurrection, when he said to them "Go ye into all the world, and preach the gospel to every creature." The same errand that Christ has respect to, John xx, 21: "As my Father hath sent me, even so send I you."

And what confirms this is, that Christ elsewhere recommends to officers in his church, that are in that respect chief among his followers, the example which he set in his abasing himself to be as a servant that ministers to guests at a table, in his giving his life for us, Matt. xx 27, 28: "Whosoever will be chief among you, let him be your servant: even as the Son of Man came not to be ministered unto, but to minister, and to give his life a ransom for many." Compare Luke xxii. 25-28.

The work and business of ministers of the gospel is as it were

that of servants, to wash and cleanse the souls of men: for this is
done by the preaching of the word, which is their main business: Eph.
v. 26, "That he might sanctify and cleanse it with the washing of water
by the word."

The words of the text thus considered, do undoubtedly lead us to
this conclusion, and teach us this doctrine, viz.,

That it is the duty of ministers of the gospel, in the work of
their ministry, to follow the example of their great Lord and Master.

And this is what I would by divine assistance make the subject of
my present discourse.

And I propose to handle this subject in the following method.

I.   I would observe wherein ministers of the gospel ought to
follow the example of Christ.

II.   Give some reasons why they should follow his example.

III.   I would endeavor to make a proper application of those
things to myself, and others that are called to this work of the
ministry.

IV.   Show what improvement should be made of them by the people of
this church and congregation.

I.   Then, I would show wherein ministers of the gospel ought, in
the work of their ministry, to follow the example of their great Lord
and Master, Jesus Christ.

And here,

1.   In general, ministers should follow their Lord and Master in
all those excellent virtues, and in that universal and eminent holiness
of life, which he set an example of in his human nature.

The ministers of Christ should be persons of the same spirit that
their Lord was of: the same spirit of humility and lowliness of heart;
for the servant is not greater than his Lord.   They should be of the
same spirit of heavenly-mindedness and contempt of the glory, wealth

and pleasures of this world: they should be of the same spirit of devotion and fervent love to God: they should follow the example of his prayerfulness; of whom we read from time to time of his retiring from the world, away from the noise and applauses of the multitudes, into mountains and solitary places for secret prayer, and holy converse with his Father; and once of his rising up in the morning a great while before day, and going and departing into a solitary place to pray, Mark i. 35;--and another time, of his going out into a mountain to pray, and continuing all night in prayer to God, Luke vi. 12. Ministers should follow Christ's example, in his strict, constant and inflexible observance of the commands which God had given him, touching what he should do and what he should say; he spake nothing of himself, but those things which the Father had commanded him, those he spake, and always did those things that pleased him, and continued in through obedience in the greatest trials, and through the greatest opposition that ever there was any instance of. Ministers should be persons of the same quiet, lamblike spirit that Christ was of, the same spirit of submission to God's will, and patience under afflictions, and meekness towards men, of the same calmness and composure of spirit under reproaches and sufferings from the malignity of evil men; of the same spirit of forgiveness of injuries; of the same spirit of

charity, of fervent love and extensive benevolence; the same disposition to pity the miserable, to weep with those that weep, to help men under their calamities of both soul and body, to hear and grant the requests of the needy, and relieve the afflicted; the same spirit of condescension to the poor and mean, tenderness and gentleness towards the weak, and great and effectual love to enemies. They should also be of the same spirit of zeal, diligence and self-denial for the glory of God, and advancement of his kingdom, and for the good of mankind; for which things' sake Christ went through the greatest labors, and endured the most extreme sufferings.

2.   More particularly should ministers of the gospel follow the example of their great Master, in the manner in which they seek the salvation and happiness of the souls of men.   They should follow his example of love to souls: though it be impossible that that should love them to so great a degree, yet they should have the same spirit of love to them, and concern for their salvation, according to their capacity. Love to men's souls in Christ was far above any regard he had to his temporal interest, his ease, his honor, his meat and drink; and so it should be with his ministers.   They should have the same spirit of compassion to men under their spiritual calamaties and miseries, that he had of whom we read, Mark vi. 34, that "when he came out and saw much people, he was moved with compassion towards them, because they were as sheep not having a shepherd; and he began to teach them many things."   The word translated "move with compassion," signifies, that he was most sensibly affected, and had his inmost bowels moved with pity.   And again we read, Luke xix. that when Christ was riding to Jerusalem, that wicked city, but a few days before his crucifixion, and was come to the descent of the Mount of Olives, where he had a fair view of the city, when he beheld it, he wept over it, on account of the misery and ruin they had brought themselves into danger of by their sin; although the sin by which especially they had made themselves thus miserable, was their vile treatment of him (for Jerusalem was a city that had been peculiarly injurious to him); and though Christ knew how cruelly he should be treated in that city before that week was past, how he there should be set at nought, and with great malignity bound, falsely accused and condemned, reviled, spit upon, scourged and crucified: yet all does not prevent his most affectionate tears of compassion towards them.   "When he was come near, he beheld the city, and wept over it, saying, If thou hadst known, even thou (thou as wicked as thou art, and as vile as thou hast been in thy treatment of me; even thou), the things which belong unto they peace!   But now they

are hid from thine eyes." (Compare Matt. xxiii. 37, and Luke xiii. 34) One would have thought he would have been more concerned for himself than Jerusalem, who had such a dreadful cup to drink, and was to suffer such extreme things by the cruelty of Jerusalem that week. But he as it were forgets his own sorrow and death, and weeps over the misery of his cruel enemies.

Ministers should imitate their great Master in his fervent prayers for the good of the souls of men. We find it to be Christ's manner when-ever he undertook any thing of special importance in the work of his ministry, first to retire and pour out his soul in extraordinary prayer to his Father. Thus when he was about to enter on a journey, and go a circuit throughout all Galilee, to preach in their synagogues, "he rose up a great while before day, and went out, and departed into a solitary place, and there prayed," Mark i. 35-39. And when he was about to choose his twelve apostles, and send them out to preach the gospel, he first went out into a mountain to pray, and continued all night in prayer to God, Luke vi. 12. And the night before his crucifixion, wherein he offered up himself a sacrifice for the souls of men, he pours out his soul in extraordinary prayer, for those he was about to die for, as we have an account in John xvii. That wonderful and most affecting prayer of his, was not so much for himself as for his people. Although he knew what amazing sufferings he was to undergo the next day, yet he seems as it were to be unmindful of himself, and to have his heart all taken up with concern about his disciples; which he manifests in his spending so much time in comforting and counselling them, and praying for them with great affection, compassion, earnest care and fatherly tenderness. And the prayers that he made in the garden of Gethsemane, under the amazing view of the cup he was to drink the next day, seem to be intercessory; especially the last of the three prayers which he there made, when being in an agony, he prayed more earnestly; and his sweat was as it were great drops of

blood falling down to the ground: when he did not pray that the cup
might pass from him, as he had done before, but that God's will might
be done. (Compare Luke xxii. 44, with Matt. xxvi. 42.) That prayer,
as the apostle teaches us, Heb. v. 6, 7, was a prayer that he put up as
our High Priest; and therefore must be a prayer of intercession for us,
a prayer offered up with his blood which he sweat in his agony; as
prayers were wont to be offered up with the blood of the sacrifices in
the temple. His prayer at that time, Thy will be done, was not only an
expression of submission, but had the form of a petition, as it is in
the Lord's prayer. He prayed that God's will might be done in his
being enabled to do the will of God, persevering in obedience unto
death; and in the success of his sufferings; which might in an eminent
manner be called the will of God, as it is in Psal, xl. 7, 8: "Then
said I, Lo, I come.--I delight to do thy will, O my God."

Ministers should follow the example of Christ in his diligence and
laboriousness in his work. "He went about doing good, and healing all
that were oppressed of the devil," Acts x. 38. So abundant was he in
labors, that oftentimes he scarcely allowed himself time to eat or
drink; insomuch that his friends sometimes went out to lay hold of him,
saying, "He is beside himself," Mark iii. 20, 21. That three years and
a half of his public ministry was so filled with action and labor, that
one of his disciples that constantly attended him, and was an eye-
witness of his activity, tells us, that if all that he did should be
written, the world would not contain the books.

Ministers should follow the example of Christ, in his readiness
not only to labor, but suffer for the salvation of souls, to spend and
be spent for them. In this respect the Apostle Paul imitated his Lord
and Master. Philip. ii. 17, "Yea, and if I be offered upon the
sacrifice and service of your faith, I joy and rejoice with you all."
Col. i. 24, "Who now rejoice in my sufferings for you, and fill up that
which is behind of the afflictions of Christ in my flesh, for his

body's sake, which is the church." 2 Cor. xii. 15, "And I will very gladly spend and be spent for you." Christ, in his prayers, labors and sufferings for the souls of men, is represented as travailing in birth with them. Isai. liii. 11, "He shall see of the travail of his soul." In like manner should ministers travail for the conversion and salvation of their hearers. They should imitate the faithfulness of Christ in his ministry, in speaking whatsoever God had commanded him, and declaring the whole counsel of God. They should imitate him in the manner of his preaching; who taught not as the Scribes, but with authority, boldly, zealously and fervently; insisting chiefly on the most important things in religion, being much in warning men of the danger of damnation, setting forth the greatness of the future misery of the ungodly; insisting not only on the outward, but also the inward and spiritual duties of religion: being much in declaring the great provocation and danger of spiritual pride, and self-righteous disposition; yet much insisting on the necessity and importance of inherent holiness, and the practice of piety. Behaving himself with admirable wisdom in all that he said and did in his ministry, amidst the many difficulties, enemies and temptations he was surrounded with, wonderfully adapting his discourses to persons, seasons and occasions. Isai. l. 4, "The Lord God hath given me the tongue of the learned, that I should know how to speak a word in season to him that is weary."

Ministers should follow their Master in his zeal, so wonderfully mixed and tempered with gentleness and condescension in his dealing with souls; preaching the gospel to the poor, and taking a gracious notice from time to time of little children. And they should imitate their Lord in his following the work of the ministry, not from mercenary views, or for the sake of worldly advantages, but for God's glory, and men's salvation; and in having his heart engaged in his work; it being his great delight, and his meat to do the will of his Father, and finish his work, John iv. 34, and having his heart set on the success of his great undertaking in the salvation of souls; this being the joy that was set before him, for which he ran his race, endured the course, and despised the shame; his delight in the prospect of the eternal salvation of souls, more than countervailing the dread he had of his extreme sufferings. Many waters could not quench his love, neither could the floods drown it, for his love was stronger than death; yea, than the mighty pains and torments of such a death.

I now proceed to the

II.   Thing proposed in the handling this subject, which was to give some reasons why ministers of the gospel should follow the example of their great Lord and Master, Jesus Christ.

1.   They should follow his example, because he is their Lord and Master Christ, as he is a divine person, is the Lord of heaven and earth, and so one of infinite dignity, to whom our supreme respect is due; and on that account he is infinitely worthy that we should regard, not only his precepts, but example. The infinite honorableness of his person recommends his virtues, and a conformity to them as our greatest dignity and honor.

Christ is more especially the Lord of Christians; who are therefore under special obligations to follow him.   He is their shepherd, and surely the flock should follow their shepherd.   He is the captain of their salvation; and it becomes soldiers to follow their captain and leader.   He is their head; not only their head of rule and authority, but their head of influence and communication, their vital head, and Christians are members of his body; but members, as partakers of the life and spirit of the head, are conformed to the head.

But Christ is still in a more peculiar manner the Lord and Master of ministers of the gospel, as they are not only members of his church, but the officers of his kingdom, and the dignified servants of his family.   It is the manner of a people to imitate their prince, but especially the ministers of his kingdom, and officers of his household.

It is the duty of the whole army to follow their general, but especially of those officers that have a commission under him.

2. Ministers of the gospel are in some respects called and devoted to the same work and business that Christ himself was appointed to. Ministers are not men's mediators; for there is but one Mediator between God and man, the Man Christ Jesus: they are not our priests to make atonement and work out righteousness for us; for Christ by one offering has perfected forever them that are sanctified; they are not lords over God's heritage; for one is their master, even Christ. But yet ministers of the gospel, as Christ's servants and officers under him, are appointed to promote the designs of that great work of Christ, the work of salvation. It is the work that ministers are devoted to; and therefore they are represented as co-workers with Christ. 2 Cor. vi. 1, "We then, as workers together with him, beseech you also that ye receive not the grace of God in vain." Christ is the Saviour of the souls of men; ministers also, are spoken of in Scripture as saving men's souls. I Tim. iv. 16, "In doing this, thou shalt both save thyself and them that hear thee." Rom x. 14, "If by any means I may provoke to emulation them which are my flesh, and might save some of them." 1 Cor. ix. 22, "That I might by all means save some." And whereas it is said, Obad, 21, "saviours shall come upon Mount Zion;" ministers of the gospel are supposed to be there intended.

The work of ministers is in many respects like the work that Christ himself was appointed to, as the Saviour of men; and especially the same with the work which Christ does in his prophetical office; only with this difference, that ministers are to speak and act wholly under Christ, as taught of him, as holding forth his word, and by light and strength communicated from him. Christ himself after his baptism, followed the work of the ministry: he was a minister of the true sanctuary, Heb. viii. 2; he spake and acted as his Father's minister; was a minister of the gospel, and as such preached and administered sacraments. Pastors of churches are ministers of the same gospel; but in their ministry they act as the ministers of Christ. Jesus Christ is the great Bishop of souls; ministers are also bishops under him. Christ came into the world that he might be the light of the world; ministers are set to be lights unto the churches and are also said to be the light of the world, Matt. v. 14. Christ is the bright and morning star; ministers are stars in Christ's hand. Christ is the messenger of the covenant; ministers are called messengers of the Lord of Hosts. Christ is his people's shepherd, the good shepherd, the great shepherd of his sheep. Ministers are also frequently called shepherds, and are directed to feed the flock of Christ, which he purchased with his own blood.

Seeing therefore it is thus, that the work that ministers are called and devoted to, is no other than the work of Christ, or the work that Christ does, certainly they ought to do his work; which they do not, unless they imitate him, and do as he does, or as he hath set them an example.

3. The example of Christ is most worthy of ministers' imitation. His example was perfect, without error, blemish or defect; and therefore worthy to be made our rule, and to be regarded and followed without exception, limitation or reserve; unless in those things which he did that were proper to his peculiar office. Christ's virtue was not only perfect, but was exercised in those circumstances, and under those trials, that rendered his virtuous acts vastly the most amiable of any that ever appeared in any creature whether man or angel. If we consider the perfection of the virtue that Christ exercised, his virtue did exceed that of most eminent saints, more than the purest gold exceeds the meanest and foulest ore: and if we consider the manner of its exercise, and the trials under which it was exercised and the blessed fruits it has brought forth, so his virtue exceeds that of all other perfectly innocent creatures, and even of the brightest angel, as

the sun in its glory exceeds the stars.

And this example was set us in our own nature, and so is especially fitted for our imitation. There was in the man Christ Jesus, who was one of us, and dwelt among us, such exercises of virtue as become our state and circumstances in the world, as those who dwell in frail flesh and blood, and as members of human society, and dwellers in such a world of sorrow and death.

And then these amiable exercises of virtue in Christ, were exhibited chiefly in the things which he did in that work wherein ministers are called to act as co-workers with him. The bright and glorious example of Christ that is set before us, is chiefly in what he did during the three years and a half of his public ministry; and in the devotion, heavenly-mindedness, humility, patience, meekness, forgiveness, self-denial and charity, which he exercised in the labors and sufferings he went through for the good of the souls of men: and therefore is especially set for the imitation of those who are set apart that they may make it the whole business of their lives to seek the same good of souls.

4. Ministers should follow that example of Christ which has been spoken of, because if they are fit for ministers, and are such as have any right to take that work upon themselves, Christ has set them this example in what he has done for their souls. "I have given you an example (says Christ in the text), that you should do as I have done to you." Ministers should be animated in this work by a great love to the souls of men, and should be ready to spend and be spent for them; for Christ loved them, and gave himself for them: he loved them with a love stronger than death. They should have compassion to men under their spiritual miseries, as Christ had pity on them. They should be much in prayer for the people of their flock, considering how Christ prayed and agonized for them, in tears of blood. They should travail in birth with the souls that are committed to their care, seeing their

own salvation is the fruit of the travail of Christ's soul. They
should exercise a meek and condescending spirit to the mean and weak
and poor, and should as it were wash the feet of Christ's disciples;
considering how Christ condescended to them, when they were wretched
and miserable and poor and blind and naked, and abased himself to wash
their feet.

The chief trials of Christ's virtue, and so their most bright and
eminent exercises, were in the abasement, labor and suffering, that he
was the subject of for our salvation. Which certainly may well endear
those virtues to us, and greatly engage us to imitate that example: so
the things whereof this example consists, were things by which we have
infinite benefit, without which we should have been unspeakably
miserable forever and ever, and by virtue of which we have the glorious
privilege of the children of God, and have a full title to the crown of
exceeding glory, and pleasures for evermore, at God's right hand.

III. I now proceed, as was proposed, in the third place, to apply
what has been said to myself, and others that are employed in this
sacred work of the gospel ministry, and to such as are about to
undertake it, or are candidates for it; and particularly to him that is
now to be solemnly set apart to this work in this place.

We are those to whom these things especially belong: we may hear
Christ saying to us this day, "I have given you an example, that ye
should do as I have done." For the words of Christ in the text were
not only spoken to the twelve, but are also spoken to us. We have now
had represented to us, though in a very imperfect manner, the example
that Christ has set, and what reasons there are that we, above all
others, should imitate it.

It is not only our great duty, but will be our greatest honor to
imitate Christ, and do the work that he has done, and so act as co-
workers with him.

There are two kinds of persons that are given to Christ, and appointed and devoted of God to be his servants, to be employed with Christ, and under him, in his great work of the salvation of the souls of men; and they are angels and ministers. The angels are all of them, even the most exalted of them, subjected of God the Father to our Redeemer, and given to him as his servants, to be subservient to the great designs of his saving and glorifying his elect; Heb. i. 14, "Are they not all ministering spirits, sent forth to minister for them who shall be heirs of salvation?" And doubtless, they were created for this very end: God made them for his Son, to be subservient to him in this great work; which seems to be the chief design of all God's works. And the employment of ministers of the gospel in this respect, is like that of the glorious angels. The principalities and powers in heavenly places, esteem it not any debasement, but their great honor, to be employed as Christ's ministers in this work; for therein they are employed as the ministers of God, in the greatest and most honorable of all God's works; that work of God wherein his glory is chiefly displayed, and which his heart was chiefly upon from eternity. It is the honor of the Son of God himself, that he is appointed to this work. It was because God the Father infinitely loved his Son, and delighted to put honor upon him, that he appointed him to be the author of that glorious work of the salvation of men. And when we consider the greatness, importance and excellency of it, we have reason to be astonished at the condescension of God, that he would ever improve mere creatures as co-workers and ministers of Christ in this affair; for who is sufficient for these things? 2 Cor. ii. 6. "Who is fit or worthy? Who is equal to a work of such dignity, and vast importance?" Especially have we reason to wonder that God will employ, not only holy and glorious angels, but feeble, frail, sinful worms of the dust, in this work, who need redemption themselves; and yet the honor that is put upon faithful ministers, is in some respects greater than that of

the angels: they seem to be that kind of servants that are the most
dignified of the two. For Christ makes his angels to be ministering
spirits unto them, unto the faithful ministers; and the angels are
their angels; as faithful ministers of the gospel are not only
ministers to the church, but dignified members of the church, that
spouse of the King of glory, on whom the most glorious angels, the
highest ministers in the court of heaven, are appointed to attend. And
then Christ seems especially to delight to carry on his work of the
salvation of souls, though the ministrations of men, who have that
nature that Christ is united to, and that are of those sons of men with
whom he had his delight before the world was made. So it is by the
ministration of men, that the Scriptures are given; they were the
penmen of the holy Bible; and by them the gospel is preached to the
world: by them ordinances are administered, and, through their
ministrations, especially, souls are converted. When Christ himself
was employed in the work of the ministry, in the time of his
humiliation, but few, comparatively, were brought home to him,
immediately by his ministrations: it pleased Christ to reserve this
honor for his disciples and ministers, after his ascension, to whom he
promised that they should, in this respect, do greater works than he,
Job. xiv. 12; and accordingly it was by their preaching that the
gentile world was converted, and Satan's kingdom overthrown. Thus God
delights "to perfect praise out of the mouths of babes and sucklings,
that he may still the enemy and the avenger."

It will be our great honor that we are called to this work of
Christ, if therein we follow him; for therein we shall be like the Son
of God: but if we are unfaithful in this office, and do not imitate
our master, our offence will be heinous in proportion to the dignity of
our office, and our final and everlasting disgrace and ignominy
proportionably great; and we, who in honor are exalted up to heaven,
shall be cast down proportionably low in hell.

Let us further consider, that our following the example of Christ in the work of the ministry, is the way to enjoy the sensible, joyful presence of Christ with us. The disciples had the comfort of Christ's presence and conversation by following him, and going where he went. When we cease to follow him he will go from us, and we shall soon lose sight of him.

Our being conformed to Christ's example, will also be the way for us to be conformed to him, and partake with him in his privileges: it is the way for us to have his joy fulfilled in us. Christ, in doing the work to which the Father appointed him, obtained a glorious victory over his enemies, and having spoiled principalities and powers, triumphed over them. If we imitate his example, it will be the way for us in like manner to conquer principalities and powers, yea, to be much more than conquerors: it will be the way for us always to triumph in Christ Jesus. It will be the way for us to obtain success in our ministry, and actually to be made the happy instruments of the eternal salvation of souls. Christ has not only told us, but shown us the way to success in our business, and the way to victory over all that oppose us in it. And our imitating Christ in our ministry, will be the way for us to be partakers with him in his glory; the way for us in like manner to be approved, and openly honored and rewarded by God; the way to be brought to sit with Christ on his throne, as he is set down with the Father on his throne. And as Christ is now exalted to shine as the bright luminary and glory of heaven, so our following his example, will be the way for us to be exalted, to shine with him, "as the stars forever and ever," Daniel xii. 3. And as Christ in heaven rejoices in his success, and will receive his church, presented to him without spot, as his everlasting crown; so our imitating Christ in our work will be the way to partake with Christ in this joy, and have the souls whose salvation we are the instruments of, to be our crown of rejoicing forever. Thus Christ and we shall rejoice together in that world of glory and joy where there is no more labor or sorrow. And we must enter into that joy and glory, in the way of following Christ in our work; there is no other way for ministers to enter there.

And that we may thus follow Christ's example, and be partakers with him in his glory, we had need to be much in prayer for his Spirit. Christ himself, though the eternal Son of God, obtained the Holy Spirit for himself in a way of prayer: Luke iii. 21, 22, "Jesus being baptized, and praying, the heaven was opened, and the Holy Ghost descended like a dove upon him." If we have the spirit of Christ dwelling in us, we shall have Christ himself thereby living in us, and then we shall undoubtedly live like him. If that fountain of light dwells richly in us, we shall shine like him, and so shall be burning and shining lights.

That we may be and behave like Christ, we should earnestly seek much acquaintance with him, and much love to him, and be much in secret converse with him. It is natural, and as it were necessary for us to imitate those whom we are much acquainted and conversant with, and have a strong affection for.

And in order to our imitating Christ in the work of the ministry, in any tolerable degree, we had need not to have our hearts overcharged, and time filled up with worldly affections, cares and pursuits. The duties of a minister that have been recommended, are absolutely inconsistent with a mind much taken up with worldly profit, glory, amusements and entertainments.

And another thing that is of very great importance, in order to our doing the work that Christ did, is, that we take heed that the religion which we promote, be that same religion that Christ taught and promoted, and not any of its counterfeits and delusive appearances, or any thing substitued by the subtle devices of Satan, or vain imaginations of men in lieu of it. If we are zealous and very diligent to promote religion, but do not take good care to distinguish true from false religion, we shall be in danger of doing much more hurt than good, with all our zeal and activity.

I come now to the

IV.   And last thing at first proposed, viz., to show what improvement should be made of what has been said, by the people of this church and congregation, who are now about solemnly to commit their souls to the charge of him they have chosen to be their pastor, and who is not about to be set apart to that office.

And YOU, MY BRETHREN, as all of you have immortal souls to save, if you have considered the things that have been spoken, cannot but be sensible, that it not only greatly concerns your elect pastor to take heed how he behaves himself in his great work, wherein he is to act as a co-worker with Christ for your salvation; but that it infinitely concerns you how you receive him, and behave towards him. Seeing that it is for your eternal salvation that he is appointed to watch and labor; and seeing his business is to do the work of Christ for you, it is natural and easy to infer, that your reception and entertainment of him should in some respect imitate the church's reception of Jesus Christ. Gal. iv. 14, "My temptation which was in my flesh, ye despised not, nor rejected; but received me as an angel of God, even as Christ Jesus." Christ, in the text, commands those whom he sends, to follow his example, and then in the 20th verse following, he directs those to whom he sends them, how to treat them. "Verily, verily, I say unto you, He that receiveth whomsoever I send, receiveth me; and he that receiveth me, receiveth him that sent me." Seeing the work of your minister is in some respects the same with the work of Christ, and he is to be appointed and devoted to do this work for your souls in particular, surely you should esteem him very highly in love for his work's sake, and do all that is in your power to help him, and put him under the best advantages to imitate his great master in this work, to give himself wholly to his work, as Christ did during the time of his

ministry, and to be successful in his work. And as it was observed
before, that it is impossible that ministers should in any tolerable
degree imitate the example of Christ in their work, if their minds are
overcharged with worldly cares and concerns, you ought so to provide
for him and support him, that he shall have no need to entangle himself
with these things; otherwise you will not only bring a great temptation
upon him, which will vastly tend to hinder him in the work of Christ
among you, but will, for the sake of sparing a little of your worldly
substance to yourselves, foolishly and miserably starve your own souls,
and the souls of your children, and will but cheat yourselves; for you
will not be in the way to prosper either in your spiritual or temporal
concerns. The way to have your houses filled with plenty, is to "honor
the Lord with your substance, and with the first fruits of all your
increase," Prov. iii. 9.

And as it is your duty and interest well to support your minister,
so it concerns you to pray earnestly for him, and each one to do what
in him lies in all respects to encourage and help him, and strengthen
his hands, by attending diligently to his ministry, receiving the truth
in love, treating him with the honor due to a messenger of Christ,
carefully avoiding all contention with him, and one with another. And
take heed in particular, that you do not forsake him to follow those,
who under pretense of extraordinary purity, are doubtless doing the
devil's work, in separating themselves, and endeavoring to draw off
others from the ministers and churches in the land in general.

If you think I have spoken something freely to you, I hope it will
be considered, that this is probably the last time you will ever hear
me speak from the pulpit, and that I shall never see you again till we
see one another in the invisible eternal world, where these things will
open to us all in their just importance.

And now nothing is left but to express my sincerest wishes and
prayers, that the God of all grace would be with you, and your elect

pastor, and that he would give you in him a great and long-lasting blessing, that you may enjoy much of the presence of Christ with you in him; that in him may be made up the great loss you sustained by the death of your former faithful and eminent pastor, whose praise was in all the churches; and that you may receive him as you ought to receive a faithful minister of Jesus Christ, and may be a great comfort to him, and may receive great spiritual and eternal benefit by his means; and that you may be each other's crown of rejoicing in the day of the Lord Jesus.

THE CONCERN OF A WATCHMAN FOR SOULS
Heb. 13:17.
"They watch for your souls, as they that must give accounts."

After the Apostle had in this epistle particularly and largely
insisted on the great doctrines of the gospel relating to the person,
priesthood, sacrifice, exaltation and intercession of Christ, and the
nature, privileges and benefits of the new dispensation of the covenant
of grace, as answering to the types of the Old Testament; He improves
all in the latter part of the epistle to enforce christian duties and
holy practice, as his manner is in most of his epistles. And after he
had recommended other duties to the christian Hebrews, in this verse he
gives them counsel with regard to their duty towards those that were
set over them in ecclesiastical authority; "Obey them that have the
rule over you, and submit yourselves."--By them that had the rule over
them, the apostle means their ecclesiastical rulers, and particularly
their ministers and pastors that preached the word of God to them; as
is evident by verse 7. "Remember them that have the rule over you, who
have spoken unto you the word of God": and also by the words of the
text, that immediately follow in the same verse, in which the
employment of those that have the rule over them, that they are to obey
and submit to, is represented. Concerning which may be observed,

1. What it was their pastors were conversant about, in the
employment they were charged with, viz. the souls of men. The
employments that many others were engaged in were about the bodies of
men; so it is with almost all the particular callings that mankind do
follow; they are in one respect or other to provide for men's bodies,
or to further their temporal interest; as the business of husbandmen,
sailors, merchants, physicians, attorneys, and civil officers and
rulers, and the innumerable trades and mechanical arts that are

----

Preached at the Ordination of the Reverend Mr. Jonathan Judd, to the
Pastoral Office over the Church of Christ, in the New Precinct at
Northampton, June 8, 1743.

practised and pursued by the children of men; but the work of the
ministry is about the soul, that part of man that is immortal, and made
and designed for a state of inconceivable blessedness, or extreme and
unutterable torments throughout all eternity, and therefore infinitely
precious; and is that part of man in which the great distinction lies
between man and all the other innumerable kinds of creatures in this
lower world, and by which he is vastly dignified above them; it is such
beings as these that the work of the ministry is immediately conversant
about.

2.   How ministers in the business they have to attend are to be
employed about men's souls, they are to watch for them; which implies
that they are committed to their care to keep, that they may be so
taken care of that they may not be lost, but eternally saved.

3.   A grand argument to induce and oblige them to faithfulness in
this employment, they must give account; i.e. they must give an account
to him that committed those souls to their care, of the souls they were
betrusted with, and of the care they have taken of them.

Therefore that we may the better understand the nature of that
work of a minister of the gospel and pastor of a church, and the grand
inducement to faithfulness in it, spoken of in the text, and know the
better what improvement we ought to make of these things, I would

I.   Show that ministers of the gospel have the souls of men committed
      to their care by the Lord Jesus Christ.

II.   I would show to what purpose Christ thus commits the precious
      souls of men to the care of ministers.

III. That the way in which Christ expects that ministers should seek
      that these purposes may be obtained, with respect to the souls
      committed to them, is by watching for them.

IV.   I would observe, how when the time of their employment is at an
      end, they must give an account to him that committed the care of
      these souls unto them.

And then make application of the whole.

1.   Ministers of the gospel have the precious and immortal souls of men committed to their care and trust by the Lord Jesus Christ.

The souls of men are his; he is the creator of them: God created all things by Jesus Christ. He created not only the material world, but also those things that are immaterial and invisible, as angels and the souls of men. Col. i. 16. "For by him were all things created that are in heaven, and that are in earth, visible and invisible; whether they be thrones or dominions, or principalities, or powers; all things were created by him and for him."

God is the creator of men in both soul and body; but their souls are in a special and more immediate manner his workmanship, wherein less use is made of second causes, instruments or means, or any thing pre-existent. The bodies of men, though they are indeed God's work, yet they are formed by him in a way of propagation from their natural parents, and the substance of which they are constituted is matter that was pre-existent; but the souls of men are by God's immediate creation and infusion, being in no part communicated from earthly parents, nor formed out of any matter or principles existing before. The Apostle observes the difference, and speaks of earthly fathers as being father of our spirits. Heb. xii.9. "Furthermore we have had fathers of our flesh, which corrected us, and we gave them reverence; shall we not much rather be in subjection to the Father of spirits and live?" Therefore God is once and again called "the God of the spirits of all flesh," Numb. xvi.22. and chap. xxvii.16. And in Eccl. xii.7. God is represented as having immediately given or implanted the soul, as in that respect differing from the body, that is of pre-existent matter; "Then shall the dust return to the earth as it was, and the spirit shall return unto God who gave it." And it is mentioned in Zech. xii.1 as one of God's glorious prerogatives, that he is he that "formeth the spirit of man within him." And indeed the soul of man is by far the greatest and most glorious piece of divine workmanship, of all the creatures on this lower creation. And therefore it was the more meet that, however second causes should be improved, in the production of meaner creatures; yet this which is the chief and most noble of all, and the crown and end of all the rest, should be reserved to be the more immediate work of God's own hands, and display of his power, and to be communicated directly from him, without the intervention of instruments, of honouring second causes so much as to improve them in bringing to pass so noble an effect. It is observable that even in the first creation of man, when his body was formed immediately by God, not in a course of nature, or in the way of natural propagation; yet the soul is represented as being in a higher, more direct and immediate manner from God, and so communicated that God did therein as it were communicate something of himself: The Lord God formed man (i.e. his body) of the dust of the ground, (a mean and vile original) and breathed into his nostrils the breath of life; (whereby something was communicated from an infinitely higher source, even God's own living spirit or divine vital fullness) and so man became a living soul.

The souls of men being thus in a special manner from God, God is represented as having a special propriety in them, Ezek. xviii.4: "Behold all souls are mine: As the soul of the father, so also the soul of the son is mine."

And as the souls of men are more directly from God, by the more special and immediate exercise of his divine power as a creator, and are what he challenges as his by a special propriety, and are the most noble part of the lower creation, and are infinitely distinguished from all other creatures here below in that they are immortal beings; so they are, above all other creatures which God hath made in this world, the subjects of God's care and special providence.

Divines are wont to distinguish between God's common and special providence. His common providence is that which he exercises towards all his creatures, rational and irrational, animate and inanimate, in preserving them, and disposing of them by his mighty power, and according to his sovereign pleasure. His special providence is that which he exercises towards his intelligent rational creatures, as moral agents: of which sort are mankind alone, of all the innumerable kinds of creatures in this lower world: and in a special manner the souls of men; for in them only is immediately seated reason and intelligence, and a capacity of moral agency; and therefore they in a peculiar manner are the subjects of God's special providence that he exercises in this lower world. And it is to be observed that God's common providence is subordinated to his special providence; and all things in this world are governed and disposed of in subordination to the great ends God has to obtain with respect to the souls of men. And it is further to be observed, that as the creation of the world was committed to the Son of God by the Father, so is the government of it; and in a peculiar manner the affairs of God's special providence, are left in his hands; and so the souls of men, that are the peculiar subjects of his special providence, are committed to his care; and more especially such souls as are of Christ's visible kingdom or church, which is often in the scripture represented as the field and vineyard that he is the owner of, and has taken the care of.--And what Christ's value is for men's souls appears by what he has done and suffered for them.

But these souls that Christ has made, and that are committed into his hand of the Father, and that are so precious in his account, he commits to the care of ministers. There is a certain order of men that are so dignified and honoured by him, as to have so great a trust reposed in them. He, as it were, brings those souls as an infinitely precious treasure, and commits them to them to take care of; as a prince commits his treasure, his jewels, and most precious things into the hands of one of the dignified servants of his household; or as the father of a family, when he goes on a journey into a far country, leaves his family to the care of a steward.

I come now in the

2nd place, to inquire to what purpose Christ commits the precious souls of men to the care of ministers.

I answer in two things,

1. He commits men's souls to ministers to keep and take care of them for him, that by their means they may answer their end in glorifying him. God has made all things for himself, he has created them for his glory; but more especially those creatures that he has endued with understanding, as he has done with souls of men: it is by them that God has his glory from all his creatures as they are the eye of the creation to behold the glory of God manifested in the other creatures, and the mouth of the creation to praise him and ascribe to him the glory that is displayed in them. The other creatures glorify God passively and eventually, as God glorifies himself in them, as they are the subjects of the exercise of his power and wisdom in their creation and preservation, and in those events that are brought to pass in his disposal of them. Thus God glorifies himself in his works that are manifest in the irrational and inanimate creation, in the view of his rational creatures that he has made capable of beholding and admiring them, and adoring, loving and praising him for them: But they only are capable of glorifying him actively and immediately; therefore all the other creatures do, as it were, bring their tribute of glory to them, through their hands, to be offered to their Creator.   And therefore the souls of men are beings that, with regard to the glory of God, the great end of all things, are of immensely greater importance than all other creatures in this lower world. But these, with respect to this their great end, are committed to the care and keeping of ministers; and therefore Christ has furnished them with proper means to bring them to this end; he has given them all needful instruction; they have a perfect rule and directory to guide them in this great affair;

and has enjoined them the duties they are to perform in their office in every particular, and the manner in which they are to perform these duties, in the charge which he has left them; and has furnished them with all needful helps for the instruction of those souls that are committed to them, to lead them to answer their great end, in duly glorifying their Creator; and all proper means for the exciting and engaging them to attend to, and follow those instructions, as also means for their help and assistance in it, that they may do it the more easily and effectually.

2. They are committed to their care and keeping that they may not be eternally lost, but may have everlasting life. These souls, as I observed before, are immortal and made for eternity; they are set in this world between two opposite eternal states, the one a state of exceeding and eternal glory and blessedness, the other a state of unutterable and unalterable misery: and as they are by nature they are liable to either; by their original guilt and corruption they are exposed to perish forever, in total and perfect destruction and misery: but Christ, from his knowledge of the infinite worth of souls, and his great compassion and love to them, has, by his own precious blood, made way for their escape, and at this infinite expense, has procured unspeakable exaltation and perfect blessedness for them in heaven to all eternity; which by this means they have opportunity to obtain. But yet it remains uncertain what will become of them, until Christ's redemption be applied to them, or they are actually cast into hell; there is an opportunity given, a time of probation, until the great and unalterable event shall determine one way or the other. In the mean time there is a space for the use of means, and the exercise of care, prudence and diligence for our own souls and the souls of others; that they may not fail of the grace of God, but may escape that infinitely dreadful destruction that they are naturally in danger of, and may indeed obtain that infinite privilege of eternal life, that is offered

through the purchase of Jesus Christ. And now in this grand affair, and to this great purpose of an escape from eternal misery, and the obtaining everlasting glory, Christ has committed the precious souls of men to the care of ministers; that by their means they may have the benefit of his redemption, and might obtain that which he has suffered so much to procure. Christ knew that notwithstanding all that he had done to procure life for souls, they would need much care to be taken of them, and many means to be used with them, in order to their being indeed preserved from eternally perishing, and actually brought to the possession of life: and therefore he has appointed a certain order of men, whose whole business it might be to take care of immortal souls; and into their hands has committed these souls, and has betrusted them with the ordinances of his house, and means that he has provided for their salvation; that nothing might be wanting that they need for their furniture for this great business; he has as it were committed to them his goods, and has given them in some respects the key of his stores and treasury; to them are committed the oracles of God and treasure of the gospel. 2 Cor. iv.7. "We have this treasure in earthen vessels." And Chap. v.18,19. "And all things are of God, who hath reconciled us to himself by Jesus Christ; and hath given to use the ministry of reconciliaton, to wit, that God was in Christ reconciling the world unto himself, not imputing their trespasses unto them, and hath committed to us the work of reconciliation."

And as the word of God, so the sacraments that he has appointed, and the discipline of his house, he has committed to them, to be administered by them; and has subjected the souls themselves that they have the care of them, as far as is necessary to put them under the greatest advantage effectually to care for their salvation, and has left a charge to their people to obey them and submit themselves, as in the verse of my text.

I now proceed

III. To observe, that the way in which he who has committed souls to ministers, expects they should seek that these purposes may be obtained with respect to them, is by watching for them.

Though great things have been done by Christ to make way for the salvation of those precious souls, and although Christ has furnished ministers with all proper means to keep them; yet they are in such circumstances in this world, that there is need of the exercise of great watchfulness, and the utmost care and diligence, in those that have the care of them, to prevent their being lost: for they are in the midst of snares, and encompassed round with dangers on every side; they are in the enemy's country, where there are multitudes every where that are strong and subtil, and exceeding blood-thirsty and cruel, that are indefatigably, day and night, seeking the destruction of these souls.

If a prince should commit some great treasure, consisting of most precious jewels, to the care of a subject, to keep for him, and carry through an enemy's country, and bring home safe to his palace, and knew that the enemies by the way would be sensible that the treasure was committed to him, and would be aware of the great value of it, and therefore would be exceeding greedy of it, and incessant in their endeavours to get it from him; would not the prince expect that he, with whom he had entrusted this treasure, should use great care in keeping it? Would he be esteemed faithful to his trust, in the care of so great a treasure, and in such circumstances, without keeping up a continual watch? They that have the care of a city in time of war, and especially at a time when the city is encompassed by enemies that lay siege to it, are wont, if faithful, to maintain incessant vigilance to defend it: the watchmen of the city in such a case had need to watch strictly, for they have the care of the lives of men.--Ministers are from time to time represented in Scripture as the watchmen that have the care of the city of God; as Cant. iii.3. and v.7. Isai. lii.8, and

lxii.6 and in other places. These watchmen have not only the care of
the lives of men's bodies, but of their souls, which are infinitely
more precious. It is expected of them that they should behave
themselves as those that both kept and built the city of Jerusalem, in
Nehemiah's time, while they were continually observed by malicious and
subtil enemies, that diligently sought by all means to circumvent them,
and to destroy the city and people; who with one hand wrought in the
work, and with the other hand held a weapon; holding spears from the
rising of the morning until the stars appeared; and had a trumpet
always at hand to sound, to give warning of any appearing danger, and
did not put off their clothes, nor lay up their weapons, day nor night,
Neh. iv. from the 16 verse to the end.

Ministers are appointed to be shepherds over Christ's flock; and
he commits his flock to their care to keep them, and lead them through
a great and howling wilderness, full of hungry wolves and roaring
lions. And is there not a need of a strict and constant watch in the
shepherds in such a case, as they would preserve the lives of the
sheep, and lead them to the land of their rest?

I come now to,

IV. The last thing in the doctrinal handling of the text, viz.
That ministers hereafter must give account to him that committed men's
precious souls to their care.

Christ's committing souls to ministers' care and charge, and
betrusting them with them as servants or stewards, necessarily supposes
them to be account able to their master with respect to the charge
committed to them.

He that has a treasure committed to him by the owner, and takes
the care and charge of it, not as his own possession, but only to
improve or keep for an appointed time, for him to whom the proper
possession belongs, must return that treasure to the owner when his
time is out, and is accountable to him how he has fulfilled that which

he undertook; and if any precious jewel be missing, he must give an account of it.--So must ministers give an account of the souls committed to their care.

The office and work of ministers is not to last always; their care of souls is but for a limited season; and when that is expired, they must return to their master to give an account.

After what manner they must be called to an account, may be shown in these two things,

1. The event of things with regard to the souls committed to them will be inquired into. As there are so many precious souls committed to their care by Christ, so hereafter it will be inquired what is become of those souls. As if a person has a number or precious jewels committed to him to keep; when the time of his betrustment is out, and he comes to return the intrusted treasure, the state of it will be examined, that it may be seen whether any jewel be lacking or not; and if any be missing, an account must be given what is become of it. The charge of a minister is in scripture represented by that of a steward, to whom the householder, when going into a far country commits his goods, and when he returns, expects that the steward should give an account of his stewardship. In such a case the householder looks into the state of his goods that he left behind under the steward's care. The master in the parable, Matt. xxv.14, &c. when he returns from his journey, has his goods, that he committed to the care of his servants, brought forth and laid before him.

2. It will be inquired how far the event that shall be found, with regard to souls committed to them, was owing to their faithfulness or unfaithfulness in that care and watch that was appointed them. If any precious soul be found lacking, it will be inquired how this comes to pass: they must give an account what they have done with this and that soul that is missing, whether they were lost through their neglect or no; they must give an account what care they have taken, and what

diligence they have used, and whether or no they can wash their hands from guilt with respect to them: it shall be examined by an eye that is as a flame of fire, whether the blood of the souls that are lost is not indeed to be found in their skirts.--We find in the parable of the great supper, that the servants that are sent out to invite guests, return from time to time to their master to give him an account both of the event in their success with respect to some that they were set to, and unsuccessfulness with regard to others; and also of their own doings and faithfulness, whereby they are clear of the guilt of their unsuccessfulness, and are commended to the gracious reward of their success. Luke xiv.20,21. I now come to the

APPLICATION

In which I shall only address myself to those who are principally concerned in the great and solemn affair of this day, viz. to him who is now solemnly to be set apart to the work of the ministry in this place, and to those whose souls are to be committed to his care.

1. I would apply myself to you, dear sir, to whose care the great Redeemer and Head of the church is this day committing a number of precious souls in this place. I beseech you now to suffer the word of exhortation on this solemn occasion; suffer me to put you in mind how great the person is, with whom you are immediately and chiefly concerned in the affair of this day; even the great Shepherd of the sheep, and glorious Lord of heaven and earth, who is to be your and our judge. You present yourself this day before him to receive at his hands a sacred depositum, a great treasure, a number of souls that are to exist throughout all eternity, each one of which is infinitely more precious than all the precious gems that the earth affords. And I beseech you to consider to how great a purpose he is about to commit them to your care and keeping; it is that they, by means of your

faithful care and watchfulness, may be saved with an everlasting salvation. You may judge how much Christ will insist upon it that you should exercise great diligence and strictness in the care you take of them, by the value he himself has manifested of the souls of men, by what he has done and suffered for them: he has shown how precious he has judged immortal souls to be, in that he, though a person of infinite glory, did not think his own blood, his life, his soul, too precious to be offered up as a price for them to redeem them, that they might obtain that salvation in order to which he now is about to commit a number of them to your care, and to betrust you with the means that he has provided for that end; committing to you his holy oracles, and the food of his house, which is his own body and blood, that therewith you might feed these souls; and in some sense committing to you the keys of his stores and treasures, that you might supply and enrich them, and be a means of their eternal wealth and glory.

Consider, dear sir, how great an honor he does you whom God the Father hath made head of the whole universe, and Lord of all things to the church; that after he has provided for the salvation of souls by his dying pains and precious blood, and the Father has committed to him all power in heaven and earth, that he might actually bestow eternal life on them that he died for; he should call you to be a co-worker with him, and should commit precious souls to your care,that you might be the instrument of bringing them home to him, and bringing that to pass with respect to them, for which his soul travailed in the agonies of death, and in ineffable conflicts with the dreadful wrath of God. You are now about to receive the precious treasure at his hands, which you are to keep for him: you present yourself here before the Lord for this end, that you may as it were reach forth your hand and take this great depositum with solemn vow diligently and faithfully to keep it, and devote yourself to that service; so that if it be possible for you to prevent it, no one of those infinitely precious jewels may be lost, but that you may return them all safe to him from whose hands you receive them.

Consider the example of your glorious Lord and master. There was a number of the souls of men committed by the father into his hands, that he might take care for their salvation. And after what manner did he execute his office? How did he lay out himself for the salvation of those souls? What great things did he do? And what great things did he suffer? How hard was the labour he went through? And how greatly did he deny himself? How did this great shepherd of the sheep behave himself when he saw the wolf coming to destroy the sheep; he did not flee to save his own life, and so leave the sheep to become a prey; but from pity and love to the sheep, interposed himself between them and their enemy, stood between them and harm, and encountered the wolf, and in the conflict gave his own life to save theirs, John x.11-15.--We read of Christ's travailing for souls, Isai, liii. 10, 11. "It pleased the Lord to bruise him; he hath put him to grief: when thou shalt make his soul an offering for sin, he shall see his seed. He shall see of the travail of his soul, and shall be satisfied." And how did he travail for this seed of his? Look into the garden of Gethsemane, and there behold him lying on the earth, with his body covered over with clotted blood, fallen down in lumps to the ground, with his soul exceeding sorrowful, even unto death, and offering up strong crying and tears together with his blood: and look to the cross, where he endured yet far more extreme agonies, and drank up the bitter cup of God's wrath, and shed the remainder of his blood, lingeringly drained out through his tortured hands and feet, and extravated out of his broken heart into his bowels, and there turned into blood and water, through the vehement fermentation occasioned by the weight of grief and extremity of agony of soul, under which he cried out with that loud and lamentable and repeated cry. Thus he travailed in birth with his seed; thus he laboured and suffered for the salvation of those souls that the

Father had committed to him. This is the example of the good shepherd.
And though it is not required of under-shepherds that they should
endure sufferings of such a degree or nature; for Christ has suffered
them to that end, that both ministers and people might escape them; yet
surely he expects that, as they would approve themselves as his
disciples and followers, and co-workers with him in seeking the
salvation of the same souls, they should not be backward to go through
any labours or sufferings which may be requisite in them, in order to
their most effectually promoting the great end of his sufferings, with
regard to the souls that he has committed to them.

And as you, dear sir, are to stand in Christ's stead towards this
people, and to act as his ambassador; should you not show the like
spirit, the like love to souls, and imitate him in his readiness to
labour and deny yourself and suffer, yea to spend and be spent for
them? like the blessed apostles. 2 Cor. xii. 15.

The case with you, sir, is as if the head of a family, that was a
great prince, with a number of children in a strange land, when going
home to receive a kingdom, should leave his children behind him, and
commit them to the care of a servant, safely to conduct them through a
dangerous wilderness, and bring them home to him; in which case, he has
their health and lives committed to his care, as well as their future
glory in his kingdom. With what care and watchfulness would it be
expected of a servant that he should execute his office in such a case!
and surely if he fails of being thoroughly careful and watchful, after
he has taken upon him so great a charge, and any sad disaster should be
the consequence of his unfaithfulness; it will most justly be required
of him that he should answer it, and he will inexcusably fall under his
master's heaviest displeasure.

And suffer me, sir, to put you in mind of the account you must
give to your master of these souls he seems this day to be about to
commit to you: You are to watch for these souls as one that must give

account. If any one of these souls should be missing hereafter, having been lost under your ministry, it will be demanded of you another day, by your great Lord, "What is become of a such a soul? Here are not all the souls that I committed to you to bring home to me; there is such an one missing; what is become of it? has it perished through your neglect?" If you are able to say at that time, "Lord, it was not through my neglect; I have done what in me lay for his salvation; I ceased not to warn and counsel and reprove him, and faithfully set before him his danger, and have not forborne to declare thy whole counsel to him; I have not neglected this and other souls that thou didst commit to me, to gratify my sloth, or pursue my worldly interest; I have given myself wholly to this work; labouring therein night and day; I have been ready, Lord, as thou knowest, to sacrifice my own ease and profit, and pleasure, and temporal convenience, and the good will of my neighbours, for the sake of the good of the souls I had the charge of; I have not led this soul into any snare by my ill example; I have neglected no means of thine appointment, either public or private, to turn him from sin to God; I sought out acceptable words, and studied for the most likely means to be used for his saving good; but he would not hearken, but turned a deaf ear; under all was stupid and obstinate, and went on carelessly and forwardly in the imagination of his heart." If you are able to say in like manner as Christ did to the Father, with respect to the souls that were committed to him; "those that thou gavest me I have kept, and one of them is lost, but the son of perdition"; you will be able to hold up your head with comfort before your Judge, your account will be accepted, you shall be acquitted, and your unsuccessful faithfulness shall be rewarded. But if when it shall be demanded of you what is become of such and such souls? You shall be dumb, having nothing to say, your conscience flying in your face, and it shall appear that it has been much owing to your unfaithfulness; O how amazing will your case be! What confusion and astonishment will

fill your soul before your great master and Judge! And remember that
the blood of such souls will be required at your hands. Ezek xxxiii.6.

And suffer me, dear brother, to tell you, that you must another
day meet these souls that you are now going to take the charge of,
before the judgment seat of Christ; and if by means of your
faithfulness towards them, in your work, you shall meet them at the
right hand of Christ in glory, how joyful a meeting will it be to you!
They will be indeed your crown of rejoicing in that day. But if you
behold them with devils at the left hand, in horror and despair, your
conscience accusing you of unfaithfulness towards them, and it appears
that they are lost through your neglect, now amazing will the sight of
them be to you!

Your master and mine is this day calling me to resign the pastoral
care of a number of souls into your hands, that have hitherto been
committed to my care: It is with cheerfulness that I can now resign
them to the care of one, concerning whom I can have so much hope that
he will be faithful in his care of them. May the Lord of the harvest
enable you to discharge your duty towards them more faithfully than I
have done, and make you a far greater blessing to them; and may you
come with them at the day of judgment before Christ with exceeding joy,
and in robes of glory,and say then as Christ himself will say to the
Father, when he shall come with all the souls that were given him of
the Father, and present them before him in perfect glory, here am I,
and the children which thou hast given me.

2.   I would apply myself to those whose souls are now about to be
committed to the care of that servant of Christ that is now to be
ordained to the pastoral office in this place.

Beloved brethren, and dear children, it is your immortal souls
that is the precious treasure that the great Creator and Saviour of
souls seems now to be about to commit to the care of him whom you have
chosen to be your pastor. And indeed it is a great charge, an high

betrustment; and he ought to use his utmost care and diligence that you may not be eternally lost. But if your pastor should exercise such care that you may be saved, surely you ought to take care for the salvation of your own souls: It nearly concerns him that you should be saved; but much more nearly does it concern you. Let your minister be never so careful and watchful, if you take no care for yourselves, his faithfulness and diligence will signify nothing, unless it be to harden you, and aggravate your damnation. In such a case, the more care and pains he takes for your salvation, the greater will your eternal misery be; for all will be only a savour of death unto death. Those people are like to sink the deepest into hell hereafter, that go to hell from under the care of the most faithful ministers, that have taken the most pains to save them from going to hell. The preciousness of your souls has now been made use of as an argument with your chosen pastor to take care for your salvation; but much more may it be used as an argument with you to seek your own salvation; for therein lies the preciousness of your souls, in their being of infinite worth to yourselves, appearing in the infinite loss you will sustain if they are lost, and your infinite gain if they are saved; herein lies that preciousness of the soul that Christ speaks of, Matt. xvi.26. "For what is a man profited, if he shall gain the whole world, and loose his own soul? Or what shall a man give in exchange for his soul?"

It is not only your minister that is concerned in the work that he is to perform among you, but also are infinitely concerned in it: And it is not only he, but you also that are infinitely concerned in the account that he has to give of the discharge of his office among you. You must all of you hereafter meet your minister before the judgment seat of Christ; and if then it shall be found that he has been faithful, and that you made an ill improvement of his ministry, and so failed of the grace of God, the sight of the devil will not be so terrible to you at that day as the sight of your minister; for he will rise up in judgment against you, and your pastor, that above all other persons in the world, excepting yourselves is concerned to endeavour your salvation, will then above all other persons appear against you before the Judge to witness against you and condemn you. But how joyful will it be to you, as well as to him, if he renders his account with joy, for these reasons that he has been both faithful and successful with respect to you, and appears with you in glory at the right hand of Christ, and has to say to the great judge concerning himself and you, Here am I, and the children which thou hast given me! What a joyful meeting of a minister and people will there be! And how will you be each other's crown of rejoicing! But if your souls perish, you will be present when it shall be required by Jesus Christ of your minister to give an account of such and such souls that are lost, which were committed to his care; and how dreadful will it be to you, if you shall then hear him boldly and truly say before the Judge, "Lord, thou knowest that I have sincerely and faithfully endeavoured their salvation, I have not been slack nor negligent towards them, I have earnestly watched for their souls, and diligently and unweariedly used all the means with them that thou didst appoint; they perished not through my neglect, but through their own obstinate negligence and wickedness!" In such a case your minister will be acquitted and justified, but you will be condemned with a most aggravated condemnation, and your blood will be upon your own head. Ezek. xxxiii.2, 3, 4. "Son of man, speak to the children of thy people, and say unto them, When I bring the sword upon a land, if the people of the land take a man of their coasts, and set him for their watchman: if when he seeth the sword come upon the land, he blow the trumpet and warn the people; then whosoever heareth the sound of the trumpet and taketh not warning; if the sword come, and take him away, his blood shall be upon his own head." The good account your minister has to give of his own faithfulness, will incense the displeasure of the Judge towards you. Luke xiv. 21. "So the servant came and showed his lord these things: Then the master of the house being angry, said to his servant, Go out quickly, &c."

And if you would have the account your minister shall have to give concerning you to be profitable and joyful to you, do not neglect your duty toward him; endeavour by all means in your power to put him under the best advantage for serviceableness and success among you: do what in you lies to encourage his heart and strengthen his hands. This I know to be a thing of vast importance, as you would have your pastor a blessing to you, and the successful instrument of the salvation of your souls and the souls of your children: therefore suffer me to be a little particular with you upon this head. I may be the more bold towards you as you hitherto have been of the flock that Christ has committed to my care, and I hope some of you my spiritual children; therefore as my beloved chidren I counsel and warn you.

If you would meet your minister with comfort another day, do not neglect doing what belongs to you comfortably to support him, so as to enable him to attend on his great work without distraction, and to give himself wholly to the business of seeking and promoting the eternal welfare and happiness of you and your children; without being disheartened by the difficulties and indigencies of straightened circumstances, or being diverted by exercising care, and taken off by involving himself in worldly business for his necessary support. While we are in the body our heavenly Father knows that we have need of these things, and the way that he hath provided for ministers' supply, is by their partaking of the temporal good things of the people to whom they minister spiritual things. 1 Cor. ix. 4, &c. "Have we not power to eat and to drink? Have we not power to lead about a sister, a wife?--Have we not power to forbear working? Who goeth a warfare any time at his own charges? Who planteth a vineyard and eateth not of the fruit thereof? Or who feedeth a flock, and eateth not of the milk of the flock? Say I these things as a man? Or saith not the law the same also? For it is written in the law of Moses, Thou shalt not muzzle the mouth of the ox that treadeth out the corn. Doth God take care for oxen? Or saith he it altogether for our sakes? For our sakes, no doubt, this is written; that he that ploweth should plow in hope, and he that thresheth in hope, should be partaker of his hope, If we have sown unto you spiritual things, is it a great thing if we shall reap your carnal things?--Do you not know that they which minister about holy things, live of the things of the temple? and they that wait at the altar, are partakers with the altar? Even so hath the Lord ordained, that they which preach the Gospel shall live of the gospel." 1 Tim. v. 17, 18. "Let the elders that rule well be counted worthy of double honour; especially they who labour in word and doctrine: For the scripture saith, Thou shalt not muzzle the ox that treadeth out the corn. And the labourer is worthy of his reward." 2 Tim. ii.6. "The husbandman that laboureth must be first partaker of the fruits." Gal. vi.6. "Let him that is taught in the word communicate to him that teacheth in all good things." Christ would not have minister's time and thoughts take up about providing temporal good things for their own support, but would have them wholly provided for by their people. Matt. x.9, 10. "Provide neither gold, nor silver, nor brass in your purses, nor script for your journey, neither two coats apiece, neither shoes, nor yet staves; for the workman is worthy of his meat." Agreeable to these directions he gave the twelve apostles, are the directions he the seventy, when he sent them out. Luke x.7. "In the same house remain, eating and drinking such things as they give; for the labourer is worthy of his hire."

You see what great care Christ has taken in this matter, and how full and abundant the scripture is in commands and directions concerning the support of ministers.

I know you are small, and in your new beginnings in this place, and not so able as many other congregations. But if we may give credit to the word of God, for you well and comfortably to support your pastor, is not the way to be poorer. Prov. iie. 9, 10. "Honour the Lord with thy substance, and with the first fruits of all thine increase; so shall thy barns be filled with plenty, and thy presses shall burst out with new wine." To give to the Lord is not the way to be poor, but the way to be supplied by the Lord. Christ now is not personally, and in his human nature, here upon earth, to be supported by temporal good things from his disciples, as once he was: but though he be now gone from hence into a far country, yet he has not left his disciples without opportunity in this way of showing their love to him; for there are two sorts of persons that he has appointed to be his receivers, viz. his indigent members, and his ministers; as of old God appointed the poor and the Levite to receive the tithes and other offerings that were made to the Lord, Deut. xvi. 11, 14. and ch. xiv. 28, 29, and xxiv. 10, 11, 12. What is given to ministers is a sacrifice to God: so the apostle represents what was sent to him for his supply from the Philippians, Phil. iv. 18. "Having received of Epaphroditus the things which were sent from you, an odour of a sweet smell, a sacrifice acceptable, well pleasing to God." And Christ, when he sent forth his disciples to preach, and had directed that they should take no provision for themselves, because the labourer is worthy of his reward, he says Matt. x.40. "He that receiveth you receiveth me, and he that receiveth me receiveth him that sent me."

And since what is given to your pastor is given to Christ, you may be assured that you cannot consult your own temporal, as well as spiritual interest better, than by liberally supplying of him; for he that lendeth to the Lord shall be repayed again with large interest. And as to your ability, if there be but a cheerful, ready mind, the greatest difficulty is got over; if you find this, there is no doubt but that God will make the duty of supporting your minister in other respects easy to you: God loves a willing offering, and a cheerful giver; if you will do your part in opening your hearts and hands, God will do his part in finding your wherewithal. But if a people grudge what they do, are always full of fears how they shall pay their rates, and excessively cautious lest they should run themselves into difficulty, and straiten themselves and families by giving to Christ, no wonder it proves difficult; it is the way to meet with nothing else but difficulties in their outward circumstances; for "there is that scattereth, and yet increaseth; but to withhold more than is meet, tends only to poverty," Prov. xi. 24.

The Jews, in the days of the prophet Haggai, were few in number, and were under difficult and straitened circumstances; and they made it an excuse why they should not be at the expense that was requisite in order to build the house of God, and set up his worship; and so for a time neglected it. And in the mean time none of their affairs prospered; they sowed much and brought in little; they eat, but they had not enough; they drank, but were not filled with drink; they clothed them, but there was none warm; and he that earneth wages, earneth wages to put it into a bag with holes; they looked for much, and lo it came to little; and the heaven was stayed from dew, and the earth was stayed from her fruit. Hag. chap. i. So in the days of the prophet Malachi it was a time of scarcity, and the people thought themselves thereby excused from paying tithes for the support of the Levites, and so robbed God of his due; but got nothing by it, but God cursed them with a curse; they made that scarcity and want the excuse for their backwardness to support God's ministers, which was its punishment; and God tells them by the prophet that if they would cheerfully do their duty in that respect it would be a sure way to have their wants plentifully supplied. Mal.iii. 1, 9, 10. "Ye are cursed with a curse, for ye have robbed me, even this whole nation. Bring ye all the tithes into the store-house, that there may be meat in mine house; and prove me now herewith, saith the Lord of Hosts, if I will not open you the windows of heaven, and pour you out a blessing, that there shall not be room enough to receive it." What can God say more to encourage a people cheerfully to run the venture of expending what is necessary for the comfortable and honourable support of the ministry?

And here let me warn you in particular, that you do not only do pretty well by your minister for a while at first, while the relation between you and him is a new thing, and then afterward, when your minister's necessities are increased, begin to fail, as it too frequently happens.

Some may be ready to say, it is no wonder ministers should be forward to urge such a duty as this, wherein their own temporal interest is so much concerned, a covetous disposition will make them love to harp upon this string.--I have not been much in insisting on this duty in my own pulpit, where it would especially concern my temporal interest; and blessed be God that I have had no occasion.--But whatever any may judge of the secrets of my heart, with regard to the principles that I have been influenced by, in what I have now said; it is enough for you to whom I have spoken it, that I have demonstrated that what I have delivered is the mind of God; and also (if there be any truth in his word) that what I have recommended is not only for the temporal interest of your minister, but also for your own both temporal and spiritual interest.

Another article of advice that I would give you, is, to beware that you do not weaken your minister's hands, and wound yourselves by contention. You are but a small people, and you will be a very foolish people indeed if you are divided against yourselves. Contention among a people hinders all manner of comfort and prosperity either of soul or body; it makes them a torment to themselves and one another; it puts them every way under disadvantages, and weakens the whole body like a consumption.

There are two sorts of contention I would warn you against.

1.   Avoid contention among yourselves about your own temporal affairs: this will exceedingly tend to render a minister's labours ineffectual; and it is what greatly damps the spirit and discourages the heart of a minister, to see his people divided into parties, and envying one another, and entertaining mutual prejudices, jealousies and grudges, and so backbiting and reproaching one another, and carrying on secret plots and designs one against the another.

2.   Avoid quarrelling with your minister in matters of church discipline. This is a common thing, but a most unchristian thing, and tends greatly to weaken the hands of a minister in the whole of his work, and render all to no purpose. The exercise of the discipline of God's house is the most difficult part of that great work that a minister has to do; and it becomes a christian people to their utmost to strengthen their minister's hands in this difficult business, and say as the people said to Ezra the priest, with respect to the affair of purging the church of Israel from the scandal of those that had married strange wives, Ezra x. 4, "Arise, for this matter belongeth to thee; we also will be with thee: Be of good courage and do it."

To conclude, If you would have your minister successful among you, and a blessing to you, and if you would be a happy people, then love one another and love your minister. There are some professors, in some of our towns, that are anti-ministerial men; they seem to have a disposition to dislike men of that order; they are apt to be prejudiced against them; and to be suspicious of them, and talk against them; and it seems to be as it were natural to them to be unfriendly and unkind towards their own ministers, and to make difficulty for them. But I do not believe there is a true christian on earth that is of this character; on the contrary the feet of them that bring good tidings, and publish the Gospel of salvation are beautiful in the eyes of all the true children of Zion; and every one that receives Christ, and whose heart is governed by a supreme love to him, has disposition to receive, love and honour his messengers.   It was the distinguishing mark by which God manifested the person he had chosen to be the wife of Isaac, that type of Christ, that it was the damsel that should give kind and friendly entertainment to Abraham's servant or steward that was sent to espouse her and bring her home to Isaac; and therein was a type of the Gospel ministry, Gen. xxiv. 14, &c.   See to it that you thus entertain the steward of the house of God that comes on this blessed errand to you.

If you and your minister thus live in peace, it will be the way for you to be a happy society, to flourish and prosper with all manner of prosperity, to have Christ dwelling among you; and for things to be brought to so blessed an event at last, as that he that is the great shepherd of the sheep, that purchased the souls of men with his blood, and your pastor that has the care of your souls committed to him, and yourselves and children, all shall rejoice together in another world, agreeable to John iv.36.   "And he that reapeth receiveth wages, and gathereth fruit unto life eternal; that both he that soweth and he that reapeth may rejoice together."

THE TRUE EXCELLENCY OF A GOSPEL MINISTER

John 5:35   "He was a burning and a shining light."

That discourse of our blessed Saviour we have an account of in
this chapter from the 17th verse to the end, was occasioned by the
Jews' murmuring against him, and persecuting him for his healing the
impotent man at the pool of Bethesda, and bidding him take up his bed
and walk on the Sabbath day. Christ largely vindicates himself in this
discourse, by asserting his fellowship with God the Father in nature
and operations, and thereby implicitly showing himself to be the Lord
of the Sabbath, and by declaring to the Jews that God the Father, and
he with him, did work hitherto, or even to this time; i.e., although it
be said that God rested on the seventh day from all his works, yet
indeed God continues to work hitherto, even to this very day, with
respect to his greatest work, the work of redemption, or new creation,
which he carries on by Jesus Christ, his Son. Pursuant to the designs
of which work was his showing mercy to fallen men by healing their
diseases, and delivering them from the calamities they brought on
themselves by sin. This great work of redemption, God carries on from
the beginning of the world to this time; and his rest from it will not
come till the resurrection, which Christ speaks of in the 21st and
following verses: the finishing of this redemption as to its
procurement, being in his own resurrection; and as to the application
in the general resurrection and eternal judgment, spoken of from verse
20 to verse 30. So that notwithstanding both the rest on the seventh
day, and also the rest that Joshua gave the children of Israel, in
Canaan; yet the great rest of the Redeemer from his work, and so of his
people with him and in him, yet remains, as the apostle observes, Heb.
chap. iv. This will be at the resurrection and general judgment;
which Christ here teaches the Jews, was to be brought to pass by the

----

Preached at Pelham, August 30, 1744, at the ordination of the Rev. Mr.
Robert Abercrombie to the work of the gospel ministry in that place.

Son of God, by the Father's appointment, and so the works of God to be finished by him.

And inasmuch as this vindication was so far from satisfying the Jews, that it did but further enrage them, because hereby he made himself equal with God, Christ therefore refers them to the witness of John the Baptist; whose testimony they must acquiesce in, or else be inconsistent with themselves; because they had generally acknowledged John to be a great prophet, and seemed for a while mightily affected and taken with it, that God, after so long a withholding the spirit of prophecy, had raised up so great a prophet among them--and it is concerning him that Christ speaks in this verse wherein the text: "He was a burning and a shining light; and ye were willing for a season to rejoice in his light."

In order to a right understanding and improvement of the words of the text, we may observe,

1.   What Christ here takes notice of in John, and declares concerning him, viz., that he was a burning and a shining light. He was a light to the church of Israel, to reveal the mind and will of God to them, after a long continued dark season, and after they had been destitute of any prophet to instruct them, for some ages: he arose on Israel, as the morning star, the forerunner of the sun of righteousness, to introduce the day-spring, or dawning of the gospel-day, to give light to them that till then had sat in the darkness of perfect night, which was the shadow of death; to give them the knowledge of salvation; as Zacharias his father declares at his circumcision, Luke i. 76-79: "And thou child shalt be called the Prophet of the Highest; for thou shalt go before the face of the Lord, to prepare his ways; to give knowledge of salvation unto his people, by the remission of their sins, through the tender mercy of our God; whereby the day-spring from on high hath visited us, to give light to them that sit in darkness, and in the shadow of death, to guide our

feet into the way of peace."

And he was a burning light, as he was full of a spirit of fervent piety and holiness, being filled with the Holy Ghost from his mother's womb, having his heart warmed and inflamed with a great love to Christ, being that friend of the bridegroom, that stood and heard him, and rejoiced greatly because of the bride groom's voice; and was glad that Christ increased, though he decreased, John ii. 29, 30. And was animated with a holy zeal in the work of the ministry: he came in this respect, in the spirit and power of Elias; as Elias was zealous in bearing testimony against the corruption, apostacies, and idolatries of Israel in his day, so was John the Baptist in testifying against the wickedness of the Jews in his day: as Elias zealously reproved the sins of all sorts of persons in Israel, not only the sins of the common people, but of their great ones, Ahab, Ahaziah, and Jezebel, and their false prophets; with what zeal did John the Baptist reprove all sorts of persons, not only the publicans and soldiers, but the Pharisees and Sadducees, telling them plainly that they were a generation of vipers, and rebuked the wickedness of Herod in his most beloved lust, though Herod sought his life for it, as Ahab and Ahaziah did Elijah's. As Elias was much in warning the people of God's approaching judgments, denouncing God's awful wrath against Ahab, Jezebel and Ahaziah, and the prophets of Baal, and the people in general: so was John the Baptist, much in warning the people to fly from the wrath to come, telling them in the most awakening manner, that the "axe was laid at the root of the tree, and that every tree that brought not forth good fruit should be hewn down and cast into the fire, and that he that came after him had his fan in his hand, and that he would thoroughly purge his floor, and gather his wheat into the garner, and burn up the chaff with unquenchable fire."

John the Baptist was not only a burning, but a shining light: he was so in his doctrine, having more of the gospel in his preaching than the former prophets, or at least the gospel exhibited with greater light and clearness, more plainly pointing forth the person that was to be the great Redeemer, and declaring his errand into the world, to take away the sin of the world, as a Lamb offered in sacrifice to God, and the necessity that all, even the most strictly moral and religious, stood in of him, being by nature a generation of vipers; and the spiritual nature of his kingdom, consisting not in circumcision, or outward baptism, or any other external performance or privileges, but in the powerful influences of the Holy Ghost in their hearts, a being baptized with the Holy Ghost and with fire.

In this clearness with which he gave knowledge of salvation to God's people, John was a bright light, and among them that had been born of women there had not arisen a greater than he. In this brightness this harbinger of the gospel-day excelled all the other prophets, as the morning star reflects more of the light of the sun than any other star, and is the brightest of all the stars.

He also shone bright in his conversation, and his eminent mortification and renunciation of the enjoyments of the world; his great diligence and laboriousness in his work, his impartiality in it, declaring the mind and will of God to all sorts without distinction; his great humility, rejoicing in the increase of the honor of Christ, though his honor was diminished, as the brightness of the morning star diminishes, as the light of the sun increases; and in his faithfulness and courage, still declaring the mind and will of God, though it cost him his own life. Thus his light shone before men.

2. We may observe to what purpose Christ declares these things of John in the text, viz., to show how great and excellent a person he was, and worthy that the Jews should regard his testimony: great are the things which Christ elsewhere says of John the Baptist, as in Matt. xi. 7-14. He speaks of him as a prophet; and more than a prophet; and one, than whom there had not risen a greater among them that had been

born of women. He observed how great and excellent a light he was in
the text, to show the Jews how inexcusable they were in not receiving
the testimony he had given of him; as you may see, verses 31, 32, 33.

Therefore that which I would observe from the text to be the
subject of my present discourse is this:

It is the excellency of a minister of the gospel to be both a
burning and a shining light.

Thus we see it is in Christ's esteem, the great prophet of God,
and the light of the world, head of the church, and Lord of the
harvest, and the great Lord and master whose messengers all ministers
of the gospel are.

John the Baptist was a minister of the gospel; and he was so more
eminently than the ancient prophets; for though God at sundry times,
and in divers manners, spake the gospel by them; yet John the Baptist
was a great minister of the gospel in a manner distinguished from them:
he is reckoned in Scripture the first that introduced the gospel day,
after the law and the prophets: Luke vi. 16, "The law and the
prophets were until John; since that time the kingdom of God is
preached." And his preaching is called the beginning of the gospel of
Jesus Christ the son of God, Mark i. 1. He came on that errand, to
give knowledge of salvation to God's people, through the remission of
their sins (as his father Zacharias observes, Luke i. 77); and to
preach these glad tidings, that the kingdom of heaven was at hand.

John being thus eminently a minister of the gospel, and a burning
and shining light, being taken notice of by Christ as his great
excellency, we may justly hence observe, that herein consists the
proper excellency of ministers of the gospel.

I would, by divine assistance, handle the subject in the following
method.

I. I would show that Christ's design, in the appointment of the
order and office of ministers of the gosepl is, that they may be lights

to the souls of men.

II.   I would show what is implied in their being burning lights.

III. I would show what is implied in their being shining lights.

IV.   I would show that it is the proper excellency of ministers of the gospel to have these things united in them, to be both burning and shining lights.

V.   I would apply these things to all that Christ has called to the work of the gospel ministry, showing how much it concerns them earnestly to endeavor that they may be burning and shining lights.

VI.   Show what ministers of the gospel ought to do that they may be so.

VII. Say something briefly concerning the duty of a people that are under the care of a gospel minister, correspondent to those things that Christ has taught us concerning the end and excellency of a gospel minister.

1. I would observe that Christ's design in the appointment of the order and office of ministers of the gospel was that they might be lights to the souls of men.

Satan's kingdom is a kingdom of darkness; the devils are the rulers of the darkness of this world. But Christ's kingdom is a kingdom of light; the designs of his kingdom are carried on by light; his people are not of the night, nor of darkness, but are the children of the light, as they are the children of God, who is the Father of lights, and as it were a boundless fountain of infinitely pure and bright light, 1 John i. 5, James i. 17.

Man by the fall extinquished that divine light that shone in this world in its first estate. The Scripture represents the wickedness of man as reducing the world to that state wherein it was when it was yet without form and void, and darkness filled it. Jer. iv. 22, 23, "For my people is foolish, they have not known me: they are sottish children; and they have none understanding: they are wise to do evil;

but to do good they have no knowledge. I beheld the earth, and lo, it was without form and void; and the heavens, and they had no light." But God in infinite mercy has made glorious provision for the restoration of light to this fallen dark world; he has sent him who is the brightness of his own glory, into the world, to be the light of the world. "He is the true light that lighteth every man that cometh into the world," i.e., every man in the world that ever has any true light. But in his wisdom and mercy, he is pleased to convey his light to men by means and instruments; and has sent forth his messengers, and appointed ministers in his church to be subordinate lights, and to shine with the communications of his light, and to reflect the beams of his glory on the souls of men.

There is an analogy between the divine constitution and disposition of things in the natural and in the spiritual world. The wise Creator has not left the natural world without light; but in this our solar system has set one great light, immensely exceeding all the rest, shining perpetually with a transcendent fulness and strength, to enlighten the whole; and he hath appointed other lesser, subordinate or dependent lights, that shine with the communications and reflections of something of his brightness. So it is in the spiritual world; there God hath appointed Jesus Christ as a Sun of righteousness: the Church of God has not the sun to be her light by day; nor for brightness, does the moon give light to her, but the Lord is her everlasting light, and her God her glory. The new Jerusalem has no need of the sun, nor the moon; for the Lamb is the light thereof. And the ministers of Christ are, as it were, the stars that encompass this glorious fountain of light, to receive and reflect his beams, and give light to the souls of men. As Christ therefore is in scripture called the sun, so are his ministers called stars. So are the twelve apostles, the chief ministers of the Christian church, called, Rev. xii.1: "And there appeared a great wonder in heaven, a woman clothed with the sun, and

the moon under her feet, and upon her head a crown of twelve stars."
And so are the ordinary ministers of the gospel called, Rev. i. 16:
"And he had in his right hand seven stars." And verse 20, "The mystery
of these seven stars which thou sawest in my right hand and the seven
golden candle sticks; the seven stars are the angels of the seven
churches." Here also ministers of the gospel are implicitly compared
to those lamps that enlightened the temple at Jerusalem, upon the tops
of the golden candlesticks; and more expressly in Zech. iv. 2: "I have
looked, and behold a candlestick, all gold, with a bowl upon the top of
it, and his seven lamps thereon."

These lamps have all their oil from Christ, and are enkindled by
his flames, and shine by his beams; and being thus dependent on him,
they are near to him, and held in his right hand, that they may receive
light from him, to communicate to others.

The use of a light is threefold; to discover, to refresh, and to
direct.

The first use of a light is to discover things or make them
manifest. Without light nothing is to be seen. Eph. v. 13,
"Whatsoever doth make manifest is light." Ministers are set to be
lights to the souls of men in this respect, as they are to be the means
of imparting divine truth to them, and bringing into their view the
most glorious and excellent objects, and of leading them to, and
assisting them in the contemplation of those things that angels desire
to look into; the means of their obtaining that knowledge is infinitely
more important and more excellent and useful, than that of the greatest
statesmen or philosophers, even that which is spiritual and divine:
they are set to be the means of bringing men out of darkness into God's
marvellous light, and of bringing them to the infinite fountain of
light, that in his light they may see light: they are set to instruct
men, and impart to them that knowledge by which they may know God and
Jesus Christ, whom to know is life eternal.

Another use of light is to refresh and delight the beholders. Darkness is dismal: the light is sweet, and a pleasant thing it is to behold the sun. Light is refreshing to those who have long sat in darkness: they therefore that watch and keep awake through a dark night, long and wait for the light of the morning; and the wise man observes, Prov. xv. 30, that "the light of the eyes rejoiceth the heart." Spiritual light is especially refreshing and joyful. Psalm xcvii. 11, "Light is sown for the righteous, and gladness for the upright in heart." They that see the light of Christ, the star that hath arisen out of Jacob, are refreshed and do rejoice, as the wise men that saw the star that showed them where Christ was: Matt. ii. 10, "And when they saw the star, they rejoiced with exceeding great joy."

Ministers are set in the church of God to be the instruments of this comfort and refreshment to the souls of men, to be the instruments of leading souls to the God of all consolation, and fountain of their happiness: they are sent as Christ was, and as co-workers with him, to preach good tidings to the meek, to bind up the broken hearted, to proclaim liberty to the captives, and the opening of the prison to them that are bound, and to comfort all that mourn: they are to lead those that "labor, and are heavy laden" to their true rest, and to speak a word in season to him that is weary: they are set to be ministers of the consolation and joy of the saints. 2 Cor. 1. 24, "We have not dominion over your faith; but are helpers of your joy."

The third use of light is to direct. 'Tis by light that we see where to go: "he that walks in darkness knows not whither he goes," and is in danger of stumbling and falling into mischief. 'Tis by light that men see what to do, and are enabled to work; in the night, Christ tells us no man can work. Ministers are set to be lights to men's souls in this respect also; as Zacharias observes of John the Baptist, Luke i. 79, "To guide our feet in the way of peace." Ministers have the record of God committed to them that they may hold that forth, which

God has given to be to man as a light shining in a dark place, to guide them in the way through this dark world, to regions of eternal light. Ministers are set to be the instruments of conveying to men that true wisdom spoken of, Job 28, "which cannot be gotten for gold, nor shall silver be weighed for the price thereof; which cannot be valued with the gold of Ophir, with the precious onyx, or the sapphire."

I proceed now to the

II.   Thing proposed, viz., to show what is implied in a minister of the gospel's being a burning light.

There are these things that seem naturally to be understood by this expression, viz., that his heart be filled with much of the holy ardor of a spirit of true piety; and that he be fervent and zealous in his administrations.

1.   That his heart be full of much of the holy ardor of a spirit of true piety. We read of the power of godliness. True grace is no dull, inactive, ineffectual principle; it is a powerful thing; there is an exceeding energy in it; and the reason is, that God is in it; it is a divine principle, a participation of the divine nature, and a communication of divine life, of the life of a risen Saviour, who exerts himself in the hearts of the saints, after the power of an endless life. They that have true grace in them, they live; but not by their own life; but Christ lives in them: his Holy Spirit becomes in them a living principle and spring of divine life: the energy and power of which is in Scripture compared to fire. Matt. iii. 11: "I indeed baptize you with water; but he that cometh after me is mightier than I, whose shoes I am not worthy to bear; he shall baptize you with the Holy Ghost, and with fire." True piety is not a thing remaining only in the head, or consisting in any speculative knowledge or opinions, or outward morality, or forms of religion; it reaches the heart, is chiefly seated there, and burns there. There is a holy ardor in every thing that belongs to true grace: true faith is an ardent

thing, and so is true repentance; there is a holy power and ardor in true spiritual comfort and joy; yea, even in true Christian humility, submission and meekness. The reason is, that divine love or charity is the sum of all true grace, which is a holy flame enkindled in the soul: it is by this therefore especially, that a minister of the gospel is a burning light: a minister that is so, has his soul enkindled with the heavenly flame; his heart burns with love to Christ, and fervent desires of the advancement of his kingdom and glory; and also with ardent love to the souls of men, and desires for their salvation.

2. The inward holy ardor of his soul is exercised and manifested in his being zealous and fervent in his administrations: for he is a burning light; which implies that his spiritual heat and holy ardor is not for himself only, but is communicative, and for the benefit of others: he is ardent, as he is a light, or in the performance of the duties of that office wherein he is set to be a light in the church of Christ. His fervent zeal, which has its foundation and spring in that holy and powerful flame of love to God and man, that is in his heart, appears in the fervency of his prayers to God, for and with his people; and in the earnestness and power with which he preaches the word of God, declares to sinners their misery, and warns them to fly from the wrath to come, and reproves, and testifies against all ungodliness; and the unfeigned earnestness and compassion with which he invites the weary and heavy laden to their Saviour; and the fervent love with which he counsels and comforts the saints; and the holy zeal, courage and steadfastness, with which he maintains the exercise of discipline in the house of God, notwithstanding all the opposition he meets with in that difficult part of the ministerial work; and in the diligence and earnestness with which he attends every duty of his ministerial function, whether public or private.

But I hasten to the

III. Thing proposed in the handling of this subject, viz, to show what is implied in a minister's being a shining light.

There are three things that seem to be naturally signified by it.

1. That he be pure, clear, and full in his doctrine. A minister is set to be a light to men's souls, by teaching, or doctrine: and if he be a shining light in this respect, the light of his doctrine must be bright and full; it must be pure without mixture of darkness: and therefore he must be sound in the faith, not one that is of a reprobate mind; in doctrine he must show uncorruptness; otherwise his light will be darkness: he must not lead his people into errors, but teach them the truth only, guiding their feet into the way of peace, and leading them in the right ways of the Lord.

He must be one that is able to teach, not one that is raw, ignorant, or unlearned, and but little versed in the things that he is to teach others; not a novice, or one that is unskillful in the word of righteousness; he must be one that is well studied in divinity, well acquainted with the written word of God, mighty in the Scriptures, and able to instruct and convince gainsayers.

And in order to be a shining light he must be one that really knows what religion is, one that is truly acquainted with that Saviour and way of salvation, that he is to teach to others, that he may speak the things that he knows, and testify the things that he has seen, and not be a blind leader of the blind: he must be one that is acquainted with experimental religion, and not ignorant of the inward operations of the Spirit of God, nor of Satan's devices; able to guide souls under their particular difficulties. Thus he must be a scribe well instructed in things that pertain to the kingdom of God; one that brings forth out of his treasures, things new and old.

And in order to his being a shining light, his doctrine must be full, he must not only be able to teach, but apt to teach, ready to instruct the ignorant, and them that are out of the way, and diligent in teaching, in public and private; and careful and faithful to declare the whole counsel of God, and not keep back any thing that may be profitable to his hearers.

Also his being a shining light implies that his instructions are clear and plain, accommodated to the capacity of his hearers, and tending to convey light to their understanding.

2.   Another thing requisite in order to a minister's being a shining light, is that he be discreet in all his administrations. The fervent zeal that thus should animate and actuate him in his administrations should be regulated by discretion: he should not only be knowing, and able to communicate knowledge and formed to do it: but also wise, and know how to conduct himself in the house of God, as a wise builder, and a wise steward. And as he is one that God hath sent forth to labor in his field, and committed the care of his vineyard to, so he should conduct himself there as one whom his God doth instruct to discretion: he should not only be as harmless as a dove, but as wise as a serpent; showing himself a workman that needs not to be ashamed, rightly dividing the word of truth; and one that knows how to govern the church of God, and to walk in wisdom towards those that are without.

3.   Another thing implied in a minister's being a shining light, is that he shines in his conversation: if he shines never so much in his doctrine and administrations in the house of God, yet if there be not an answerable brightness in his conversation, it will have a tendency to render all ineffectual. Christ, in Matt. v. 14, 15, 16, says to his disciples (having undoubtedly a special respect to those of them that were sent forth to preach the gospel), "Ye are the light of the world:--men do not light a candle, and put it under a bushel, but on a candlestick, and it giveth light unto all that are in the house." And how does Christ direct them to give light to others? "Let your light," says he, "so shine before men, that others seeing your good works, may glorify your Father which is in heaven." And he tells the

same disciples again, John xv. 8, "Herein is my Father glorified, that ye bear much fruit." And how should they bring forth fruit? Christ tells them, verse 10, "If you keep my commandments, ye shall abide in my love," and verse 14, "Ye are my friends if ye do whatsoever I command you."

God sent his Son into the world to be the light of the world these two ways, viz., by revealing his mind and will to the world, and also by setting the world a perfect example. So ministers are set to be lights, not only as teachers, but as ensamples to the flock, 1 Peter v. 3.

The same things that ministers recommend to their hearers in their doctrine, they should also show them an example of in their practice Thus the apostle says to Timothy, 1 Tim. iv. 11, "These things command and teach;" and then adds in the next verse, "Be thou an example of the believers, in word, in conversation, in charity, in spirit, in faith, in purity." So he directs Titus, in his teaching, to recommend sobriety, gravity, temperance, patience, and other virtues, in the beginning of the 2nd chapter of Titus. But then adds in the 7th verse, "In all things showing thyself a pattern of good works."

We see in natural bodies, that when heat is raised in them to a high degree, at length they begin to shine: and, as I observed before, a principle of true grace in the soul is like an inward heat, a holy ardor of a heavenly fire enkindled in the soul: this in ministers of the gospel ought to be to that degree, as to shine forth brightly in all their conversation; and there should as it were be a light about them wherever they go, exhibiting to all that behold them, the amiable, delightful image of the beauty and brightness of their glorious master.

I proceed to the

IV. Thing proposed, which is to show that the excellency of a minister of the gospel consists in his being thus both a burning and a shining light.

This is manifest in two things:

1. Herein his ministry is acceptable and amiable in the sight of God and men.

When light and heat are thus united in a minister of the gospel, it shows that each is genuine, and of a right kind, and that both are divine. Divine light is attended with heat; and so, on the other hand, a truly divine and holy heat and ardor is ever accompanied with light.

It is the glory of the sun that such a bright and glorious light, and such a powerful, refreshing, vivifying heat, are both together diffused from that luminary. When there is light in a minister, consisting in human learning, great speculative knowledge and the wisdom of this world, without a spiritual warmth and ardor in his heart, and a holy zeal in his ministrations, his light is like the light of an _ignis fatuus_, and some kinds of putrifying carcasses that shine in the dark, though they are of a stinking savor. And if on the other hand a minister has warmth and zeal, without light, his heat has nothing excellent in it, but is rather to be abhorred; being like the heat of the bottomless pit; where, though the fire be great, yet there is no light. To be hot in this manner, and not lightsome, is to be like an angel of darkness. But ministers by having light and heat united in them, will be like the angels of light; which for their light and brightness are called morning stars. Job xxviii. 7, "When the morning stars sang together, and all the sons of God shouted for joy." And because of that holy ardor of divine love and zeal with which they burn, they are compared to a flaming fire: Psal. civ. 4, "Who maketh his angels spirits, and his ministers a flaming fire," and are therefore called seraphim, which is a word that is derived from a root that signifies to burn. So that by ministers of the gospel being a burning and shining lights, the angels of the churches will become like the angels of heaven, and those stars held in the right hand of Christ here below, will be like those morning stars above, and which is much more, hereby ministers will be like their glorious Lord and Master; who is not only the Master of ministers of the gospel, but is the head and Lord of the glorious luminary and sun of the heavenly world, from whence all the inhabitants of that world have their light and life, and all their glory.   In this Sun of righteousness is that light, whose brightness is such that the light of the sun in the firmament in comparison of it is as darkness, yea, black as sackcloth of hair: for he is the infinite brightness of God's glory; and of him it is said, Isai. xxiv. 23, "Then the moon shall be confounded, and the sun ashamed, when the Lord of Hosts shall reign in Mount Zion, and in Jerusalem, before his ancients, gloriously."   And accompanying this bright light in him, is the infinitely intense flame of love.   There is no love to be compared to his; nor ever was love both to God and man so manifested, as has been in what Christ has done and suffered; for herein was love!   Ministers, by being burning and shining lights, become the sons of God, of whom we read that he is light, and that he is love.   1 John i. 5, "this then is the message which we have heard of him, and declare unto you, that God is light, and in him is no darkness at all,"   And chap. iv.   16, "And we have known and believed the love that God hath to us: God is love, and he that dwelleth in love, dwelleth in God, and God in him."

Therefore it must needs be that the ministers, by being burning and shining lights, are acceptable and amiable in the sight of God, as he delights in his own image and in the image of his Son: and hereby also they will be honorable and amiable in the sight of men, all such as have any sense of that which is truly excellent and beautiful; and it is the way to have their ministry pleasant and delightful to those of this character that sit under it.

2.   Herein a minister of the gospel will be likely to answer the ends of his ministry: by this means his ministry will not only be amiable, but profitable.   If a minister has light without heat, and

entertains his auditory with learned discourses, without a savor of the power of godliness, or any appearance of fervency of spirit, and zeal for God and the good of souls, he may gratify itching ears, and fill the heads of his people with empty notions; but it will not be very likely to reach their hearts, or save their souls. And if, on the other hand, he be driven on with a fierce and intemperate zeal, and vehement heat, without light, he will be likely to kindle the like unhallowed flame in his people, and to fire their corrupt passions and affections; but will make them never the better, nor lead them a step towards heaven, but drive them apace the other way.

But if he approves himself in his ministry, as both a burning and a shining light, this will be the way to promote true Christianity amongst his people, and to make them both wise, good, and cause religion to flourish among them in the purity and beauty of it.

When divine light and heat attend each other in ministers of the gospel, their light will be like the beams of the sun, that do not only convey light, but give life; and converts will be likely to spring up under their ministry, as the grass and plants of the field under the influence of the sun; and the souls of the saints will be likely to grow, and appear beautiful as the lily, and to revive as the corn, and grow as the vine, and their scent to be as the wine of Lebanon; and their light will be like the light of Christ, which is the light of life, John viii. 12.

If the sun should shine upon the earth, with the same brightness that it doth now, yet if it were without any heat, it would give life to nothing; the world would be a desolate wilderness, with nothing growing in it; the death of every living thing must be the consequence; and the sun's light could be of no service to us, but to cause us to see our own and others' misery, without being able to help ourselves or them. On the other hand, if the sun diffused the same heat that now it does, but the world was destitute at the same time of any light, it would be equally unserviceable; mankind having no light to guide them in their business, in tilling the field, or gathering the produce of the earth, we should be like the Egyptians in the three days' darkness, who saw not one another, nor rose from their places: and thus also death would be the unavoidable consequence. But by light and heat accompanying one another, the whole face of the earth becomes fruitful, and is adorned, and all things are quickened and flourish, and mankind enjoy both life and comfort.

I proceed to the

V. Thing proposed in handling the doctrine, to apply these things to all here present, that Christ has called to the work of the gospel ministry, observing how much it concerns such to endeavor to be burning and shinging lights.

Our office and work is most honorable, in that we are set by Christ to be lights or luminaries in the spiritual world. Light is the most glorious thing in the material world, and there are, it may be, no parts of the natural world that have so great an image of the goodness of God, as the lights or luminaries of heaven; and especially the sun, who is constantly communicating his benign influence to enlighten, quicken and refresh the world by his beams; which is probably the reason that the worship of the sun was (as is supposed) the first idolatry that mankind fell into. But so are ministers honored by their great Lord and Master, that they are set to be that to men's souls, that the lights of heaven are to their bodies; and that they might be the instruments and vehicles of God's greatest goodness, and the most precious fruits of his eternal love to them, and means of that life, and refreshment and joy, that are spiritual and eternal, and infinitely more precious than any benefit received by the benign beams of the sun in the firmament. And we shall be likely indeed to be the instruments of those unspeakable benefits to the souls of our fellow creatures, if we have those qualifications, which have been shown to be the true and proper excellency of ministers of the gospel. Herein our glory will answer the honorable station Christ has set us in. And hereby our ministry will be likely to be as beneficial as our office is honorable: we shall be like Christ, and shall shine with his beams; Christ will live in us, and be seen in his life and beauty in our ministry, and in our conversation, and we shall be most likely to be the means of bringing others to him, and of their receiving of his light, and being made partakers of his life, and having his joy fulfilled in them. And this will be the way for us hereafter to be as much advanced and distinguished in our reward, as we are honored in the office and business we are called to here. In this way, those whom Christ has set to be lights in his church, and to be stars in the spiritual world here, shall be lights also in the church triumphant, and shine as stars forever in heaven. Daniel xii. 3, "And they that be wise shall shine as the brightness of the firmament, and they that turn many to righteousness, as the stars forever and ever."

But if we fail of the proper excellency of ministers of the gospel, we shall not be in the sight of God the more worthy or honorable for our high office, but the more abominable and inexcusable; our wickedness being aggravated by God's great goodness and condescension to us, and the peculiar obligations that he laid upon us; and instead of being eminently beneficial and great blessings, as lights to reflect the beams of Christ's glory and love, we shall be so much the more hurtful and pernicious, for our being in such a station; and so shall be likely hereafter to suffer a so much more dreadful punishment. The devils in hell are so much the more odious to God, and more the objects of his wrath, because he set them in the dignity and glory of angels, the excellency of which state they are fallen from. And it is likely that those in hell that will be nearest to the fallen angels, in their state of misery, will be those that Christ once set to be angels of the churches, but through their unfaithfulness, failed of their proper excellency and end.

Here I would apply myself in a few words to the person whose intended ordination, this day, to the great work of the gospel ministry, is the occasion of this discourse.

You have now, dear sir, heard something of the nature and design of that office to which you are this day, in the name of Christ, to be solemnly set apart. You are therein called to be a light to the souls of men, a lamp in God's temple, and a star in the spiritual world. And you have heard wherein, in Christ's esteem, consists the proper excellency of one in that office, and how in this a minister of the gospel becomes like his glorious master, and glorifies him, and is likely to be the instrument of the salvation and happiness of the souls of men, and to receive a glorious reward from the hands of God.

These, sir, are the motives that you are to be influenced by, to endeavor to be a burning and shining light in the work of the minstry. As to the things of this world, you are not to expect outward ease, pleasure and plenty: nor are you to depend on the friendship and respect of men; but should prepare to endure hardness, as one that is going forth as a soldier to war.   But they are higher things than these, more excellent benefits than the world can afford, that Christ offers to those that approve themselves to him in this work.

God in his providence has brought you far from your native land, and from your friends and acquaintance there; but you will have reason notwithstanding to acknowledge the good hand of his providence towards you, if he is pleased to make you a burning and shining light in this part of his church, and by the influence of your light and heat (or rather by his divine influence, with your ministry) to cause this wilderness to bud and blossom as the rose, and give it the excellency of Carmel and Sharon, and to cause you to shine in the midst of this people with warm and lightsome, quickening and comforting beams, causing their souls to flourish, rejoice and bear fruit like a garden of pleasant fruits, under the beams of the sun.

By this means you will be to their souls the vehicle of the influences and blessings of the heavenly world, which is a world of light and love, shall be ever held in Christ's right hand, and shall be terrible to the powers of darkness and shall see more and more of the light of Christ's glory and grace in this place, with you and this people, and shall hereafter not only shine yourself, as the brightness of the firmament, but shall meet with them in glory also, who shall shine there around you, as a bright constellation in the highest heaven; where they shall be your everlasting crown of rejoicing.

But I hasten to the

VI. Thing proposed, which was to show that course ministers of the gospel ought to take, or what things they should do, that they may be burning and shining lights.

And here I shall but just mention things, without enlarging.

And in order to this, ministers should be diligent in their studies, and in the work of the ministry to which they are called; giving themselves wholly to it; taking heed to themselves, that their hearts be not engaged, and their minds swallowed up, and their time consumed, in pursuits after the profits and vainglory of the world.

And particularly, ministers should be very conversant with the holy Scriptures; making it very much their business, with the utmost diligence and strictness, to search those holy writings: for they are as it were the beams of the light of the sun of righteousness; they are the light by which ministers must be enlightened, and the light they are to hold forth to their hearers; and they are the fire whence their hearts and the hearts of their hearers must be enkindled.

They should earnestly seek after much of the spiritual knowledge of Christ, and that they may live in the clear views of his glory. For by this means they will be changed into the image of the same glory and brightness, and will come to their people as MOSES came down to the congregation of ISRAEL, after he had seen God's back parts in the mount, with his face shining.   If the light of Christ's glory shines upon them, it will be the way for them to shine with the same kind of light on their hearers, and to reflect the same beams, which have heat, as well as brightness.   The light of the knowledge of the glory of God in the face of Jesus Christ, is the treasure the apostle speaks of, that ministers have, as in earthen vessels: 2.   Cor. iv. 6, 7, "For God, who commanded the light to shine out of the darkness, hath shined into your hearts, to give the light of the knowledge of the glory of God, in the face of Jesus Christ.   But we have this treasure in earthen vessels."   This was probably typified of old, by the burning lights and lamps which GIDEON's soldiers had in one hand in earthen pitchers, while they held a trumpet in the other, with which they sounded (typifying the preaching of the gospel).   And thus with the sounds of these trumpets, and these burning lights or earthen vessels, they overcame the enemies of God and his people.

Ministers, in order to their being burning and shining lights, should walk closely with God, and keep near to Christ; and they may ever be enlightened and enkindled by him.   And they should be much in seeking God, and conversing with him by prayer, who is the fountain of light and love: and knowing their own emptiness and helplessness should be ever dependent on Christ; being sensible with JEREMIAH that they are children, should sit as children at Christ's feet to hear his word, and be instructed by him; and being sensible with ISAIAH that they are men of unclean lips, should seek that their lips may be, as it were, touched with a live coal from the altar, as it were by the bright and burning seraphim.

I come now to the

VII.   And last thing proposed, to say something very briefly concerning the duties of a people that are under the care of a minister corresponding with these things that Christ has taught us concerning the nature and end of this sacred office. And here I would have a special respect to the people of God in this place, who are about to have the care of their souls committed to him, that is now solemnly to be set apart to the work of the ministry.

If it be, as you have heard, the proper excellency of a minister of the gospel to be a burning and shining light, then it is your duty earnestly to pray for your minister, that he may be filled with divine light, and with the power of the Holy Ghost, to make him so.   For herein you will be praying for the greatest benefit to yourselves; for if your minister burns and shines, it will be for your light and life. That which has been spoken of, as it is the chief excellency of a minister, so it renders a minister the greatest blessing of any thing in the world that ever God bestows on a people.

And as it is your duty to pray that your minister may by this means become such a blessing to you, so you should do your part to make him so, by supporting him, and putting him under the best advantage, with a mind free from worldly cares, and the pressure of outward wants and difficulties, to give himself wholly to his work; and by all proper acts of respect and kindness and assistance to encourage his heart, and strengthen his hands: and to take heed that instead of this you do not take a course to obscure and extinguish the light that would shine among you, and to smother and suppress the flame, by casting dirt upon it; by necessitating your minister by your penuriousness towards him, to be involved in worldly care; and by discouraging his heart by disrespect and unkindness. And particularly when your minister shows himself to be a burning light by burning with a proper zeal against any wickedness that may be breaking out amongst his people, and manifests it by bearing a proper testimony against it in the preaching of the word, or by a faithful exercise of the discipline of God's house, instead of taking it thankfully, and yielding to him in it, as you ought, does not raise another fire of a contrary nature against it, viz., the fire of your unhallowed passions, reflecting upon and reproaching him for his faithfulness. Herein you will act very unbecoming a Christian people, and show yourselves very ungrateful to your minister, and to Christ, who has bestowed upon you so faithful a minister, and will also, while you fight against him, and against Christ, fight most effectually against your own souls. If Christ gives you a minister that is a burning and shining light, take heed that you do not hate the light, because your deeds are reproved by it; but love and rejoice in his light; and that not only for a season, like John the Baptist's apostatizing hearers: and come to the light.   Let your frequent resort be to your minister for instruction in soul cases, and under all spiritual difficulties; and be open to the light and willing to receive it; and be obedient to it. And thus walk as the children of the light, and follow your minister wherein he is a follower of Christ, i.e., wherein he is as a burning and shining light. If you continue so to do, your path will be the path of the just, which shines more and more to the perfect day, and the end of your course shall be in those blissful regions of everlasting light above, where you shall shine forth with your minister, and both with Christ, as the sun, in the kingdom of the heavenly Father.

THE CHURCH'S MARRIAGE TO HER SONS, AND TO HER GOD

Isaiah lxii. 4, 5.   "Thy land shall be married.   For as a young man marrieth a virgin, so shall thy sons marry thee: and as the bridegroom rejoiceth over the bride, so shall thy God rejoice over thee."

In the midst of many blessed promises that God makes to his church in this and the preceding and following chapters, of advancement of a state of great peace, comfort, honor and joy, after long continued affliction, we have the sum of all contained in these two verses.   In the 4th verse God says to his church, "Thou shalt no more be termed Forsaken; neither shall they land any more be termed Desolate: but thou shalt be called Hephzibah, and thy land, Beulah: for the Lord delighteth in thee, and thy land shall be married."   When it is said, "Thy land shall be married," we are, by thy land, to understand "the body of thy people, thy whole race;" the land, by a metonymy very usual in Scripture, being put for the people that inhabit the land.

The 5th verse explains how this that is promised in the last words of verse 4, should be accomplished in two things, viz., in being married to her sons, and married to her God.

1.   It is promised that she should be married to her sons, or that her sons should marry her: "For as a young man marrieth a virgin, so shall thy sons marry thee."   Or, as the words might have been more literally translated from the original: "As a young man is married to a virgin, so shall thy sons be married to thee."   Some by this understand a promise, that the posterity of the captivated Jews should return again from Babylon to the land of Canaan, and should be, as it were, married or wedded to their own land; i.e., they should be reunited to their own land, and should have great comfort and joy in it, as a young man in a virgin that he marries.   But their thus

----

Preached at the instalment of the Rev. Mr. Samuel Buel, as pastor of the church and congregation at East Hampton, on Long Island, September 19, 1746.

interpreting the words seems to be through inadvertence; not carefully
observing the words themselves, how that when it is said, "So shall thy
sons marry thee," God does not direct his speech to the land itself,
but to the church whose land it was; the pronoun thee being applied to
the same mystical person in this former part of the verse, as in the
words immediately following in the latter part of the same sentence,
"And as the bridegroom rejoiceth over the bride, so shall thy God
rejoice over thee." It is the church, and not the hills and valleys of
the land of Canaan, that is God's bride, or the Lamb's wife. It is
also manifest, that when God says, "So shall thy sons marry thee," he
continues to speak to her to whom he had spoken in the three preceding
verses; but there it is not the ground or soil of the land of Canaan,
but the church, that he speaks to when he says, "The Gentiles shall see
thy righteousness, and all kings thy glory: and thou shalt be called
by a new name, which the mouth of the Lord shall name. Thou shalt also
be a crown of glory in the hand of the Lord, and a royal diadem in the
hand of thy God. Thou shalt no more be termed Forsaken," &c. And to
represent the land itself as a bride, and the subject of espousals and
marriage, would be a figure of speech very unnatural, and not known in
Scripture; but for the church of God to be thus represented is very
usual throughout the Scripture from the beginning, to the end of the
Bible. And then it is manifest that the return of the Jews to the land
of Canaan from the Babylonish captivity, is not the event mainly
intended by the prophecy of which these words are a part. The time of
that return was not the time when that was fulfilled in the 2nd verse
of this chapter, "And the Gentiles shall see thy righteousness, and all
kings thy glory and thou shalt be called by a new name, which the mouth
of the Lord shall name." That was not the time spoken of in the two
preceding chapters, with which this chapter is one continued prophecy.
That was not the time spoken of in the last words of the foregoing
chapter, when the Lord would cause righteousness and praise to spring

forth before all nations; nor was it the time spoken of in the 5th,
6th, and 9th verses of that chapter, when "strangers should stand and
feed the flocks of God's people, and the sons of the alien should be
their ploughmen, and vine dressers; but they should be named the
priests of the Lord, and men should call them the ministers of God;
when they should eat the riches of the Gentiles, and in their glory
boast themselves, and their seed should be known among the Gentiles,
and their offspring among the people; and all that should see them
should acknowledge them, that they are the seed which the Lord hath
blessed." Nor was that the time spoken of in the chapter preceding
that, "when the abundance of the sea should be converted unto the
church; when the isle should wait for God, and the ships of Tarshish to
bring her sons from far, and their silver and gold with them; when the
forces of the Gentiles and their kings should be brought; when the
church should suck the milk of the Gentiles, and suck the breast of
kings; and when that nation and kingdom that would not serve her should
perish and be utterly wasted; and when the sun should be no more her
light by day, neither for brightness should the moon give light unto
her, but the Lord should be unto her an everlasting light, and her God
her glory; and her sun should no more go down, nor her moon withdraw
itself, because the Lord should be her everlasting light, and the days
of her mourning should be ended." These things manifestly have respect
to the Christian church in her most perfect and glorious state on earth
in the last ages of the world; when the church should be so far from
being confined to the land of Canaan, that she should fill the whole
earth, and all lands should be alike holy.

So that the children of Israel's being wedded to the land of
Canaan, being manifestly not the meaning of these words in the text,
"As a young man marrieth a virgin, so shall thy sons marry thee," as
some suppose; I choose rather, with others, to understand the words of
the church's union with her faithful pastors, and the great benefits

she should receive from them. God's ministers though they are set to be the instructors, guides, and fathers of God's people, yet are also the sons of the church: Amos ii, 11, "I raised up of your sons for prophets, and of your young men for Nazarites." Such as these, when faithful, are those precious sons of Zion comparable to fine gold spoken of, Lam. iv. 2: spoken of again, verse 7: "Her Nazarites were purer than snow, they were whiter than milk." And as he that marries a young virgin becomes the guide of her youth; so these sons of Zion are represented as taking her by the hand as her guide: Isai. li. 18, "There is none to guide her among all the sons whom she hath brought forth: neither is there any that taketh her by the hand of all the sons that she hath brought up." That by these sons of the church is meant ministers of the gospel, is confirmed by the next verse to the text: "I have set watchmen upon thy walls, O Jerusalem."

That the sons of the church should be married to her as a young man to a virgin, is a mystery or paradox not unlike many others held forth in the word of God, concerning the relation between Christ and his people, and their relation to him and to one another; such as that Christ is David's Lord and yet his son, and both the root and offspring of David; that Christ is a son born and a child given, and yet the everlasting Father; that the church is Christ's mother, as she is represented, Cant. iii. 11, and viii.1--and yet that she is his spouse, his sister, and his child; that ministers are the sons of the church, and yet that they are her fathers, as the apostle speaks of himself, as the father of the members of the church of Corinth, and also the mother of the Galatians, travailing in birth with them, Gal. iv. 19.

2.   The second and chief fulfilment here spoken of, of that promise of the church's being married, is in her being married to Christ. "And as the bridegroom rejoiceth over the bride, so shall thy God rejoice over thee." Not that we are to understand that the church has many husbands, or that Christ is one husband, and ministers are

other husbands that she hath; for though ministers are here spoken of
as being married to the church, yet it is not as being his fellows or
competitors, or as husbands of the church standing in a conjugal
relation to his bride in any wise parallel with his: for the church
has but one husband; she is not an adulteress, but a virgin, that is
devoted wholly to the Lamb, and follows him whithersoever he goes. But
ministers espouse the church entirely as Christ's ambassadors, as
representing him and standing in his stead, being sent forth by him to
be married to her in his name, that by this means she may be married to
him. As when a prince marries a foreign lady by proxy, the prince's
ambassador marries her, but not in his own name, but in the name of his
master, that he may be the instrument of bringing her into a true
conjugal relation to him. This is agreeable to what the apostle says,
2 Cor. xi. 2: "I am jealous over you with a godly jealousy; for I have
espoused you to one husband, that I may present you as a chaste virgin
to Christ." Here the apostle represents himself as being, as it were,
the husband of the church of Corinth; for it is the husband that is
jealous when the wife commits adultery; and yet he speaks of himself as
having espoused them not in his own name, but in the name of Christ,
and for him and him only, and as his ambassador, sent forth to bring
them home a chaste virgin to him. Ministers are in the text
represented as married to the church in the same sense that elsewhere
they are represented as fathers of the church: the church has but one
father, even God, and ministers are fathers as his ambassadors; so the
church has but one shepherd. John x. 16, "There shall be one fold and
one shepherd;" but yet ministers, as Christ's ambassadors, are often
called the church's shepherds or pastors. The church has but one
Saviour; but yet ministers, as his ambassadors and instruments, are
called her saviours. 1 Tim. iv. 16, "In doing this thou shalt both
save thyself and them that hear thee." Obad. 21, "And saviours shall
come upon Mount Zion." The church has but one priest; but yet in Isai.

lxvi. 21, speaking of the ministers of the Gentile nations, it is said, "I will take of them for priests and Levites." The church has but one Judge, for the Father hath committed all judgment to the Son; yet Christ tells his apostles, that they shall sit on twelve thrones, judging the twelve tribes of Israel.

When the text speaks first of ministers marrying the church, and then of Christ's rejoicing over her as the bridegroom rejoiceth over the bride; the former is manifestly spoken of as being in order to the latter, even in order to the joy and happiness that the church shall have in her true bridegroom. The preaching of the gospel is in this context spoken of three times agoing, as the great means of bringing about the prosperity and joy of the church; that is foretold; once in the first verse, "For Zion's sake will I not hold my peace, and for Jerusalem's sake I will not rest, until the righteousness thereof go forth as brightness, and the salvation thereof as a lamp that burneth;" and then again in the text, and lastly in the two following verses, "I have set watchmen upon thy walls, O Jerusalem, which shall never hold their peace day nor night, ye that make mention of the Lord, keep not silence; and give him no rest, till he establish, and till he make Jerusalem a praise in the earth."

The text thus opened affords these two propositions proper for our consideration on the solemn occasion of this day.

I.   The uniting of faithful ministers with Christ's people in the ministerial office, when done in a due manner, is like a young man's marrying a virgin.

II.   This union of ministers with the people is in order to their being brought to the blessedness of a more glorious union, in which Christ shall rejoice over them, as a bridegroom rejoiceth over the bride.

I.   The uniting of a faithful minister with Christ's people in the ministerial office, when done in a due manner, is like a young man's marrying a virgin.

I say, the uniting of a faithful minister with Christ's people, and in a due manner: for we must suppose that the promise God makes to the church in the text, relates to such ministers, and such a manner of union with the church; because this is promised to the church as a part of her latter day glory, and as a benefit that should be granted her by God, as the fruit of his great love to her, and an instance of her great spiritual prosperity and happiness in her purest and most excellent state on earth. But it would be no such instance of God's great favor and the church's happiness, to have unfaithful ministers entering into office in an undue and improper manner. They are evidently faithful ministers that are spoken of in the next verse, where the same are doubtless spoken of as in the text, "I have set watchmen on thy walls, O Jerusalem, which shall never hold their peace day nor night." And they are those that shall be introduced into the ministry at a time of its extraordinary purity, order, and beauty, wherein (as is said in the first, second, and third verses) her righteousness should go forth as brightness, and the Gentiles should see her righteousness, and all kings her glory, and she should be a crown of glory in the hand of the Lord, and a royal diadem in the hand of her God.

When I speak of the uniting of a faithful minister with Christ's people in a due manner, I do not mean a due manner only with regard to external order; but its being truly done in a holy manner, with sincere, upright aims and intentions, with a right disposition, and proper frames of mind in those that are concerned; and particularly in the minister that takes the office, and God's people to whom he is united, each exercising in this affair a proper regard to God and one another.

Such a uniting of a faithful minister with the people of God in the ministerial office, is in some respect like a young man's marrying a virgin.

1.   When a duly qualified person is properly invested with the ministerial character, and does in a due manner take upon him the sacred work and office of a minister of the gospel, he does, in some sense, espouse the church of Christ in general: for though he do not properly stand in a pastoral relation to the whole church of Christ through the earth, and is far from becoming a universal pastor; yet thenceforward he has a different concern with the church of Christ in general, and its interests and welfare, than other persons have that are laymen, and should be regarded otherwise by all the members of the Christian church.   Wherever he is providentially called to preach the word of God, or minister in holy things, he ought to be received as a minister of Christ, and the messenger of the Lord of Hosts to them. And every one that takes on him the office of a minister of Christ as he ought to do, espouses the church of Christ, as he espouses the interest of the church in a manner that is peculiar.   He is under obligations, as a minister of the Christian church, beyond other men, to love the church, as Christ, her true bridegroom, hath loved her, and to prefer Jerusalem above his chief joy, and to imitate Christ, the great shepherd and bishop of souls and husband of the church, in his care and tender concern for the church's welfare, and earnest and constant labors to promote it, as he has opportunity.   And as he, in taking office, devotes himself to the service of Christ in his church; so he gives himself to the church, to be hers, in that love, tender care, constant endeavor, and earnest labor for her provision, comfort, and welfare, that is proper to his office, as a minister of the church of Christ, by the permission of divine Providence, as long as he lives; as a young man gives himself to a virgin when he marries her.   And the church of Christ in general, as constituted of true saints through the world, (though they do not deliver up themselves to any one particular minister, as universal pastor, yet) do cleave to, and embrace the

ministry of the church with endeared affection and high honor, and
esteem, for Christ's sake; and do joyfully commit and subject
themselves to them to cleave to, honor, and help them, to be guided by
them and obey them so long as in the world; as the bride doth in
marriage cleave and deliver up herself to her husband. And the
ministry in general, or the whole number of faithful ministers, being
all united in the same work as fellow laborers, and conspiring to the
same design as fellow helpers to the grace of God, may be considered as
one mystical person, that espouses the church as a young man espouses a
virgin. As the many elders of the church of Ephesus are represented as
one mystical person, Rev. ii. 1, and all called the angel of the church
of Ephesus; and as the faithful ministers of Christ in general, all
over the world, seem to be represented as one mystical person, and
called an angel: Rev. xiv. 6, "And I saw another angel fly in the
midst of heaven, having the everlasting gospel to preach unto them that
dwell upon the earth, and to every nation, and kindred, and tongue, and
people." But,

2. More especially is the uniting of a faithful minister with a
particular Christian people, as their pastor, when done in a due
manner, like a young man's marrying a virgin.

It is so with respect to the union itself, the concomitants of the
union, and the fruits of it.

(1.) The union itself is, in several respects, like that which is
between a young man and a virgin whom he marries.

It is so with respect to mutual regard and affection. A faithful
minister, that is in a Christian manner united to a Christian people as
their pastor, has his heart united to them in the most ardent and
tender affection: and they, on the other hand, have their hearts
united to him, esteeming him very highly in love for his works' sake,
and receiving him with honor and reverence, and willingly subjecting
themselves to him, and committing themselves to his care, as being,

under Christ, their head and guide.

And such a pastor and people are like a young man and virgin united in marriage, with respect to the purity of their regard one to another. The young man gives himself to his bride in purity, as undebauched by meretricious embraces; and she also presents herself to him a chaste virgin. So in such a union of a minister and people as we are speaking of, the parties united are pure and holy in their affection and regard one to another. The minister's heart is united to the people, not for filthy lucre, or any worldly advantage, but with a pure benevolence to them, and desire of their spiritual welfare and prosperity, and complacence in them as the children of God and followers of Christ Jesus. And, on the other hand, they love and honor him with a holy affection and esteem; and not merely as having their admiration raised, and their carnal affections moved by having their ears tickled, and their curiosity, and other fleshly principles, gratified by a florid eloquence, and the excellency of speech and man's wisdom; but receiving him as the messenger of the Lord of Heaven, coming to them on a divine and infinitely important errand, and with those holy qualifications that resemble the virtues of the Lamb of God.

And as the bridegroom and bride give themselves to each other in covenant; so it is in that union we are speaking of between a faithful pastor and a Christian people. The minister, by solemn vows, devotes himself to the people, to improve his time and strength, and spend and be spent for them, so long as God in his providence shall continue the union: and they, on the other hand, in a holy covenant commit the care of their souls to him, and subject themselves to him.

(2.) The union between a faithful minister and a Christian people, that we are speaking of, is like that between a young man and virgin in their marriage, with respect to the concomitants of it.

When such a minister and such a people are thus united, it is attended with great joy. The minister joyfully devoting himself to the service of his Lord in the work of the ministry, as a work that he delights in; and also joyfully uniting himself to the society of the saints that he is set over, as having complacence in them, for his dear Lord's sake, whose people they are; and willingly and joyfully, on Christ's call, undertaking the labors and difficulties of the service of their souls. And they, on the other hand, joyfully receiving him as a precious gift of their ascending Redeemer. Thus a faithful minister and a Christian people are each other's joy: Rom. xv. 32, "That I may come unto with joy by the will of God, and may with you be refreshed." 2 Cor. i. 14, "As you have acknowledged us in part, that we are your rejoicing, even as ye are ours."

Another concomitant of this union, wherein it resembles that which becomes a young man and virgin united in marriage, is mutual helpfulness, and a constant care and endeavor to promote each other's good and comfort. The minister earnestly and continually seeks the profit and comfort of the souls of his people, and to guard and defend them from every thing that might annoy them, and studies and labors to promote their spiritual peace and prosperity. They, on the other hand, make it their constant care to promote his comfort, to make the burden of his great and difficult work easy, to avoid those things that might add to the difficulty of it, and that might justly be grievous to his heart; and do what in them lies to encourage his heart, and strengthen his hand in his work; and are ready to say to him, when called to exert himself in the more difficult parts of his work, as the people of old to Ezra the priest, when they saw him bowed down under the burden of a difficult affair: Ezra x. 4, "Arise, for this matter belongeth to thee: we also will be with thee: be of good courage, and do it." They spare no pains nor cost to make their pastor's outward circumstances easy and comfortable, and free from pinching necessities and distracting cares, and to put him under the best advantages to follow his great work fully and successfully.

Such a pastor and people, as it is between a couple happily united in a conjugal relation, have a mutual sympathy with each other, a fellow feeling of each other's burdens and calamities, and a communion in each other's prosperity and joy. When the people suffer in their spiritual interests, the pastor suffers: he is afflicted when he sees their souls in trouble and darkness: he feels their wounds; and he looks on their prosperity and comfort as his own. 2 Cor. xi. 29, "Who is weak, and I am not weak? Who is offended, and I burn not?" 2 Cor. vii. 13, "We were comforted in your comfort." And, on the other hand, the people feel their pastor's burdens, and rejoice in his prosperity and consolations; see Phil. vi. 14, and 2 Cor. ii. 3.

(3.) This union is like that which is between a young man and a virgin in its fruits.

One of it is mutual benefit: they become meet-helps one for another. The people receive great benefit by the minister, as he is their teacher to communicate spiritual instructions and counsels to them, and is set to watch over them to defend them from those enemies and calamities they are liable to; and so is, under Christ, to be both their guide and guard, as the husband is of the wife. And as the husband provides the wife with food and clothing; so the pastor, as Christ's steward, makes provision for his people, and brings forth out of his treasure things new and old, gives every one his portion of meat in due season, and is made the instrument of spiritually clothing and adorning their souls. And, on the other hand, the minister receives benefit from the people, and they minister greatly to his spiritual good by that holy converse to which their union to him as his flock leads them. The conjugal relation leads the persons united therein to the most intimate acquaintance and conversation with each other; so the union there is between a faithful pastor and a Christian people, leads them to intimate conversation about things of a spiritual nature: it leads the people most freely and fully to open the case of their souls to the pastor, and leads him to deal most freely, closely, and thoroughly with them in things pertaining thereto. And this conversation not only tends to their benefit, but also greatly to his.

And the pastor receives benefit from the people outwardly, as they take care of and order his outward accommodations for his support and comfort, and do, as it were, spread and serve his table for him.

Another fruit of this union, wherein it resembles the conjugal union, is a spiritual offspring. There is wont to arise from the union of such a pastor and people, a spiritual race of the children of the congregation that are new-born. These new-born children of God are in the Scripture represented both as the children of ministers, as those that have begotten them through the gospel, and also as the children of the church, who is represented as their mother that hath brought them forth, and at whose breasts they are nourished; as in Isaiah liv. 1, and lxvi. 11, Gal. iv. 26, 1Pet. ii. 2, and many other places.

Having thus briefly shown how the uniting of faithful ministers with Christ's people in the ministerial office, when done in a due manner, is like a young man's marrying a virgin,

I now proceed to the

II.   PROPOSITION, viz., that this union of ministers with the people of Christ, is in order to their being brought to the blessedness of a more glorious union, in which Christ shall rejoice over them as the bridegroom rejoiceth over the bride.

1. The saints are, and shall be the subjects of this blessedness. Of all the many various kinds of union of sensible and temporal things that are used in Scripture to represent the relation there is between Christ and his church; that which is between bridegroom and bride, or husband and wife, is much the most frequently made use of both in the Old and New Testament. The Holy Ghost seems to take a peculiar delight in this, as a similitude fit to represent the strict, intimate, and blessed union that is between Christ and his saints. The apostle

intimates, that one end why God appointed marriage, and established so near a relation as that between husband and wife, was, that it might be a type of the union that is between Christ and his church, in Eph. v. 30, 31, 32: "For we are members of his body, of his flesh, and of his bones. For this cause shall a man leave his father and mother, and shall be joined to his wife; and they two shall be one flesh."--For this cause, i.e., because we are members of Christ's body, of his flesh, and of his bones: for this cause, God appointed that man and wife should so be joined together as to be one flesh, to represent this high and blessed union between Christ and his church: the apostle explains himself in the next words, "This is a great mystery, but I speak concerning Christ and the church." This institution of marriage, and making the man and his wife one flesh, is a great mystery; i.e., it contains in it a great mystery; that is, a great and glorious mystery hid in the design of it: and the apostle tells us what that glorious mystery is: "I speak concerning Christ and the church;" as much as to say, the mystery I speak of, is that blessed union that is between Christ and his church, which I spoke of before.

This union is a blessed union indeed; of which that between a faithful minister and a Christian people is but a shadow. Ministers are not the proper husbands of the church, though their union to God's people, as Christ's ambassadors, in several respects resembles the conjugal relation: but Christ is the true husband of the church, to whom the souls of the saints are espoused indeed, and to whom they are united as his flesh and his bones, yea, and one spirit; to whom they have given themselves in an everlasting covenant, and whom alone they cleave to, love, honor, obey, and trust in, as their spiritual husband, whom alone they reserve themselves for as chaste virgins, and whom they follow whithersoever he goeth. There are many ministers in the church of Christ, and there may be several pastors of one particular church: but the church has but one husband, all others are rejected and

despised in comparison of him; he is among the sons as the apple tree
among the trees of the wood; they all are barren and worthless, he only
is the fruitful tree; and therefore, leaving all others, the church
betakes herself to him alone, and sits under his shadow with great
delight, and his fruit is sweet to her taste; she takes up her full and
entire rest in him, desiring no other. The relation between a minister
and people shall be dissolved, and may be dissolved before death: but
the union between Christ and his church shall never be dissolved,
neither before death nor by death, but shall endure through all
eternity: "The mountains shall depart, and the hills be removed; but
Christ's conjugal love and kindness shall not depart from his church;
neither shall the covenant of his peace, the marriage covenant, be
removed," Isa. liv. 10.--The union between a faithful minister and a
Christian people is but a partial resemblance even of the marriage
union, it is like marriage only in some particulars: but with respect
to the union between Christ and his church, marriage is but a partial
resemblance, yea, a faint shadow of that; everything that is desirable
and excellent in the union between an earthly bridegroom and bride, is
to be found in the union between Christ and his church; and that in an
infinitely greater perfection and more glorious manner: there is
infinitely more to be found in it than ever was found between the
happiest couple in a conjugal relation; or could be found if the bride
and bridegroom had not only the innocence of Adam and Eve, but the
perfection of angels.

Christ and his saints, standing in such a relation as this one to
another, the saints must needs be unspeakably happy. Their mutual joy
in each other is answerable to the nearness of their relation and
strictness of their union. Christ rejoices over the church as the
bridegroom rejoiceth over the bride, and she rejoices in him as the
bride rejoices in the bridegroom. My text has respect to the mutual
joy that Christ and his church should have in each other. For though

the joy of Christ over his church only is mentioned, yet it is evident that this is here spoken of and promised as the great happiness of the church, and therefore supposes her joy in him.

The mutual joy of Christ and his church is like that of a bridegroom and bride, in that they rejoice in each other, as those that they have chosen above others, for their nearest, most intimate, and everlasting friends and companions. The church is Christ's chosen: Isaiah xli. 9, "I have chosen thee, and not cast thee away:" chapt, xlviii. 10, "I have chosen thee, in the furnace of affliction." How often are God's saints called his elect or chosen ones? He has chosen them, not to be mere servants, but friends: John xv. 15, "I call you not servants, but I have called you friends." And though Christ be the Lord of glory, infinitely above men and angels, yet he has chosen the elect to be his companions; and has taken upon him their nature; and so in some respect, as it were, levelled himself with them, that he might be their brother and companion. Christ as well as David, calls the saints his brethren and companions; Psalm cxxii. 8, "For my brethren and companions' sake I will now say, Peace be within thee." So in the book of Canticles, he calls his church his sister and spouse. Christ hath loved and chosen his church as his peculiar friend, above others: Psalm cxxxv. 4, "The Lord hath chosen Jacob unto himself, and Israel for his peculiar treasure." As the bridegroom chooses the bride for his peculiar friend, above all others in the world, so Christ has chosen his church for a peculiar nearness to him, as his flesh and his bone, and the high honor and dignity of espousals above all others, rather than the fallen angels, yea, rather than the elect angels. For verily, in this respect, "he taketh not hold of angels, but he taketh hold of the seed of Abraham;" as the words are in the original, in Heb. ii. 16. He has chosen his church above the rest of mankind, above all the Heathen nations, and those that are without the visible church, and above all other professing Christians: Cant. vi. 9, "My dove, my undefiled is but one; she is the only one of her mother, she is the choice one of her that bare her." Thus Christ rejoices over his church, as obtaining in her that which he has chosen above all the rest of the creation, and as sweetly resting in his choice. Psal. cxxxii. 13, 14, "The Lord hath chosen Zion; he hath desired it. This is my rest forever."

On the other hand, the church chooses Christ above all others: he is in her eyes the chief among ten thousands, fairer than the sons of men: she rejects the suit of all his rivals for his sake: her heart relinquishes the whole world: he is her pearl of great price, for which she parts with all; and rejoices in him, as the choice and rest of her soul.

Christ and his church, like the bridegroom and bride, rejoice in each other, as having a special propriety in each other. All things are Christ's; but he has a special propriety in his church. There is nothing in heaven or earth, among all the creatures, that is his, in that high and excellent manner that the church is his: they are often called his portion and inheritance; they are said, Rev. xiv. 4, "to be the first fruits to God and the Lamb." As of old, the first fruit was that part of the harvest that belonged to God, and was to be offered to him; so the saints are the first fruits of God's creatures, being that part which is in a peculiar manner Christ's portion, above all the rest of the creation. James i. 18, "Of his own will begat he us by the word of truth, that we should be a kind of first fruits of his creatures." And Christ rejoices in his church, as in that which is peculiarly his: Isai. lxv. 19, "I will rejoice in Jerusalem, and joy in my people." The church has also a peculiar propriety in Christ: though other things are hers, yet nothing is hers in that manner that her spiritual bridegroom is hers: as great and glorious as he is, yet he, with all his dignity and glory, is hers; all is wholly given to her, to be fully possessed and enjoyed by her, to the utmost degree that she is capable of: therefore we have her so often saying in the language of exultation and triumph, "My beloved is mine, and I am his," in the book of Canticles, chap. ii. 16, and vi. 3, and vii. 10.

Christ and his church, like the bridegroom and bride, rejoice in each other, as those that are the objects of each other's most tender and ardent love. The love of Christ to his church is altogether unparalleled: the height and depth and length and breadth of it pass knowledge; for he loved the church, and gave himself for it; and his love to her proved stronger than death. And on the other hand, she loves him with a supreme affection: nothing stands in competition with him in her heart: she loves him with all her heart: her whole soul is offered up to him in the flame of love. And Christ rejoices and has sweet rest and delight in his love to the church. Zeph. iii. 17, "The Lord thy God in the midst of thee is mighty: he will save: he will rejoice over thee with joy: he will rest in his love: he will joy over thee with singing." So the church, in the exercises of her love to Christ rejoices with unspeakable joy. 1 Pet. i. 7, 8, "Jesus Christ; whom, having not seen, ye love: in whom, though now he see him not, yet believing, ye rejoice with joy unspeakable, and full of glory."

Christ and his church rejoice in each other's beauty. The church rejoices in Christ's divine beauty and glory. She, as it were, sweetly solaces herself in the light of the glory of the Sun of righteousness; and the saints say one to another, as in Isai. ii. 5, "O house of Jacob, come ye, let us walk in the light of the Lord." The perfections and virtues of Christ are as a perfumed ointment to the church, that make his very name to be to her as ointment poured forth. Cant. i. 3, "Because of the savor of thy good ointments, thy name is as ointment poured forth, therefore do the virgins love thee." And Christ delights and rejoices in the beauty of the church, and the beauty which he hath put upon her: her Christian graces are ornaments of great prices in his sight, 1 Pet. iii. 4. And he is spoken of as greatly desiring her beauty, Psal. xlv. 11. Yea, he himself speaks of his heart as ravished with her beauty. Cant. iv. 9, "Thou hast ravished my heart, my sister, my spouse; thou hast ravished my heart with one of thine eyes, with one chain of thy neck."

Christ and his church, as the bridegroom and bride, rejoice in each other's love. Wine is spoken of, Psal. civ. 15, as that which maketh glad man's heart: but the church of Christ is spoken of as rejoicing in the love of Christ, as that which is more pleasant and refreshing than wine. Cant. i. 4, "The king hath brought me into his chambers: we will be glad and rejoice in thee, we will remember thy love more than wine." So on the other hand Christ speaks of the church's love as far better to him than wine. Cant. iv. 10, "How fair is thy love, my sister, my spouse! How much better is thy love than wine!"

Christ and his church rejoice in communion with each other, as in being united in their happiness, and having fellowship and a joint participation in each other's good: as the bridegroom and bride rejoice together at the wedding feast, and as thenceforward they are joint partakers of each other's comforts and joys. Rev. iii. 20, "If any man hear my voice, and open the door, I will come in to him, and sup with him, and he with me." The church has fellowship with Christ in his own happiness, and his divine entertainments; his joy is fulfilled in her, John xv. 11, and xvii. 13. She sees light in his light; and she is made to drink at the river of his own pleasures, Psal. xxxvi. 8, 9. And Christ brings her to eat and drink at his own table to take her fill of his own entertainments. Cant. v. 1, "Eat, O friends, drink, yea, drink abundantly, O beloved." And he, on the other hand, has fellowship with her; he feasts with her, her joys are his; and he rejoices in that entertainment that she provides for him. So Christ is said to feed among the lilies, Cant. ii. 16, and chap. vii. 13; she

speaks of all manner of pleasant fruits, new and old, which she had
laid up for him; and say to him, chap. iv. 16, "Let my beloved come
into his garden, and eat his pleasant fruit." And he makes answer in
the next verse, "I am come into my garden, my sister, my spouse; I have
gathered my myrrh with my spice, I have eaten my honeycomb with my
honey, I have drunk my wine with my milk."

And lastly, Christ and his church, as the bridegroom and bride,
rejoice in conversing with each other. The words of Christ, by which
he converses with his church, are most sweet to her; and therefore she
says of him, Cant. v. 16, "His mouth is most sweet." And on the other
hand, he says of her, chap. ii. 14, "Let me hear thy voice; for sweet
is thy voice." And chapt. iv. 11, "Thy lips, O my spouse, drop as the
honeycomb; honey and milk are under they tongue.

Christ rejoices over his saints as the bridegroom over the bride
at all times: but there are some seasons wherein he doth so more
especially. Such a season is the time of the soul's conversion; when
the good shepherd finds his lost sheep,then he brings it home
rejoicing, and calls together his friends and neighbors, saying,
Rejoice with me. The day of a sinner's conversion is the day of
Christ's espousals; and so eminently the day of his rejoicing.
Canticles iii. 11, "Go forth, O ye daughters of Zion, and behold king
Solomon with the crown wherewith his mother crowned him in the day of
his espousals, and in the day of the gladness of his heart." And it is
oftentimes remarkably the day of the saints' rejoicing in Christ: for
then God turns again the captivity of his elect people, and, as it
were, fills their mouth with laughter, and their tongue with singing;
as in Psal. cxxvi. at the beginning. We read of the jailer, that when
he was converted, "he rejoiced, believing in God, with all his house,"
Acts xvi. 34.

And there are other seasons of special communion of the saints
with Christ, wherein Christ doth in an especial manner rejoice over his

saints, and as their bridegroom brings them into his chambers, that they also may be glad and rejoice in him, Cant. i. 4.

But the time wherein this mutual rejoicing of Christ and his saints will be in its perfection, is the time of the saints' glorification with Christ in heaven; for that is the proper time of the saints' entering in with the bridegroom into the marriage, Matt. xxv. 10. The saints' conversion is rather like the betrothing of the intended bride to her bridegroom before they come together; but the time of the saints' glorification is the time when that shall be fulfilled in Psal. xiv. 15, "With gladness and rejoicing shall they be brought; they shall enter into the kings' palace." That is the time when those that Christ loved, and gave himself for, that he might sanctify and cleanse them, as with the washing of water by the word, shall be presented to him in glory, not having spot, or wrinkle, or any such thing. The time wherein the church shall be brought to the full enjoyment of her bridegroom, having all tears wiped away from her eyes; and there shall be no more distance or absence. She shall then be brought to the entertainments of an eternal wedding feast, and to dwell eternally with her bridegroom; yea, to dwell eternally in his embraces. Then Christ will give her his love; and she shall drink her fill, yea, she shall swim in the ocean of his love.

And as there are various seasons wherein Christ and particular saints do more especially rejoice in each other; so there are also certain seasons wherein Christ doth more especially rejoice over his church collectively taken. Such a season is a time of remarkable outpouring of the Spirit of God: it is a time of the espousal of many souls to Christ; and so a time of much of the joy of espousals: and also it is a time wherein Christ is wont more especially to visit his saints with his loving-kindness, and to bring them near to himself, and especially to refresh their hearts with divine communications: on which account, such a time becomes a time of great joy to the church of

Christ. So when the Spirit of God was so wonderfully poured out on the city of Samaria, with the preaching of Philip, we read that there was great joy in that city, Acts viii. 8. And the time of that wonderful effusion of the Spirit at Jerusalem, begun at the feast of Pentecost, was a time of holy feasting and rejoicing, and a kind of wedding day to the church of Christ; wherein "they continuing daily, with one accord, in the temple, and breaking bread from house to house, did eat their meat with gladness, and singleness of heart," as Acts ii. 46.

But more especially is the time of that great outpouring of the Spirit of God in the latter days, so often foretold in the Scriptures, represented as the time of the marriage of the Lamb, and of the rejoicing of Christ and his church in each other, as the bridegroom and the bride. This is the time prophesied of in our text and context; and this is the time foretold in Isai. lxv. 19, "I will rejoice in Jerusalem, and joy in my people; and the voice of weeping shall no more be heard in her, nor the voice of crying." This is the time spoken of Rev. xix. 6, 7, 8, 9, where the apostle John tells us, he "heard as it were the voice of a great multitude, and as the voice of many waters, and as the voice of mighty thunderings, saying, Alleluia: for the Lord God omnipotent reigneth. Let us be glad and rejoice, and give honor to him; for the marriage of the Lamb is come, and his wife hath made herself ready." And adds, "To her was granted, that she should be arrayed in fine linen, clean and white; for the fine linen is the righteousness of saints. And he saith unto me, Write, Blessed are they which are called into the marriage supper of the Lamb."

But above all, the time of Christ's last coming, is the time of the consummation of the church's marriage with the Lamb, and the time of the complete and most perfect joy of the wedding. In that resurrection morning, when the Sun of righteousness shall appear in our heavens, shining in all his brightness and glory, he will come forth as a bridegroom; he shall come in the glory of his Father, with all his

holy angels. And at that glorious appearing of the great God, and our
Saviour Jesus Christ, shall the whole elect church, complete as to
every individual member, and each member with the whole man, both body
and soul, and both in perfect glory, ascend up to meet the Lord in the
air, to be thenceforth forever with the Lord. That will be a joyful
meeting of this glorious bridegroom and bride indeed.   Then the
bridegroom will appear in all his glory without any veil: and then the
saints will shine forth as the sun in the kingdom of their Father, and
at the right hand of their Redeemer; and then the church will appear as
the bride, the Lamb's wife. It is the state of the church after the
resurrection, that is spoken of, Rev. xxi. 2: "And I John saw the holy
city, the new Jerusalem, coming down from God out of heaven, prepared
as a bride adorned for her husband." And verse 9, "Come hither, I will
show thee the bride, the Lamb's wife." Then will come the time, when
Christ will sweetly invite his spouse to enter in with him into the
palace of his glory, which he had been preparing for her from the
foundation of the world, and shall, as it were, take her by the hand,
and lead her in with him: and this glorious bridegroom and bride
shall, with all their shining ornaments, ascend up together into the
heaven of heavens; the whole multitude of glorious angels waiting upon
them: and this son and daughter of God shall, in their united glory
and joy, present themselves together before the Father; when Christ
shall say, "Here am I, and the children which thou hast given me:"   and
they both shall, in that relation and union, together receive the
Father's blessing; and shall thenceforward rejoice together, in
consummate, uninterrupted, immutable, and everlasting glory, in the
love and embraces of each other, and joint enjoyment of the love of the
Father.

    2.   That forementioned union of faithful ministers with the people
of Christ, is in order to this blessedness.

    1.   It is only with reference to Christ, as the true bridegroom of

his church, that there is any union between a faithful minister and a Christian people, that is like that of a bridegroom and bride.

As I observed before, a faithful minister espouses a Christian people, not in his own name, but as Christ's ambassador. He espouses them, that in their being espoused to him, they may be espoused to Christ; and not that the church may commit adultery with him. It is for his sake that he loves her, with a tender conjugal affection, as she is the spouse of Christ, and as he, as the minister of Christ, has his heart under the influence of the Spirit of Christ; as Abraham's faithful servant, that was sent to fetch a wife for his master's son, was captivated with Rebekah's beauty and virture; but not with reference to a union with himself, but with his master Isaac. It was for his sake he loved her, and it was for him that he desired her, and set his heart upon her, that she might be Isaac's wife. And it was for this that he greatly rejoiced over her, and for this he wooed her, and for this he obtained her, and she was for a season united to him; but it was but as a fellow traveller, that by him she might be brought to Isaac in the land of Canaan; and for this he adorned her with ornaments of gold; it was to prepare her for Isaac's embraces. All that tender care which a faithful minister takes of his people as a kind of spiritual husband, to provide for them, to lead and feed them, and comfort them, is not as looking upon them as his own bride, but his master's.

And on the other hand, the people receive him, and unite themselves to him in covenant, and honor him and subject themselves to him, and obey him, only for Christ's sake, and as one that represents him, and acts in his name towards them. All this love, and honor, and submission, is ultimately referred to Christ. Thus the apostle says, Gal. iv. 14, "Ye received me as an angel, or messenger of God, even as Christ Jesus." And the children that are brought forth in consequence of the union of the pastor and people, are not properly the minister's

children, but the children of Christ; they are not born of man, but of
God.

2.   The things that appertain to that forementioned union of a
faithful minister and Christian people, are the principal appointed
means of bringing the church to that blessedness that has been spoken
of.   As Abraham's servant, and the part he acted as Isaac's agent
towards Rebekah, were the principal means of his being brought to enjoy
the benefits of her conjugal relation to Isaac.   Ministers are sent to
woo the souls of men for Christ: 2 Cor. v. 20, "We are then
ambassadors for Christ, as though God did beseech you by us; we pray
you in Christ's stead, be ye reconciled to God."   We read in Matt.
xxii. of a certain king, that made a marriage for his son, and sent
forth his servants to invite and bring in the guests.   It is ministers
that are these servants.   The labors of faithful ministers are the
principal means God is wont to make use of for the conversion of the
children of the church, and so of their espousals unto Christ.   I have
espoused you to one husband, says the apostle, 2 Cor. xi. 2.   The
preaching of the gospel by faithful ministers, is the principal means
that God makes use of for the exhibiting Christ and his love and
benefits to his elect people, and the chief means of their being
sanctified, and so fitted to enjoy their spiritual bridegroom.   Christ
loved the church, and gave himself for it, that he might sanctify and
cleanse it, as by the washing of water by the word, i.e., by the
preaching of the gospel, and so might present it to himself, a glorious
church.   The labors of faithful ministers are ordinarily the principal
means of the joy of the saints in Christ Jesus, in their fellowship
with their spiritual bridegroom in this world: 2 Cor. i. 24, "We are
helpers of your joy." They are the instruments that God makes use of
for the bringing up the church, as it were, from her childhood, till
she is fit for her marriage with the Lord of glory; as Mordecai brought
up Hadassah, or Esther, whereby she was fitted to be queen in

Ahasuerus's court. God purifies the church under their hand, as
Esther, to fit her for her marriage with the king, was committed to the
custody of Hagai the keeper of the women, to be purified six months
with oil of myrrh, and six months with sweet odors. They are made the
instruments of clothing the church in her wedding garments, that fine
linen, clean and white, and adorning her for her husband; as Abraham's
servant adorned Rebekah with golden earrings and bracelets. Faithful
ministers are made the instruments of leading the people of God in the
way to heaven, conducting them to the glorious presence of the
bridegroom, to the consummate joys of her marriage with the Lamb; as
Abraham's servant conducted Rebekah from Padanaram to Canaan, and
presented her to Isaac, and delivered her into his embraces. For it is
the office of ministers, not only to espouse the church to her husband,
but to present her a chaste virgin to Christ.

I would now conclude this discourse with some exhortations,
agreeable to what has been said. And,

1. The exhortation may be to all that are called to the work of
the gospel ministry. Let us who are honored by the glorious bridegroom
of the church, to be employed as his ministers, to so high a purpose,
as has been represented, be engaged and induced by what has been
observed, to faithfulness in our great work; that we may be, and act
towards Christ's people that are committed to our care, as those that
are united to them in holy espousals, for Christ's sake, and in order
to their being brought to the unspeakable blessedness of that more
glorious union with the Lamb of God, in which he shall rejoice over
them, as the bridegroom rejoiceth over the bride. Let us see to it
that our hearts are united to them, as a young man to a virgin that he
marries, in the most ardent and tender affection; and that our regard
to them be pure and uncorrupt, that it may be a regard to them, and not
to what they have, or any worldly advantages we hope to gain of them.
And let us behave ourselves as those that are devoted to their good;

being willing to spend and be spent for them; joyfully undertaking and enduring the labor and self-denial that is requisite in order to a thorough fulfilling the ministry that we have received; continually and earnestly endeavoring to promote the prosperity and salvation of the souls committed to our care; and, as those that are their bone and their flesh, looking on their calamities and their prosperity as our own; feeling their spiritual wounds and griefs, and refreshed with their consolations; and spending our whole lives in diligent care and endeavor to provide for, nourish, and instruct our people, as the intended spouse of Christ, yet in her minority, that we may form her mind and behavior, and bring her up for him, and that we may cleanse her, as with the washing of water by the word, and purify her as with sweet odors, and clothed in such raiment as may become Christ's bride; that when the appointed wedding day comes, we may have done our work as Christ's messengers; and may then be ready to present Christ's spouse to him, a chaste virgin, properly educated and formed, and suitably adorned for her marriage with the Lamb; that he may then present her to himself, a glorious church, not having spot, or wrinkle, or any such thing, and may receive her into his eternal embraces, in perfect purity, beauty, and glory.

Here I would mention three or four things tending to excite us to this fidelity.

1. We ought to consider how much Christ has done to obtain that joy that has been spoken of, in order to which we have been called to the work of the ministry, viz., that wherein Christ rejoices over his church, as the bridegroom rejoiceth over the bride.

The creation of the world seems to have been especially for this end, that the eternal Son of God might obtain a spouse towards whom he might fully exercise the infinite benevolence of his nature, and to whom he might, as it were, open and pour forth all that immense fountain of condescension, love, and grace that was in his heart, and that in this way God might be glorified. Doubtless the work of creation is subordinate to the work of redemption: that is called the creation of the new heavens and new earth, and is represented as so much more excellent that the old, that that, in comparison of it, is not worthy to be mentioned, or come into mind.

But Christ has done greater things than to create the world, to obtain his bride and the joy of his espousals with her: for he was incarnate, and became man for this end; which was a greater thing than his creating the world. For the Creator to make the creature was a great thing, but for him to become a creature was a greater thing. And he did a much greater thing still to obtain this joy; in that for this he laid down his life, and suffered even the death of the cross: for this he poured out his soul unto death; and he that is the Lord of the universe, God over all blessed for evermore, offered himself a sacrifice, in both body and soul, in the flames of divine wrath. Christ obtains his elect spouse by conquest; for she was a captive in the hands of dreadful enemies; and her Redeemer came into the world to conquer these enemies, and rescue her out of their hands that she might be his bride: and he came and encountered these enemies in the greatest battle that ever was beheld by men or angels: he fought with principalities and powers: he fought alone with the powers of darkness, and all the armies of hell; yea, he conflicted with the infinitely more dreadful wrath of God, and overcame in this great battle; and thus he obtained his spouse. Let us consider at how great a price Christ purchased this spouse: he did not redeem her with corruptible things, as silver and gold, but with his own precious blood; yea, he gave himself for her. When he offered up himself to God in those extreme labors and sufferings, this was the joy that was set before him, that made him cheerfully to endure the cross, and despise the pain and shame in comparison of this joy; even that rejoicing over his church, as the bridegroom rejoiceth over the bride that the Father had promised him, and that he expected when he should present her to himself in perfect beauty and blessedness.

The prospect of this was what supported him in the midst of the dismal prospect of his sufferings, at which his soul was troubled; as appears by the account we have, John xii. 27: "Now is my soul troubled; and what shall I say? Father, save me from this hour: but for this cause came I unto this hour." These words show the conflict and distress of Christ's holy soul in the view of his approaching sufferings. But in the midst of his trouble, he was refreshed with the joyful prospect of the success of those sufferings, in bringing home his elect church to himself, signified by a voice from heaven, and promised by the Father: on which he says, in the language of triumph, verse 31, 32, "Now is the judgment of this world: now shall the prince of this world be cast out. And I, if I be lifted up, will draw all men unto me."

And ministers of the gospel are appointed to be the instruments of bringing this to pass; the instruments of bringing home his elect spouse to him, and her becoming his bride; and the instruments of her sanctifying and cleansing by the word, that she might be meet to be presented to him on the future glorious wedding day. How great a motive then is here to induce us that are called to be these instruments, to be faithful in our work, and most willingly labor and suffer, that Christ may see of the travail of his soul and be satisfied? Shall Christ do such great things, and go through such great labors and sufferings to obtain this joy, and then honor us sinful worms, so as to employ us as his ministers and instruments to bring this joy to pass; and shall we be loth to labor, and backward to deny ourselves for this end?

2. Let us consider how much the manner in which Christ employs us in this great business has to engage us to a faithful performance of it. We are sent forth as his servants; but it is as highly dignified

servants, as stewards of his household, as Abraham's servant; and as his ambassadors, to stand in his stead, and in his name, and represent his person in so great an affair as that of his espousals with the eternally beloved of his soul. Christ employs us not as mere servants, but as friends of the bridegroom; agreeable to the style in which John the Baptist speaks of himself, John iii. 29, in which he probably alludes to an ancient custom among the Jews at their nuptial solemnities, at which one of the guests that was most honored and next in dignity to the bridegroom, was styled the friend of the bridegroom.

There is not an angel in heaven, of how high an order soever, but what looks on himself honored by the Son of God and Lord of glory, in being employed by him as his minister in the high affair of his espousals with his blessed bride. But we are not only thus honored, but such an honor as this has Christ put upon us, that his spouse should in some sort be ours; that we should marry, as a young man marries a virgin, the same mystical person that he himself will rejoice over, as the bridegroom rejoiceth over the bride; that we should be his ministers to treat and transact for him with his dear spouse, that he might obtain this joy; and to transact in such a manner with her as in our treaty with her, to be married to her in his name, and sustain an image of his own endearing relation to her; and that she should receive us, in some sort, as himself, and her heart be united to us in esteem, honor, and affection, as those that represent him; and that Christ's and the church's children should be ours, and that the same that is the fruit of the travail of Christ's soul should be also the fruit of the travail of our souls; as the apostle speaks of himself as travailing in birth with his hearers, Gal. iv. 19. The reason why Christ puts such honor on faithful ministers, even above the angels themselves, is, because they are of his beloved church, they are select members of his dear spouse, and Christ esteems nothing too much for her, no honor too great for her. Therefore Jesus Christ, the King of angels and men,

does as it were cause it to be proclaimed concerning faithful
ministers, as Ahasuerus did concerning him that brought up Esther, his
beloved queen; "Thus shall it be done to the man that the king delights
to honor."

And seeing Christ hath so honored us, that our relation to his
people imitates his; surely our affection to them should resemble his,
and we should imitate him in seeking their salvation, spiritual peace,
and happiness, as Christ sought it. Our tender care, labors, self-
denial, and readiness to suffer for their happiness, should imitate
what hath appeared in him, that hath purchased them with his own blood.

3. Let it be considered, that if we faithfully acquit ourselves
in our office, in the manner that hath been represented, we shall
surely hereafter be partakers of the joy, when the bridegroom and bride
shall rejoice in each other in perfect and eternal glory.

God once gave forth a particular command, with special solemnity,
that it should be written for the notice of all professing Christians
through all ages, that they are happy and blessed indeed, who are
called to the marriage supper of the Lamb: Rev. xix. 9, "And he saith
unto me, Write, Blessed are they which are called unto the marriage
supper of the Lamb. And he saith unto me, These are the true sayings
of God." But if we are faithful in our work, we shall surely be the
subjects of that blessedness; we shall be partakers of the joy of the
bridegroom and bride, not merely as friends and neighbors that are
invited to be occasional guests, but as members of the one and the
other. We shall be partakers with the church, the blessed bride, in
her joy in the bridegroom, not only as friends and ministers to the
church, but as members of principal dignity; as the eye, the ear, the
hand, are principal members of the body. Faithful ministers in the
church will hereafter be a part of the church that shall receive
distinguished glory at the resurrection of the just, which, above all
other times, may be looked on as the church's wedding day: Dan. xii.

2, 3, "Many of them that sleep in the dust of the earth shall awake,
some to everlasting life; and they that be wise shall shine as the
brightness of the firmament, and they that turn many to righteousness,
as the stars forever and ever."   They are elders that are represented
as that part of the church triumphant that sit next to the throne of
God: Rev. iv. 4, "And round about the throne were four and twenty
seats; and upon the seats I saw four and twenty elders sitting, clothed
in white raiment; and they had on their heads crowns of gold."

And we shall also be partakers of the joy of the bridegroom in his
rejoicing   over   his   bride.   We,   as   the   special   friends   of   the
bridegroom, shall stand by the bridegroom, and hear him express his joy
on that day, and rejoice greatly because of the bridegroom's voice; as
John the Baptist said of himself, John iii. 29:   "He that hath the
bride is the bridegroom: but the friend of the bridegroom, which
standeth and heareth him, rejoiceth greatly because of the bridegroom's
voice."   Christ, in reward for our faithful service, in winning and
espousing his bride to him, and bringing her up from her minority, and
adorning her for him, will then call us to partake with him in the joy
of his marriage.   And she that will then be his joy, shall also be our
crown of rejoicing.   1 Thess. ii. 19, "What is our hope, or joy, or
crown of rejoicing?   Are not ye in the presence of our Lord Jesus
Christ at his coming?"   What a joyful meeting had Christ and his
disciples together, when the disciples returned to their Master, after
the faithful and successful performance of their appointed service,
when Christ sent them forth to preach the gospel; Luke x. 17, "And the
seventy returned with joy, saying, Lord, even the devils are subject
unto us through thy name."   Here we see how they rejoice: the next
words show how Christ also rejoiced on that occasion: "And he said
unto them, I behold Satan as lightning fall from heaven."   And in the
next verse but two, we are told that, "in that hour Jesus rejoiced in
spirit, and said, I thank thee, O Father, Lord of Heaven and earth,

that thou hast hid these things from the wise and prudent, and hast
revealed them unto babes." So if we faithfully acquit ourselves, we
shall another day return to him with joy; and we shall rejoice with him
and he with us. Then will be the day when Christ, that has sown in
tears and in blood, and we that have reaped the fruits of his labors
and sufferings, shall rejoice together agreeable to John iv. 35, 36,
37. And that will be a happy meeting indeed, when Christ and his
lovely and blessed bride, and faithful ministers that have been the
instruments of wooing and winning her heart to him, and adorning her
for him, and presenting her to him, shall all rejoice together.

4. Further to stir us up to faithfulness in the great business
that is appointed us, in order to the mutual joy of this bridegroom and
bride, let us consider what reason we have to hope that the time is
approaching when this joy shall be to a glorious degree fulfilled on
earth, far beyond whatever yet has been; I mean the time of the
church's latter day glory. This is what the words of our text have a
more direct respect to; and this is what is prophesied of in Hos. ii.
19, 20: "And I will betroth thee unto me forever, yea, I will betroth
thee unto me in righteousness, and in judgment, and in loving-kindness,
and in mercies I will even betroth thee unto me in faithfulness, and
thou shalt know the Lord." And this is what is especially intended by
the marriage of the Lamb, in Rev. xix.

We are sure this day will come: and we have many reasons to think
that it is approaching; from the fulfilment of almost every thing that
the prophecies speak of as preceding it, and their having been
fulfilled now of a long time; and from the general earnest expectations
of the church of God, and the best of her ministers and members, and
the late extraordinary things that have appeared in the church of God,
and appertaining to the state of religion, and the present aspects of
Divine Providence, which the time will not allow me largely to insist
upon.

As the happiness of that day will have a great resemblance of the glory and joy of the eternal wedding day of the church after the resurrection of the just; so will the privileges that faithful ministers shall be the subjects of at that time, much resemble the blessed privileges that they shall enjoy, as partaking with the bridegroom and bride, in their honor and happiness, in eternal glory. This is the time especially intended in the text, wherein it is said, "as a young man marrieth a virgin, so shall thy sons marry thee." And it is after in the prophecies spoken of as a great part of the glory of that time, that then the church should be so well supplied with faithful ministers. So in the next verse to the text, "I have set watchmen on thy walls, O Jerusalem, that shall never hold their peace, day nor night." So, in Isai. xxx. 20, 21, "Thy teachers shall not be removed into a corner any more, but thine eyes shall see thy teachers; and thine ears shall hear a word behind thee, saying, This is the way, walk ye in it, when ye turn to the right hand, and when ye turn to the left." Jer. iii. 15, "And I will give you pastors according to mine heart, which shall feed you with knowledge and understanding." And chap. xxiii. 4, "And I will set up shepherds over them, which shall feed them." And the great privilege and joy of faithful ministers at that day is foretold in Isai. lii. 9: "Thy watchmen shall lift up the voice, with the voice together shall they sing: for they shall see eye to eye, when the Lord shall bring again Zion."

And as that day must needs be approaching, and we ourselves have lately seen some things that we have reason to hope are forerunners of it; certainly it should strongly excite us to endeavor to be such pastors as God has promised to bless his church with at that time; that if any of us should live to see the dawning of that glorious day, we might share in the blessedness of it, and then be called, as the friends of the bridegroom, to the marriage supper of the Lamb, and partake of that joy in which heaven and earth, angels and saints, and

Christ and his church, shall be united at that time.

But here I would apply the exhortation in a few words to that minister of Christ, who above all others is concerned in the solemnity of this day, who is now to be united to, and set over this people as their pastor.

You have now here, Reverend Sir, the great importance, and high ends of the office of an evangelical pastor, and the glorious privileges of such as are faithful in this office, imperfectly represented. May God grant that your union with this people, this day, as their pastor, may be such, that God's people here may have the great promise God makes to his church in the text, now fulfilled unto them. May you now, as one of the precious sons of Zion, take this part of Christ's church by the hand, in the name of your great Master, the glorious bridegroom, with a heart devoted unto him with true adoration and supreme affection, and for his sake knit to this people, in a spiritual and pure love, and as it were a conjugal tenderness; ardently desiring that great happiness for them, which you have now heard Christ has chosen his church unto, and has shed his blood to obtain for her; being yourself ready to spend and be spent for them; remembering the great errand on which Christ sends you to them, viz., to woo and win their hearts, and espouse their souls to him, and to bring up his elect spouse, and to fit and adorn her for her embraces; that you may in due time present her a chaste virgin to him, for him to rejoice over, as the bridegroom rejoiceth over the bride. How honorable is this business that Christ employs you in! And how joyfully should you perform it! When Abraham's faithful servant was sent to take a wife for his master's son, how engaged was he in the business; and how joyful was he when he succeeded! With what joy did he bow his head and worship, and bless the Lord God of his master, for his mercy and his truth in making his way prosperous! And what a joyful meeting may we conclude he had with Isaac, when he met him in the field, by the well of Lahai-roi, and there presented his beauteous Rebekah to him, and told him all things that he had done!   But this was but a shadow of that joy that you shall have, if you imitate his fidelity, in the day when you shall meet your glorious Master, and present Christ's church in this place, as a chaste and beautiful virgin unto him.

We trust, dear sir, that you will esteem it a most blessed employment, to spend your time and skill in adorning Christ's bride for her marriage with the Lamb, and that it is work that you will do with delight; and that you will take heed that the ornaments you put upon her are of the right sort, what shall be indeed beautiful and precious in the eyes of the bridegroom, that she may be all glorious within, and her clothing of wrought gold; that on the wedding day, she may stand on the King's right hand in gold of Ophir.

The joyful day is coming, when the spouse of Christ shall be led in unto the King with raiment of needle-work; and angels and faithful ministers will be the servants that shall lead her in. And you, sir, if you are faithful in the charge that is now to be committed to you, shall be joined with glorious angels in that honorable and joyful service; but with this difference, that you shall have the higher privilege. Angels and faithful ministers shall be together in bringing in Christ's bride into his palace, and presenting her to him: but faithful ministers shall have a much higher participation of the joy of that occasion: they shall have a greater and more immediate participation with the bride in her joy; for they shall not only be ministers to the church as the angels are but parts of the church, principal members of the bride.   And as such, at the same time that angels do the part of ministering spirits to the bride, when they conduct her to the bridegroom, they shall also do the part of ministering spirits to faithful ministers. And they shall also have a higher participation with the bridegroom than the angels, in his rejoicing at that time; for they shall be nearer to him than they; for they are also his members, and are those that are honored as the principal instruments of espousing the saints to him, and fitting them for the enjoyment of him; and therefore they will be more the crown of rejoicing of faithful ministers, than of the angels of heaven.

So great, dear sir, is the honor and joy that is set before you, to engage you to faithfulness in your pastoral care of this people; so glorious the prize that Christ has set up to engage you to run the race that is set before you.

I would now conclude with a few words to the people of this congregation, whose souls are now to be committed to the care of that minister of Christ, whom they have chosen as pastor.

Let me take occasion, dear brethren, from what has been said, to exhort you, not forgetting the respect, honor, and reverence, that will ever be due from you to your former pastor, that has served you so long in that work, but by reason of age and growing infirmities, and the prospect of his place being so happily supplied by a successor, has seen meet to relinquish the burden of the pastoral charge over you: I say, let me exhort you (not forgetting due respect to him as a father) to perform the duties that belong to you, in your part of that relation and union, now to be established between you and your elect pastor: to receive him as the messenger of the Lord of Hosts, one that in his office represents the glorious bridegroom of the church, to love and honor him, and willingly submit yourselves to him, as a virgin when married to a husband. Surely the feet of that messenger should be beautiful, that comes to you on such a blessed errand as that which you have heard, to espouse you to the eternal Son of God, and to fit you for, and lead you to him as your bridegroom. Your chosen pastor comes to you on this errand, and he comes in the name of the bridegroom, so empowered by him, and representing him, that in receiving him, you will receive Christ, and in rejecting him, you will reject Christ.

Be exhorted to treat your pastor as the beautiful and virtuous

Rebekah treated Abraham's servant: she most charitably and hospitably entertained him, provided lodging and food for him and his company, and took care that he should be comfortably entertained and supplied in all respects, while he continued in his embassy; and that was the note or mark of distinction which God himself gave him, by which he should know the true spouse of Isaac from all others of the daughters of the city. Therefore in this respect approve yourselves as the true spouse of Christ, by giving kind entertainment to your minister that comes to espouse you to the antitype of Isaac. Provide for his outward subsistence and comfort, with the like cheerfulness that Rebekah did for Abraham's servant. You have account of her alacrity and liberality in supplying him, in Gen. xxiv. 18, 19, 20, and 25. Say as her brother did, verse 31, "Come in, thou blessed of the Lord."

Thus you should entertain your pastor. But this is not that wherein your duty towards him chiefly lies: the main thing is to comply with him in his great errand, and to yield to the suit that he makes to you in the name of Christ, to go to be his bride. In this you should be like Rebekah: she was, from what she heard of Isaac, and God's covenant with him, and blessing upon him, from the mouth of Abraham's servant, willing forever to forsake her own country, and her father's house, to go into a country she had never seen, to be Isaac's wife, whom also she never saw. After she had heard what the servant had to say, and her old friends had a mind she should put off the affair for the present, but it was insisted on that she should go immediately, and she was inquired of, "whether she would go with this man," she said, "I will go." And she left her kindred, and followed the man through all that long journey, till he had brought her unto Isaac, and they three had that joyful meeting in Canaan. If you will this day receive your pastor in that union that is now to be established between him and you, it will be a joyful day in this place, and the joy will be like the joy of espousals, as when a young man marries a virgin; and it will not only be a joyful day in East Hampton, but it will doubtless be a joyful day in heaven, on your account. And your joy will be a faint resemblance, and a forerunner of that future joy, when Christ shall rejoice over you as the bridegroom rejoiceth over the bride, in heavenly glory.

And if your pastor be faithful in his office, and you hearken and yield to him in that great errand on which Christ sends him to you, the time will come, wherein you and your pastor will be each other's crown of rejoicing, and wherein Christ, and he, and you, shall all meet together at the glorious marriage of the Lamb, and shall rejoice in and over one another, with perfect, uninterrupted, never ending and never fading joy.

BIBLIOGRAPHY

Primary Sources—Manuscripts and Typescripts

This study draws upon several kinds of unpublished primary sources in Yale's Edwards Manuscript Collection. Using the Beinecke Rare Book and Manuscript Library card index to Edwards' sermons (an index listing each sermon by text), I chose several hundred manuscript sermons for initial reading and then narrowed my focus to twenty-one selected "ministerial" sermons. I also had the good fortune at Beinecke to use Thomas Schafer's typed transcripts of Edwards' unpublished "Miscellanies." Scanning each of the eight boxes of Schafer typescripts, I noted the miscellanies particularly related to gospel ministry. Finally I examined Edwards' unpublished scriptural annotations written in the blank pages of his personal, interleaved Bible.

I. Manuscript Sermons. Sermons cited directly in this study are listed here by text:

Psalm 95:7-8	Acts 6:1-3
Canticles 1:3(1)	Acts 14:23
Canticles 1:3(2)	Acts 16:19
Isaiah 3:1-2	Acts 17:30
Isaiah 27:13	Acts 20:28
Ezekiel 44:9	Romans 12:4-8
Micah 2:11	I Corinthians 2:11-13
Zechariah 4:12-14	II Corinthians 2:15-16
Luke 10:17-18	II Corinthians 4:7
Luke 10:38-42	Hebrews 2:11
Luke 11:27-28	

II. "Miscellanies." A typed transcription by Thomas Schafer of Edwards' unpublished miscellaneous notes. I cited the following in my study:

40   # 72   #460

#636	#652	#681
#689	#764	#765

III. Edwards' personally annotated interleaved Bible.

Primary Sources--Published Works

Apocalyptic Writings. Ed. Stephen Stein. New Haven: Yale University
    Press, 1977.

Freedom of Will. Ed. Paul Ramsey. New Haven: Yale University Press,
    1957.

History of Redemption. New York: T. & J. Swords, 1793.

Images or Shadows of Divine Things. Ed. Perry Miller. New Haven:
    Yale University Press, 1948.

Jonathan Edwards: Representative Selections. E. Clarence H. Faust
    and Thomas H. Johnson. Rev. ed. New York: Hill & Wang, 1962.

Original Sin. Ed. Clyde Holbrook. Hew Haven: Yale University Press,
    1970.

Religious Affections. Ed. John E. Smith. New Haven: Yale University
    Press, 1959.

Selections from Unpublished Writings of Jonathan Edwards.   Ed.
    Alexander B. Grosart. Edinburgh: Ballantyne & Co., 1965.

Scientific and Philosophical Writing. Ed. Wallace E. Anderson. New
    Haven: Yale University Press, 1980.

The Great Awakening. Ed. C. C. Goen. New Haven: Yale University
    Press, 1972.

The Life of David Brainerd.   Ed. Norman Pettit. New Haven: Yale
    University Press, 1985.

"The Mind" of Jonathan Edwards: A Reconstructed Text. Ed. Leon
     Howard. Berkeley: Univ. of California Press, 1963.

The Works of Jonathan Edwards, A. M. Ed. Edward Hickman. 2 vols.
     London: William Tegg & Co., 1879.

The Works of President Edwards. Ed. Sereno E. Dwight. 10 vols. New
     York: S. Converse, 1829–1830.

The Works of President Edwards. Reprint of Worchester Edition. 4
     vols. New York: Leavitt & Allen, 1843.

Treatise on Grace and Other Writings Posthumously Published. Ed. Paul
     Helm. London: James Clarke & Co. Ltd., 1971.

Secondary Sources

Ainslie, James L. The Doctrines of Ministerial Order in the Reformed
     Churches of the Sixteenth and Seventeenth Centuries. Edinburgh,
     1940.

Aldridge, Alfred Owen. Jonathan Edwards. New York: Washington Square
     Press, 1964.

Allen, Alexander. Jonathan Edwards. Edinburgh: T. & T. Clark, 1889.

Altizer, Thomas J. J. The Self-Embodiment of God. New York: Harper
     and Row Publishers, 1977.

Angoff, Charles, ed. Jonathan Edwards: His Life and Influence.
     Leverton Lecture Series. Cranbury, New Jersey: Association of
     University Presses, 1973.

Augustine. On Christian Doctrine. Trans. D. W. Robertson, Jr.
     Indianapolis, Indiana: Bobbs–Merrill Company, Inc., 1958.

Austin, J. L. How To Do Things With Words. Cambridge: Harvard
     University Press, 1962.

Bainton, Roland H. Yale and the Ministry: A History of Education for
     the Christian Ministry at Yale from the Founding in 1701. New
     York: Harper, 1957.

Baumgartner, Paul R. "Jonathan Edwards: The Theory Behind His Use of Figurative Language." PMLA, 78 (September, 1963), 321-325.

Baxter, Richard. The Reformed Preacher. New York: n.p., 1860.

Bercovitch, Sacvan. The American Jeremiad. Madison: University of Wisconsin Press, 1978.

_____. The Puritan Origins of the American Self. New Haven: Yale University Press, 1975.

_____. "Typology of America's Mission," American Quarterly, 30 (Summer 1979), 135-155.

_____. Typology and Early American Literature. University of Massachusetts Press, 1972

Berkhouwer, Gerrit C. Man in the Image of God. Grand Rapids: Eerdmans Publishing Co., 1962.

Berner, Robert L. "Grace and Works in America: The Role of Jonathan Edwards." Southern Quarterly, 15, 125-134.

Bogue, Carl W. Jonathan Edwards and the Covenant of Grace. Cherry Hill, New Jersey, 1975.

Breen, T. H. The Character of the Good Ruler: Puritan Politics Before the Great Awakening, 1630-1730. New Haven: Yale University Press, 1970.

Buckingham, Willis J. "Stylistic Artistry in the Sermons of Jonathan Edwards." Papers on Language and Literature, 6, 136-151.

Burke, Kenneth. The Rhetoric of Religion: Studies on Logology. Berkeley, California: University of Calif. Press, 1970.

Burggraaff, W. J. "Jonathan Edwards: A Bibliographic Essay," Reformed Review, 18 (March, 1965), 13-19.

Bushman, Richard L. From Puritan to Yankee: Character and the Social Order in Connecticut, 1690-1765. New York, 1967.

_____. "Jonathan Edwards and Puritan Consciousness." Journal for the Scientific Study of Religion, 5 (Fall 1966), 383-395.

_____. "Jonathan Edwards as Great Man: Identity, Conversion, and Leadership in the Great Awakening." Soundings, 52 (Spring, 1969), 15-46.

Butterfield, Herbert. Christianity and History. New York: Scribner, 1950.

Cadman, S. Parkes. Ambassadors of God. New York: Macmillan Co., 1920.

Cairns, David. The Image of God in Man. London: Camelot Press, 1953.

Calvin, John. Institutes of the Christian Religion. 2 vols. Ed. John T. McNeill. Trans. Ford Lewis Battles. Philadelphia: Westminster Press, 1960.

_____. Commentaries on the Epistles of Paul the Apostle to the Corinthians. Trans. John Pringle. Edinburgh, 1848-1849.

Carse, James. Jonathan Edwards and the Visibility of God. New York: Scribner's Sons, 1967.

Cherry, Conrad. Nature and Religious Imagination: From Edwards to Bushnell. New York: Fortress Press, 1980.

_____. Theology of Jonathan Edwards: A Reappraisal. New York: Doubleday, 1966.

Crabtree, A. B. Jonathan Edwards' View of Man: A Study in Eighteenth Century Calvinism. Wallington, England: Religious Education Press, 1948.

Daane, James. Preaching With Confidence: A Theological Essay on the Power of the Pulpit. Grand Rapids, Mich.: Eerdmans Publishing Co., 1980.

Davidson, Edward H. Jonathan Edwards: The Narrative of a Puritan Mind. Boston: Houghton Mifflin, 1966.

De Jong, Peter Y. The Covenant Idea in New England Theology, 1660-1847. Grand Rapids, Mich.: Eerdmans Publishing Co., 1945.

Delattre, Roland. Beauty and Sensibility in the Thought of Jonathan Edwards: An Essay in Aesthetics and Theological Ethics. New Haven: Yale University Press, 1968.

Dowey, Edward A. The Knowledge of God in Calvin's Theology. New
    York: Columbia University Press, 1952.

Dwight, Timothy. Travels in New England and New York. 4 Vols. Ed.
    Barbara Miller Solomon. Cambridge: Belnap Press, 1967.

Elliot, Emory. Power and the Pulpit in Puritan New England.
    Princeton: Princeton University Press, 1975.

Elwood, Douglas J. The Philosophical Theology of Jonathan Edwards.
    New York: Columbia University Press, 1960.

Emerson, Everett H.   "Jonathan Edwards," Fifteen American Authors
    Before 1900: Bibliographic Essays on Research and Criticism.
    Edited by Robert A. Reese and Earl N. Harbert, Madison:
    University of Wisconsin Press, 1971.

Erdt, Terrence. Jonathan Edwards: Art and the Sense of the Heart.
    Amherst: University of Mass. Press, 1980.

_____. "The Calvinist Psychology of the Heart and 'Sense' of
    Jonathan Edwards." Early American Literature, 13, 165-180.

Evans, Donald. The Logic of Self-Involvement: A Philosophical Study
    of Everyday Language With Special Reference to the Christian Use
    of Language About God the Creator. New York: Herder and Herder,
    1969.

Emerson, Everett. Puritanism in America, 1620-1750. Boston: Twayne
    Publishers, 1977.

Gambrell, Mary. Ministerial Training in 18th Century New England.
    New York: Columbia University Press, 1937.

Gardiner, H. Norman, ed. Jonathan Edwards: A Retrospect. Boston:
    Riverside Press, 1901.

Gaustad, Edwin Scott. The Great Awakening in New England. New York:
    Harper, 1957.

Gerstner, John H. Jonathan Edwards on Heaven and Hell. Grand Rapids,
    Michigan: Baker Book House, 1980.

_____. Steps to Salvation: The Evangelical Message of Jonathan
    Edwards. Philadelphia: Westminster Press, 1960.

Goen, C. C. "Jonathan Edwards: A New Departure in Eschatology."
    Church History, 28 (1959), 25-40.

Golden, Morris. The Self Observed. Baltimore: Johns Hopkins Press,
    1972.

Goodykuntz, Harry G. The Minister in the Reformed Tradition.
    Richmond, Va.: John Knox Press, 1963.

Grabo, Norman S. "Jonathan Edwards' Personal Narrative: Dynamic
    Stasis," LWU, 2 (1969), 141-148.

Griffith, John. "Jonathan Edwards as a Literary Artist." Criticism,
    15, 156-173.

Haims, Lynn. "The Face of God: Puritan Iconography in Early American
    Poetry, Sermons, and Tombstone Carving." Early American
    Literature, 14 (1979), 15-47.

Hall, David. The Faithful Shepherd: A History of the New England
    Ministry in the Seventeenth Century. Chapel Hill: U. of North
    Carolina Press, 1972.

Haller, William. The Rise of Puritanism. New York: Harper, 1957.

Hanson, Anthony Tyrrell. The Pioneer Ministry. London: SMC Press,
    1961.

Harnack, Adolph. The Mission and Expansion of Christianity. New
    York: Harper and Bros., 1960.

Haroutunian, Joseph G. "Jonathan Edwards: Theology of the Great
    Commandment." Theology Today, I (October, 1944), 361-377.

_____. Piety Versus Moralism. New York: Holt & Co., 1932.

Hatch, Nathan O. The Sacred Cause of Liberty: Republican Thought and
    the Millennium in Revolutionary New England. New Haven: Yale
    University Press, 1977.

Heam, Rosemary, "Stylistic Analysis of the Sermons of Jonathan
    Edwards." Dissertation, Indiana, 1973.

Heimert, Alan. Religion and the American Mind: From the Great
    Awakening to the Revolution. Cambridge: Harvard University
    Press, 1966.

_____ and Perry Miller, eds. The Great Awakening: Documents Illustrating the Crisis and Its Influence. New York: Bobbs-Merrill Co., 1967.

Hendry, George S. "The Glory of God and the Future of Man." Reformed World, 34 (December, 1976), 147-157.

Holbrook, Clyde A. The Ethics of Jonathan Edwards: Morality and Aesthetics. Ann Arbor: University of Michigan Press, 1973.

Howard, Leon. "The Creative Imagination of a College Rebel: Jonathan Edwards' Undergraduate Writings." Early American Literature, 5 (1971), 50-56.

Jenson, Robert. Visible Words: Interpretation and Practice of Christian Sacraments. Philadelphia: Fortress Press, 1978.

Johnson, Thomas H. "Jonathan Edwards' Background of Reading." Publications of the Colonial Society of Massachusetts, 28 (December 1931), 216-217.

Jones, James, Shattered Synthesis: New England Puritanism Before the Great Awakening. New Haven: Yale University Press, 1973.

Jones, Phyllis M. and Nicholas R., eds. Salvation in New England: Selections from the Sermons of the First Preachers. Austin: University of Texas Press, 1977.

Kahler, Erich. "The Nature of the Symbol" in Symbolism in Religion and Literature. Ed. Rollo May. New York, 1960.

Katz, Joseph. Plotinus' Search for the Good. New York: King's Crown Press, 1950.

Kimnach, Wilson H. "Jonathan Edwards' Early Sermons: New York, 1722-1723." Journal of Presbyterian History, 55 (Fall 1977), 225-266.

_____. "Jonathan Edwards' Sermon Mill." Early American Literature, 10 (1975), 167-178.

_____. "The Brazen Trumpet: Jonathan Edwards' Conception of the Sermon," in Jonathan Edwards: His Life and Influence. Ed. Charles Angoff. Leverton Lecture Series. Cranburg, N. J.: Association of University Presses, 1973.

_____. "The Literary Techniques of Jonathan Edwards."
     Dissertation, University of Pennsylvania, 1971.

Kohl, Manfred Waldemar. Congregationalism in American. Oak Creek,
     Wisconsin: Congregational Press, 1977.

Kolodny, Annette. "Imagery in the Sermons of Jonathan Edwards."
     Early American Literature, 7, 172-182.

Ladriere, Jean. Language and Belief. Trans. Garett Barden. Notre
     Dame: University of Notre Dame Press, 1972.

Lee, Marc F. "A Literary Approach to Selected Writings of Jonathan
     Edwards." Dissertation, University of Wisconsin, Milwaukee
     1974.

Lee, Sang. "Mental Activity and the Perception of Beauty in Jonathan
     Edwards." Harvard Theological Review, 69 (July, 1976), 369-396.

_____. "Jonathan Edwards' Theory of the Imagination." Michigan
     History, 5, 233-241.

Lesser, M. X. Jonathan Edwards: A Reference Guide. Boston: G. K.
     Hall & Co., 1981.

Loewinsohn, Ronald. "Jonathan Edwards' Opticks: Images and Metaphors
     of Light in Some of His Major works." Early American Literature,
     8 (1973), 21-32.

Logan, Samuel T., Jr. "The Hermeneutics of Jonathan Edwards."
     Westminster Theological Journal, 43 (Fall 1980), 79-96.

Love, W. DeLoss, Jr. The Fast and Thanksgiving Days of New England.
     Boston, 1895.

Lynen, John, The Design of the Present. New Haven: Yale University
     Press, 1969.

Lyttle, David. "Sixth Sense of Jonathan Edwards." Church Quarterly
     Review, 167 (January, 1966), 50-59.

_____. "Jonathan Edwards on Personal Identity." Early American
     Literature, 7 (1972), 165.

Manspeaker, Nancy. Jonathan Edwards: Bibliographical Synopses. New
     York: Edwin Mellen Press, 1981.

Martz, Louis. Paradise Within. New Haven: Yale, 1964.

Mather, Cotton. Magnalia Christi Americana. 2 Vols. London, 1702, ed.
      Hartfort, 1853-1855.

_____. Manuductio ad Ministerium: Directions for a Candidate of
      the Ministry. Boston: Printed for Thomas Hancock, 1726.

McDonald, James. Kerygma and Didache. Cambridge: Harvard University
      Press, 1980.

McGiffert, Arthur Cushman. Jonathan Edwards. New York, 1932.

McGiffert, Michael, ed. God's Plot: the Paradoxes of Puritan Piety,
      Being the Autobiography and Journal of Thomas Shepard. Amherst:
      University of Massachusetts Press, 1972.

McNeill, John T. A History of the Cure of Souls. New York: Harper &
      Row, 1951.

Meade, Sidney E. "The Rise of the Evangelical Conception of the
      Ministry in American (1607-1850)" in The Ministry in Historical
      Perspectives. Ed. H. Richard Niebuhr and Daniel D. Williams.
      New York: 1956.

Miller, Perry. Errand into the Wilderness. Cambridge: Belknap Press
      of Harvard University Press, 1956.

_____. Jonathan Edwards. New York: Meridan Books, 1959.

_____. "Jonathan Edwards on the Sense of the Heart." Harvard
      Theological Review, 41 (April, 1948), 123-129.

_____. The New England Mind: From Colony to Province.
      Cambridge: Harvard University Press, 1953.

_____. The New England Mind: The Seventeenth Century. Boston:
      Beacon Press, 1961.

Miller, Perry and Thomas H. Johnson, eds. The Puritans. New York:
      American Book Co., 1938.

Mitchell, W. Fraser. English Pulpit Oratory. New York: Russell,
      Inc., 1962.

Moore, William. The New Testament Concept of the Ministry. St. Louis: Bethany Press, 1956.

Morgan, Edmund. Visible Saints: The History of a Puritan Idea. New York: New York University Press, 1963.

Murdock, Kenneth B. Literature and Theology in Colonial New England. Cambridge: Harvard University Press, 1949.

Niebuhr, H. Richard. The Kingdom of God in America. New York: Harper, 1937.

_____. The Ministry in Historical Perspectives. Eds. H. Richard Niebuhr and Daniel Williams. New York: Harpers, 1956.

Olney, James, Metaphors of Self: The Meaning of Autobiography. Princeton: Princeton University Press, 1972.

Osborne, Ronald. In Christ's Place. St. Louis: Augsburg Press, 1967.

Perkins, William. The Art of Prophecying: Or A Treatise Concerning the Sacred and Onely True Manner and Method of Preaching. First written in Latine by Mr. William Perkins: and now faithfully translated into English . . . by Thomas Tuke. Newly corrected according to his own copies. The Workes. London: John Legatt, 1617, II, 643-673.

Pettit, Norman. The Heart Prepared: Grace and Conversion in Puritan Spiritual Life. New Haven: Yale University Press, 1966.

Piercy, Josephine. Studies in Literary Types in Seventeeth Century America (1607-1710). New Haven: Yale University Press, 1939.

Prince, Thomas. The Christian History. Boston, n.d.

Rasmussen, David. Symbol and Interpretation. The Hague: Martinue Nijhoff, 1974.

Ridderbos, Jan. De Theologie Van Jonathan Edwards. s'-Gravenhage [The Hague]: Johan A Nederbragt, 1907.

Rogers, C. A. "John Wesley and Jonathan Edwards." Duke Divinity Review, 31 (Winter, 66), 20-38.

Schafer, Thomas Anton. "Jonathan Edwards' Conception of the Church." Church History, 24 (March, 1955), 51-66.

_____. "Manuscript Problems in the Yale Edition Jonathan Edwards." Early American Literature, (Winter, 1969), 159-168.

Scheick, William, ed. Critical Essays on Jonathan Edwards. Boston: G. K. Hall & Co., 1980.

_____. The Writings of Jonathan Edwards: Theme, Motif, and Style. College Station: Texas A. & M. University Press, 1975.

Shea, Daniel B. Jr. "Jonathan Edwards: The First Two Hundred Years." Journal of American Studies. 14 (1980), 181-198.

_____. Spiritual Autobiography in Early America. Princeton: Princeton University Press, 1968.

Shepard, Thomas. Works of Thomas Shepard. 3 vols. Boston: Doctrinal Tract and Book Society, 1853.

Simonson, Harold. "Jonathan Edwards and the Imagination." Andover Newton Quarterly (1975), 109-118.

_____. Jonathan Edwards: Theologian of the Heart. Grand Rapids: Eerdmans Publishing Co., 1974.

Sliwoski, Richard, "Doctrinal Dissertations on Jonathan Edwards." Early American Literature, 14 (1979-80), 318-327.

Stalker, James. The Preacher and His Models. Yale Lectures on Preaching, 1891. Intro. by Ralph Turnbull. Grand Rapids: Baker Book House; reprint, 1967.

Stein, Stephen. "Jonathan Edwards and the Rainbow: Biblical Exegesis and Poetical Imagination." New England Quarterly, 47 (September, 1974), 440-456.

_____. "Providence and the Apocalypse in the Early Writings of Jonathan Edwards." Early American Literature, 13, 250-267.

Stob, Henry. Ethical Reflections: Essays on Moral Themes. Grand Rapids: Eerdmans Publishing Co., 1978.

Stout, Harry S. "Puritanism Considered as a Profane Movement." Christian Scholars Review, 10 (1980), 156-169.

_____. "Religion, Communication, and the Ideological Origins of the American Revolution." William and Mary Quarterly, 34 (1977), 519-541.

Suter, Rufus. "A Note on Platonism in the Philsophy of Jonathan Edwards." Harvard Theological Review, 52 (October, 1959), 283-284.

_____. "The Concept of the Morality in the Philosophy of Jonathan Edwards." The Journal of Religion, (1934), 265-272.

Tallon, John W. "Flight Into Glory: The Cosmic imagination of Jonathan Edwards." Dissertation, University of Pennsylvania, 1973.

Tomas, Vincent. "The Modernity of Jonathan Edwards." The New England Quarterly, 25 (1952), 60-84.

Tracy, Patricia. Jonathan Edwards, Pastor: Religion And Society in Eighteenth-Century Northampton. New York: Hill and Wang, 1980.

Trumbull, James. The History of Northampton. 2 vols. Northampton, Mass., 1989.

Trumbull, Benjamin. A Complete History of Connecticut, Civil and Ecclesiastical. 2 vols. New Haven: Maltby, Goldsmith and Co., 1819.

Trumbull, Ralph. Jonathan Edwards, the Preacher. Grand Rapids, Michigan: Baker Publishing Co., 1958.

Upham, William P. "On the Shorthand Notes of Jonathan Edwards." Massachusetts Historical Society Proceedings (second series), 15 (February, 1902), 514-521.

Waanders, David. "Pastoral Sense of Jonathan Edwards." Reformed Review, 29 (Winter, 1976), 123-132.

Wakefield, Gordon S. Puritan Devotion: Its Place in the Development of Christian Piety. London, 1957.

Walker, Williston. Creeds and Platforms of Congregationalism. Boston: Pilgrim Press, 1960.

Watkins, Owen C. The Puritan Experience: Studies in Spiritual Autobiography. New York, 1972.

Watson, Philip S. "Introduction" to Anders Nygren's Agape and Eros,
    I. London: Society for Promoting Christian Knowledge, 1938.

Webber, Joan. The Eloquent I. Madison, Wisconsin: University of
    Wisconsin, 1968.

Weddle, David L. "Beauty of Faith in Jonathan Edwards." Ohio Journal
    of Religious Studies, 4 (Oct., 1976), 42-52.

Wendel, Francois. Calvin: Origins and Development of His Religious
    Thought. Translated by Philip Mairet. New York: Harper and
    Row, 1963.

Werge, Thomas. "Jonathan Edwards and the Puritan Mind in America;
    Directions in Textual and Interpretative Criticism." Reformed
    Review, 28 (Spring, 1980), 153-156, 173-183.

White, Eugene E. Puritan Rhetoric: The Issue of Emotion in Religion.
    Carbondale, Ill." Southern Illinois University Press, 1972.

Wilson-Kastner, Patricia. Coherence in a Fragmented World: Jonathan
    Edwards' Theology of the Holy Spirit. Washington, D. C.:
    University Press of America, 1978.

Winslow, Ola Elizabeth. Meetinghouse Hill, 1630-1783. New York, 1952.

_____. Jonathan Edwards, 1703-1758: A Biography. New York:
    Macmillan, 1940.

Youngs, J. William T., Jr. God's Messengers: Religious Leadership in
    ColonialNew England, 1700-1750. Baltimore: Johns Hopkins Press,
    1976.

INDEX

191-194, 218-222, 225,
229, 231-232, 234
Miracles, 67, 68
"Miscellanies," ii, v, 43,
  48
  entry #10, 29
  entry #40, 22, 28, 31-33,
    70
  entry #72, 57
  entry #460, 58
  entry #539, 48; #636, 69
  entry #652, 154; #681, 131
  entry #689, 24
  entry #764, 127
  entry #765, 157
  entry #1340, 61
  entry qq, 29
Mitchell, W. Fraser, 16

Narrative of Surprising
  Conversions, 70
Nature of True Virtue,
  2, 27, 148, 196
Newark, New Jersey, 192
New Haven, 192
Northampton, i, iv, vii,
  viii, 25, 32, 38-39,
  77, 112-113, 119-120,
  126, 133-134, 145, 147,
  151, 161, 180, 191-192,
  199-201, 203, 206-207,
  210, 219, 225, 227,
  235, 238
Norton, John, 11
Notes on the Bible, 55

Office of Minister, iv, v,
  1-3, 5, 12-13, 19, 22, 24,
  56, 66, 119-120, 123-126,
  139-141, 143, 160, 175,
  204
Officers, 55, 108-109, 116,
  144, 232
Olive Branch, xi, 174, 234
Olive Trees, 173
Onlooks, Ministerial, 10,
  11, 27, 130, 132, 162-163,
  166-167, 171, 173, 230
Ordinances, 60-61, 65, 179
Ordination Sermons, xi, 3,

5, 64, 66, 78, 81, 119,
123, 152, 159, 160, 164,
171, 178, 203, 218, 222,
227, 234, 238

Paradox, 76, 100, 116, 131,
159, 169-171, 236
Parker, Robert, 11
Pastoral Theology, v, vi,
14, 49, 191
Peace Which Christ Gives
98
Performative Force, 6, 14,
18, 21, 26, 31, 49, 59,
60, 84, 88, 112, 116
Perkins, William, 16, 56
Perpetuity and Change
of the Sabbath, 13, 61
Personal Narrative, 81,
104
Pettit, Norman, ii, 106
Philosophical Writings,
ii
Portsmouth, 167, 239
Preaching, 48, 57-58, 60,
68, 72, 75, 80, 85-86, 90,
96, 99, 117-118, 124, 130,
148, 157, 175, 195, 196
Pressing into the
Kingdom of God, 9, 16
Preston, John, 56
Prince, Thomas, 17
Princeton College, 58
Prophets, 67
Providence, 2, 20, 40
Public Profession, 108, 111
Puritan Sermon Form, viii,
15, 91, 133, 207

Ramsey, Paul, ii
Rand, William, 148
Reason, 72-73, 99-104, 148,
152-154, 157, 159
Religious Affections ii,
47, 57, 59, 61-63, 71,
103, 192-193, 234
Revelation, 101-103, 148,
155

Sacrament, 106-107, 112, 230

STUDIES IN AMERICAN RELIGION